Fifty Minerals

That Changed the Course of

History

First published in the UK in 2013 by Apple Press
74-77 White Lion Street
London N1 9PF
UK

www.apple-press.com

ISBN: 978-1-84543-507-3
N90646

Conceived, designed and produced by
Quid Publishing
Level 4, Sheridan House
114 Western Road
Hove BN3 1DD
UK

www.quidpublishing.com

Design by Lindsey Johns

Printed in China by 1010 Printing International Ltd

10 9 8 7 6 5 4 3 2 1

Fifty Minerals

That Changed the Course of

History

written by Eric Chaline

APPLE

Contents

Introduction

How long can men thrive between walls of brick, walking on asphalt pavements, breathing the fumes of coal and of oil, growing, working, dying, with hardly a thought of wind, and sky, and fields of grain, seeing only machine-made beauty, the mineral-like quality of life? *Charles Lindbergh (1902–74)*

The history of human civilization can be told in different ways. So far in this series, it has been told with plants (*Fifty Plants that Changed the Course of History*) and animals (*Fifty Animals that Changed the Course of History*), and in this third volume, we focus on minerals. Minerals, in the broadest sense of the term, encompass a huge variety of natural and man-made materials, including metals and alloys, rocks, crystals, gemstones, organic minerals, salts and ores.

THE RISE OF MAN

The history of how and when our hominid ancestors became human is still a matter of debate among anthropologists and archaeologists. The capacities that were once thought to differentiate humans from the 'lower' animals – language, social organization, emotions, tool use and manufacture, symbolic reasoning and self-consciousness – have been shown to be present in other species such as birds, cetaceans and apes. However, no other species has developed these capacities to the same extent as humans to transform the natural environment and effectively remove itself from the processes of evolution. Humanity's transformation of the environment began with the domestication of plants and animals, but as civilization moved from subsistence farming to urban living, the manufacture of goods and trade, the emphasis shifted to minerals: stone for building; metals for tools and weapons, and later machinery; hydrocarbons for energy; earths, ores and salts for industry; and precious and semi-precious stones and metals for currency and adornment.

Anthropologists believe that morphological and behavioural changes triggered the process that turned our ape-like ancestors into modern humans. While it is impossible to reconstruct how our pre-human ancestors thought, felt or related to one another, we have practical evidence of their level of development from their tools – at least those made from durable materials such as stone – the earliest of which are estimated to be around 2.6 million years old. It is possible

BIG BANG
The awesome power of uranium was unleashed in 1945.

ARTISTIC IMPRESSION
Clay was the first
material used by humans
to produce representative
art such as this ancient
Maltese figurine.

that humanity's relationship with tools goes even further back, but it may be that these earlier 'tools' were found rather than fashioned objects, like those used by chimpanzees today. But once our ancestors started fashioning tools, they radically transformed their relationship with the natural world.

THE AGE OF METALS

For most of the past 2.6 million years, the human toolset consisted of ever more sophisticated tools made principally of wood, bone, flint and obsidian. In around 10,000 years BP (Before Present), during what is called the 'Neolithic Revolution', humans established permanent settlements, and agriculture and animal husbandry replaced hunter-gathering as the main human lifestyle. Central to these developments was the technological revolution that affected every area of daily life.

DRIVING FORCE
The lure of gold has
driven humans to explore
and conquer the furthest
corners of the globe.

The Stone Age made way for the Age of Metals: copper, bronze and iron. The precious metals gold and silver have modern industrial applications, but their main historical uses have been as currency, and jewellery, and lay and religious ornamentation, when they were combined with gems such as diamonds, amber, coral, jade and pearls. For all their technological sophistication, humans still depend for their energy needs on coal, the mineral fuel that powered the First Industrial Revolution, and also petroleum, the power source of the Second Industrial Revolution, now supplemented by the nuclear fuels, uranium and plutonium. Industrial processes from antiquity to the present day have made use of a wide range of metals, ores, alloys and salts, including alum, aluminium, asphalt, arsenic, sodium, mercury and steel.

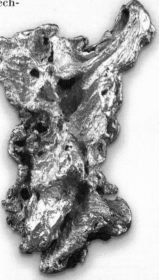

Diamond

Adamas

Type: Crystal; gemstone

Origin: Deep in Earth's mantle

Chemical formula: C

+ **INDUSTRIAL**
+ **CULTURAL**
+ **COMMERCIAL**
+ SCIENTIFIC

A model for beauty and hardness, the diamond, combined with never-tarnishing gold in an engagement ring, is the stone of choice to symbolize the purity and longevity of love and marriage. The rarity of large diamonds has made them the favourite gemstone of royalty – a noted part of the regalia of many royal houses of East and West.

FIT FOR A QUEEN

The 1786 'Affair of the Diamond Necklace' was pure soap opera, involving a queen, a cardinal, a con artist and a prostitute. The necklace in question had been ordered by the previous king of France, Louis XV (1710–74), for his mistress, but had never been delivered or paid for. The fall guy in the affair was the lecherous cleric, the Cardinal de Rohan, whom the con artist, the Countess of Lamotte, persuaded to obtain the fabulous necklace for Queen Marie-Antoinette (1755–93), impersonated by a prostitute. When the jewellers demanded payment, the queen denied all knowledge of the affair and the plot was exposed. Rohan was cleared but disgraced; Lamotte was imprisoned but escaped. Although innocent, the queen found that her reputation had been fatally compromised. The affair was one of the many scandals that precipitated the downfall of the French monarchy in the revolution of 1789.

A DIAMOND AS BIG AS THE RITZ

BRILLIANT
Of all the gemstones, none can match the allure of the flawless diamond.

Late one afternoon in January 1905, a miner unearthed a large crystal in the rock wall of the Premier diamond mine in South Africa. The crystal was so large that when he first saw it, the mine's superintendent Frederick Wells thought it was a worthless piece of natural glass. However, upon closer inspection it turned out to be the largest gem-quality diamond ever found, weighing a spectacular 621.35 g (1.36 lb) with a mass of 3,106.75 carats. The owner of the mine, Sir Thomas Cullinan, happened to be visiting that day, and the extraordinary find was named after him. Although not quite the mountain-sized diamond imagined by F. Scott Fitzgerald (1896–1940) in his 1922 novella *The Diamond as Big as the Ritz*, the Cullinan was a diamond beyond price.

The mine sold it to the government of the Transvaal (modern-day South Africa), which in turn presented it to its colonial master, the British King Edward VII (1841–1910).

To foil thieves who might try to steal the gem while it was being transported to England, a heavily guarded fake was sent by ship while the real stone was dispatched to the king by registered mail. Once safely in Edward's hands, the rough gem had to be cleaved, cut and polished. He entrusted the delicate task to the Asscher Diamond Company of Amsterdam. Joseph Asscher succeeded in cleaving the Cullinan in two on his second attempt, and further cuts yielded nine major gems and a further 96 smaller stones. The massive 530.20–carat Cullinan I, the 'King Edward VII', is mounted on the British monarch's sceptre, and the 317.40–carat Cullinan II is mounted on the band of the Imperial State Crown used in the coronation of Britain's kings and queens. The Cullinan III to IX are variously mounted on crowns or worn as jewellery by Queen Elizabeth II.

Royal rocks
The largest Cullinan stones are the crowning glories of British royal regalia.

The Cullinan, while it produced the largest regal diamonds, is a very late addition to the gems worn by royalty. The 105-carat *Koh-i-Noor* ('Mountain of Light') was the world's largest diamond prior to the discovery of the Cullinan. It was mined in northern India for Hindu kings between the eleventh and thirteenth centuries, who had it mounted as the eye of a goddess. When India fell to Muslim invaders from Central Asia, the gem became the property of the country's many Islamic dynasties, until they, in turn, succumbed to British power. In the mid-nineteenth century, the British seized the stone as war booty and presented it to Queen Victoria (1819–1901). Legend has it that the stone is cursed and will destroy any male ruler who wears it. The curse, however, does not affect women, and the British have wisely mounted it in the crowns of their queens and queen consorts.

No gold-digging for me.... I take diamonds! We may be off the gold standard someday. *Mae West, actress*

Although diamonds have adorned the bodies of kings and nobles for centuries, the increase in diamond production in the nineteenth century and the rise in living standards in the twentieth have made diamond jewellery accessible to a much greater proportion of the population. The first attested use of a diamond engagement ring dates back to fifteenth-century Europe, but the custom only became widespread in the 1930s. Today the gold-and-diamond solitaire ring, symbolizing the strength and durability of the love bond, remains the most popular engagement token in the U.S. and Europe.

COAL UNDER PRESSURE

For all its superlative qualities, 'A diamond', as Henry Kissinger (b. 1923) correctly observed, 'is a chunk of coal that is made good under pressure'. The chemical formula of diamond, C, shows that it is composed of pure carbon, like coal and graphite, but it is carbon on steroids created deep below the surface of Earth in the mantle while subject to huge pressures. Volcanic eruptions of diamond-bearing rock bring diamonds to the surface where, over millions of years, erosion by wind and rain, the gemstones are dispersed over a wide area.

Diamonds owe their hardness and translucency to their octahedral crystalline structure (imagine two perfect pyramids stuck base to base). Although colourless diamonds are traditionally the most prized for jewellery, chemical impurities can give them different colours, the most common being yellow and brown, and the rarest, blue, black, pink and red. In recent years, the top auction prices for diamonds have been paid for blue and pink stones. The traditional unit of measure for diamonds is the carat, which is a unit of mass equivalent to 0.2 g (200 mg; 0.007055 oz). The metric carat, which was adopted as the international standard in 1907, is subdivided into 100 'points' of 2 mg each.

A selection of the world's most famous diamonds:
1. Great Mogul
2 & 11. Regent
3 & 5. Florentine
4. Star of the South
6. Sancy
7. Dresden Green
8. *Koh-i-Noor* (original form)
9. Hope
10 & 12. *Koh-i-Noor* (current form)

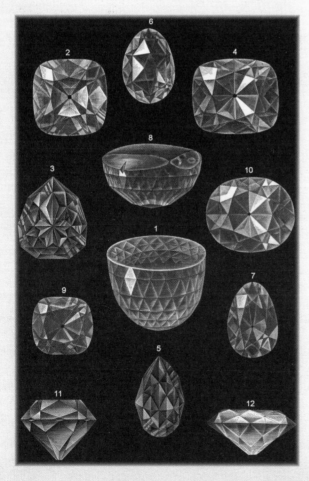

Known for their hardness, diamonds could historically only be cut by other diamonds, and now by lasers. The first guild of diamond cutters in Europe was formed in the fourteenth century, and Antwerp in Belgium remains the world centre for diamond cutting. The process of producing a gem from a rough stone must ensure the retention of its maximum quality, size and colour.

FLAWLESS
Microscopic view of an uncut natural diamond with few internal inclusions.

Once the stone has been cleaved or sawed along internal faults, it is 'bruted' by grinding against another diamond to give it a rounded shape. The facets are then cut into the stone, giving it its final shape, and the gem is polished to full brilliance. Ancient stones, such as the *Koh-i-Noor*, could be less than impressive because their original cut did not bring out their full luster. In 1852, Prince Albert, Queen Victoria's consort, supervised the re-cutting of the *Koh-i-Noor*, reducing its size by over 40 percent from 186 carats to 105.602 carats. Although the stone's brilliance was greatly increased, Albert was disappointed by the result and had the stone mounted on a brooch for the queen.

The increase in the supply of natural diamonds in the nineteenth century and the discovery of how to manufacture gem-quality synthetic and simulant diamonds in the twentieth century have reduced the rarity, cost and therefore the allure of the stone in the modern day. However, in 2011, astronomers discovered an extraterrestrial diamond large enough to satisfy even the most jaded of collectors. The remnants of a collapsed star 4,000 light-years away across the galaxy, this planet-sized diamond is five times the size of Earth.

BLOOD AND TEARS

For centuries, diamonds have been fought over and killed for, but recent decades have seen the emergence of a new class of diamonds mined in areas afflicted by war or serious civil unrest – 'blood' or 'conflict' diamonds. The majority of these come from African countries, including Angola, Sierra Leone, the Democratic Republic of the Congo, and Zimbabwe. The proceeds of the sales of conflict diamonds go to fund further wars and insurgency, triggering a cycle of destruction that leaves the affected areas devastated and impoverished.

Copper

Aes cyprium

Type: Metal

Origin: Native copper and copper-bearing ores

Chemical formula: Cu

+ *INDUSTRIAL*
+ CULTURAL
+ *COMMERCIAL*
+ SCIENTIFIC

The Stone Age lasted 2.6 million years, but once humans had established their first permanent settlements, they began to exploit a new material to make their tools, weapons and ornaments: copper. Unlike stone, which is plentiful and available to all, copper had to be mined or traded, and its working created a caste of specialist coppersmiths and a class of wealthy and powerful men and women who could afford to commission and purchase metal artifacts.

THE ICEMAN COMETH

On September 19, 1991, when two German tourists hiking on the high Alpine glaciers on the border between Italy and Austria took a shortcut away from the marked track, they came across a deep gully in which they saw something that they first took to be some rubbish discarded by an earlier visitor. As they got closer, however, they realized that the object was a human head and upper torso sticking out of the ice. The corpse was so well preserved that the hikers and the mountain rescue team and police who attended the scene thought that it was a modern

COLD WORK
Humans first worked pure native copper by cold hammering.

fatality – a lost hiker who had met an unfortunate end in the treacherous Alps. It was only when the body had been removed from the ice and taken to the local morgue that the authorities realized that the corpse, soon to be named Ötzi (named for the Ötz Valley where he was found), was the mummi-fied remains of a man who had lived in the area some 5,300 years BP (Before Present), during a period of European prehistory known as the Chal-colithic – the Copper Age.

The Chalcolithic occurred between the Neolithic ('New Stone Age', 10,000–7000 years BP) and the Bronze Age, which began around 5,300 BP in the Near East and a century later in Europe. The Chalcolithic is defined as the period when humans discovered how to work copper while they continued to use stone implements. During the Neolithic, humans developed a sedentary lifestyle based on agriculture and communal life in towns and villages. This presented them with new opportunities and difficulties. Among the latter was how to obtain foodstuffs and raw materials not available in their immediate vicinity. The answer was the development of the first trading links between different communities and cultures. Among the advantages settle-ment brought were an increase in living standards and leisure time, which allowed the development of new technologies, the most important of which was metallurgy.

Archaeologists point to the Chalcolithic as the period when social stratification began in human societies. Compared to stone, copper was more difficult to source and to use. It had then to be worked by specialists, who might have been leaders themselves as a result of their expertise, or who sold what they made to an elite of powerful and wealthy individuals. Copper on its own did not create social divisions, but it promoted certain trends initiated by human settlement. From his clothing and equipment, archaeologists believe that Ötzi the Iceman was a high-status individual, possibly a chieftain or a coppersmith. Typi-cally for the period, he carried both a fine flint dagger imported from

PROSPECTOR
It is possible that Ötzi was prospecting for copper when he met his icy end.

TREASURE
Ötzi's most treasured possession was his copper axe – both tool and fearsome weapon.

Italy and a metal axe. The axe is 60 cm (23.5 in) in length and tipped with a cast-copper blade 9.5 cm (3.7 in) long. A formidable weapon in its own right, the axe could also be used to cut down a tree in 30 minutes without blunting.

THE CYPRUS CONNECTION

In antiquity, the island of Cyprus was one of the most important sources of copper in the Mediterranean world, hence the Latin name for the metal *aes Cyprium*, the 'Cypriot metal', later abbreviated to *cuprum*, from which we derive our own word, 'copper'. There are several reasons why copper, along with gold, was one of the first metals to be worked by humans: it is extremely plentiful on Earth, being the eighth most common metallic element in Earth's crust, and it is found in several rock ores; unlike most metals, which are grey, copper has an attractive red, yellow or orange hue or, when corroded, the green caused by a patina of copper carbonate; lastly, it is also found in pure form on the ground as 'native copper'. Native copper, although its supplies were soon exhausted in the most populated areas, was easily worked into small objects by cold hammering.

Although it was once thought that copper working was discovered in the Near East and exported to Europe, archaeological evidence has shown that the technology was developed independently in the Near East and Europe, as well as in other parts of the world. Once the easily accessible deposits of native copper had been exhausted, humans had to extract the metal from copper-bearing ores. The central Alpine region that was home to Ötzi the Iceman is rich in copper-bearing ores, and it was the centre of a thriving Chalcolithic civilization. One theory is that Ötzi was on a prospecting trip for copper ores when he met his end in the high Alps.

Cyprus is second to none of the islands of the Mediterranean; it is rich in wine and oil, produces grain in abundance and possesses extensive copper mines at Tamassos.

Strabo (64 BCE–24 CE), Geography *(23 CE)*

Extracting copper from ore is a far more complex process than prospecting for copper nuggets on the ground. It is probable that humans discovered that rocks were a source of copper and other metallic elements when they crushed and heated coloured mineral ores to use as pigments and decorative glazes for pottery.

Once the copper-bearing ores had been extracted from the ground, they had to be crushed and smelted in charcoal furnaces at over 1,000°C (1,832°F) several times to remove the impurities and produce rough blocks of the pure copper, which was done at the mining site. The blocks would then be transported to settlements for further processing or traded directly with other communities. Copper is relatively soft and can be worked into small objects, such as beads and pins, by cold hammering, but this technique is not suitable for larger objects as the metal will crack. The first technological stage is to heat the copper to make it easier to work, but more complex objects need to be made by casting. The copper blocks would be melted in ceramic or metal containers, then poured into stone or clay moulds, and then finished by cold hammering. Ötzi's axe blade was cast in such a way, with the cutting end shaped by cold hammering.

The social and cultural changes wrought by the Metal Age were far-reaching. Externally, it obliged communities to interact with one another as never before. Internally, it encouraged the development of proto-writing systems as a means to keep records of production, ownership and commercial transactions, and began the process of social stratification that would lead to the division of society into different castes or classes: specialist craftsmen and a political, social and economic elite, and their subordinates. As we will learn in the next chapter, copper continued to be a central material in the early development of human civilization as one of the main ingredients in the first alloy to be made by humans: bronze.

LADY IN GREEN
The trademark patina of copper protects the metal from further corrosion.

COPPER PLATED

✦

New York City's emblematic Statue of Liberty, dedicated in 1886, is the largest copper statue in the world. The statue, designed by the French sculptor Frederic Bartholdi (1834–1904), originally had a cast-iron armature to which the copper skin was attached. Copper was the ideal material, as it resists corrosion from water and seawater. The statue's trademark green colour, known in French as *verdigris*, is a layer of copper carbonate that forms in contact with the air and protects the metal from further corrosion. The statue was extensively restored between 1984 and 1986, when the badly corroded cast-iron armature was replaced with stainless steel, and repairs were made to the outer skin.

Bronze
Aes brundisium

Type: Metallic alloy of copper and tin or arsenic

Origin: Man-made

Chemical formula: $90Cu10Sn$

✦ Industrial
✦ **Cultural**
✦ **Commercial**
✦ Scientific

Although metallurgy began with the working of copper and gold, the metal that transformed civilization and set humanity on the road to ever more sophisticated technological developments was bronze. Bronze is an alloy of tin and copper, and its production necessitated the creation of large trading networks and the development of new technologies to cast and work metals. Although it was replaced by iron for tools and weapons in the first millennium BCE, bronze remains to this day the preferred metal for casting sculptures.

THE THIRD AGE

According to the Greek poet Hesiod (fl. 8th century BCE), the Bronze Age succeeded the far happier Gold and Silver Ages. Although there is no historical evidence for the first two ages, the term Bronze Age was adopted by archaeologists and historians to describe the period in human history when the primary technology, and the ultimate source of wealth and power, was bronze metallurgy. The period lasted from the end of the fourth millennium BCE to the first millennium BCE, though in the most advanced areas of the world, including India and the Near East, bronze had been replaced by iron by the end of the second millennium BCE. For Hesiod, the Bronze Age was a period of strife, when humans were devoted to the god of war, Ares (Mars to the Romans). This description is borne out by the historical and archaeological record. The Bronze Age witnessed the rise of the first great imperial civilizations in Egypt, Mesopotamia, Syria, Anatolia, Crete, Greece, India and China.

MYTHMAKER
The ancient Greek poet Hesiod first described the Gold, Silver and Bronze Ages.

Bronze is not a metal found in nature but an alloy, consisting of around 90 percent copper and 10 percent tin. The earliest bronze did not contain tin but arsenic, and is known as 'arsenical bronze'. However, arsenical bronze, although more pliable than tin bronze, needs more hardening to achieve the same strength, with the added drawback that arsenic is toxic to those who work it. Bronze replaced copper and stone for tools and weapons because, although it was more difficult to obtain its raw materials and to manufacture, it was stronger, easier to cast and more versatile. Bronze allowed the production of much

more complex castings for statuary, musical instruments and decorative objects, as well as for new types of tools and weapons. Bronze was also stronger than the wrought-iron tools and weapons of the early Iron Age, and it was not completely phased out until the introduction of steel. Another advantage of bronze over iron is that, like copper, it resists oxidation once a layer of green copper carbonate has sealed the surface of the metal.

Tin and copper are rarely found together; therefore, tin had to be imported over large distances to be alloyed with copper to make bronze. The tin used in much of the Mediterranean world is thought to have come from the tin mines of Devon and Cornwall in southwest Britain, as well as from mines in northern Spain and northern France, while the tin used in the Near East and India was imported from Central Asia; China and Southeast Asia had their own tin deposits. This far-flung trade demanded the creation of extensive networks across the ancient world and established direct contact between completely different cultures. In other words, the manufacture of bronze triggered the first major phase of economic globalization. Seafarers from the eastern Mediterranean traveled to the British Isles, then considered to be the ends of the earth, and tin was imported into the Near East and India along what would later become the Silk Road.

> **Zeus the Father made a third generation of mortal men, a brazen race, sprung from ash-trees; and it was in no way equal to the silver age, but was terrible and strong. They loved the lamentable works of Ares and deeds of violence [....] Their armour was of bronze, and their houses of bronze, and of bronze were their implements.**
>
> *Hesiod (fl. 8th c. BCE)*, Works and Days

In the later periods, tin bronze was joined by a number of other bronze alloys, including aluminium bronze, manganese bronze, naval brass and silicon bronze, which took advantage of the metal's resistance to corrosion and good electrical conductivity for a wide range of domestic, industrial, military and maritime applications. Bronze remains the most popular material for cast-metal sculptures, which are often called 'bronzes'. The Romans called bronze *aes Brundisium* (the Brundisium metal) after one of the major importation and production sites in the Roman Empire, the port of Brundisium (now Brindisi) on the Apulian coast of southern Italy.

THE IMPERIAL METAL

Although it is impossible to reconstruct the political and social organization of the states and cities of the Neolithic period (10,000–7000 BCE) because there are no written sources from the era, archaeologists have suggested that these cultures might have been relatively democratic and egalitarian, with few social divisions based on gender, status, wealth and property. The large Neolithic city of Çatalhöyük in Turkey, for example, has no public buildings or temples, and its citizens appear to have led a communal existence, sharing their resources equitably.

As we learned in the previous chapter, the beginning of the Metal Age with the working of copper during the Chalcolithic (7000–c. 5300 BCE) began a process of social stratification that divided metallurgists, along with a class of wealthy and powerful individuals who could afford to commission and buy metal artifacts, from the rest of the population, who continued to use stone tools. These trends became even more pronounced during the Bronze Age, which witnessed the development of major imperial civilizations across the whole of the Old World, in Egypt, Mesopotamia, Minoan Crete, Mycenaean Greece, Syria, Hittite Anatolia, Elamite Iran, Harappan India and China.

CHOP, CHOP
A bronze battle-axe kept a much better edge than a copper axe.

All these cultures were highly centralized monarchies, ruled by kings who controlled the bulk of available resources, which they lavished on the construction of palaces, temples and monumental tombs. More than the control of gold or silver, their power and wealth depended on the control of the trade in tin, copper and bronze, and the manufacture of bronze artifacts, the most important of which were weapons. While copper had been suitable for the manufacture of axes, knives, chisels and arrow heads, the stronger yet more pliable bronze allowed for the production of an entirely new weapon: the sword, which appeared across the world from Celtic Europe to China. Along with the sword came bronze armour, helmets and shields, which afforded much better protection to the warrior and gave him a huge advantage over foes armed with Stone Age weapons. Another worldwide military development of the Bronze Age is the appearance of the chariot after the earlier domestication of the horse in Central Asia.

CHINESE BLING
Ancient Chinese bronze vessels demonstrated an individual's wealth and power.

DING DONG!
This set of 65 bronze bells found in a Chinese tomb indicates the royal status of its occupant.

Together these two inventions of the Bronze Age transformed warfare. The greatest work of Greek epic poetry, Homer's *Iliad* (c. 8th century BCE), describes a conflict between two mighty Bronze Age powers: Mycenaean Greece and Troy. Mounted on their horse-drawn chariots, encased in their bronze armour, and fighting with bronze-tipped lances, arrows and swords, Achilles, Hector, Paris and Odysseus fought duel-like encounters on the battlefields of Troy.

The superpowers of the period – the Minoans, Mycenaeans, Egyptians, Hittites, Phoenicians, Babylonians, Elamites, Harappans and Chinese – acquired extensive territories through their control of bronze technology and trade, and as they expanded they came into conflict with one another. Centralization and international trade also brought about more peaceful developments, including the evolution of writing, which began in Egypt with hieroglyphs, in Mesopotamia with cuneiform, and in China with the early versions of Chinese characters found on oracle bones and bronze vessels. Writing was not only needed to record the mighty deeds of god-kings but also for the far more mundane purposes of keeping inventories and writing trading contracts.

Another important economic function of bronze, although it wasn't widely used until the Bronze Age, is the use of the metal for the first types of coinage. The earliest bronze coins were made in China in the tenth century BCE in the shape of cowry shells, which had been used as an earlier form of currency. Later Chinese bronze 'coins' were shaped like shovels, hoes and knives, before they took the shape of the round coinage we are familiar with today. Bronze coinage was also minted in India in the sixth century BCE, and in ancient Turkey and Greece, where it was used alongside electrum, gold and silver coinage.

SYSTEM HISTORY

✦

Although the terms 'Bronze' and 'Iron' Ages existed in ancient Greek literature, as well as in the traditions of other Old World cultures, these referred to mythological rather than historical periods. The formal use of the three-age system, dividing early European history into the Stone, Bronze and Iron Ages, dates from the early nineteenth century. In 1816, the Danish antiquarian Christian Thomsen (1788–1865) was appointed director of what would later become the National Museum of Denmark. When he organized the artifacts in the collection for display, rather than presenting them stylistically or as an undated evolution from stone to iron implements, he attempted to arrange them chronologically. In considering all the objects in an archaeological find to establish its date, he laid the foundations of scientific archaeology.

THE ART OF BRONZE

Bronze has played a significant role in the developments of the arts, notably sculpture, the decorative arts and music. Among the earliest cast decorative pieces are the bronzes of China's Shang Dynasty (1600–1046 BCE). Chinese bronzes include highly ornate vessels for food, water and wine and musical instruments, which were used for ritual purposes, and were buried as grave goods. Many of these pieces were produced by the lost-wax casting process, which was used in later periods in India, Egypt and Greece to produce statuary. Few ancient Greek bronze statues have survived, but many are known from later Roman copies. Variations on the lost-wax process are still used to produce bronze sculpture today. The ancient Chinese cast bronze zhong bells as ceremonial musical instruments (see box, p. 18), and in the Western world a bronze alloy known as bell metal (consisting of 78 percent copper and 22 percent tin) was the favoured material for making church bells because of its resistance to corrosion and reverberation when struck.

The end of the eastern Mediterranean Bronze Age, in the twelfth century B.C., was one of history's most frightful turning points. For those who experienced it, it was a calamity. The End of the Bronze Age *(1995) by Robert Drews*

Bronze and its related alloy, brass, has survived into the modern age, but the Bronze Age, and the civilizations it created, disappeared in a cataclysm known as the 'Bronze Age Collapse' (c. 1200–1150 BCE). The mighty empires and kingdoms of the eastern Mediterranean, Egypt, Syria, Mycenae, Cyprus, the Hittite Empire and Babylonia, were all extinguished, and the great trading networks they had created to procure tin and copper were lost. The Mediterranean world entered a first Dark Age, which, according to archaeologists, was a period far bleaker than the centuries following the collapse of the Roman Empire in Western Europe that we now call the Dark Ages. When civilization arose once more in the Near East and Southern Europe, it would be based not on bronze but on another metal: iron.

SURVIVOR
A rare surviving Greek bronze of an athlete shows the skill of ancient craftsmen.

Alabaster

Alabastrum

Type: Crystal; carbonate mineral

Origin: Found in sedimentary rocks and mineral deposits in hot springs

Chemical formula: $CaCO_3$

✦ Industrial
✦ **Cultural**
✦ Commercial
✦ Scientific

Now when Jesus was in Bethany, in the house of Simon the leper, There came unto him a woman having an alabaster box of very precious ointment, and poured it on his head, as he sat at meat.

Matthew 26:6–7, King James Bible

In modern usage, alabaster refers to two distinct minerals: gypsum alabaster, which is covered in a separate entry (see pp. 96–99), and calcite alabaster, which is the subject of this entry. Long admired for its translucency and fine grain, alabaster was used in antiquity to make grave goods, statuary and containers.

Grave concerns

The ancient Egyptians developed extremely complex customs for the burial and aftercare of the dead. At first, the elaborate mummification process and its associated magical rituals – the construction of magnificent tombs, and the provision of lavish grave goods – were reserved for the pharaoh and his immediate family, but in later periods, mummification became democratized, and nobles and commoners were embalmed and buried in sarcophagi in preparation for the afterlife. Central to these beliefs was the idea that the physical body had to be preserved to ensure the survival of the deceased's spirit in the afterlife. We will examine the process of mummification in detail in the entry on natron (see pp. 114–119), but in addition to preserving the body – the musculature, skeleton and skin – the embalmers removed and preserved the major internal organs that would otherwise have decayed and led to the gradual deterioration of the corpse. These were placed in containers known as canopic boxes or jars, which were often made of alabaster.

Egyptian medical knowledge, whatever their modern New Age admirers may claim, was limited. They believed that the centre of human consciousness was located in the heart, which was left inside the mummified body to be judged in the afterlife by the god Thot. The remaining internal organs were removed, embalmed and placed in four separate containers, each dedicated to deities known as the Sons of Horus: the falcon-headed Qebhsenuef looked after

Skin deep
A beautiful complexion is often compared to the luster of alabaster.

the intestines; the jackal-headed Duamutef looked after the stomach; the baboon-headed Hapy looked after the lungs; and Imsety, who had a human head, looked after the liver. Other alabaster artifacts found in Egyptian tombs include statues, vases and cosmetics bottles and jars.

MUMMY DEAREST

Some of the most extraordinary objects found in ancient Egypt are sarcophagi hollowed out of giant blocks of alabaster. One of the finest,

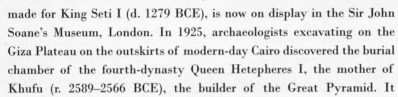

made for King Seti I (d. 1279 BCE), is now on display in the Sir John Soane's Museum, London. In 1925, archaeologists excavating on the Giza Plateau on the outskirts of modern-day Cairo discovered the burial chamber of the fourth-dynasty Queen Hetepheres I, the mother of Khufu (r. 2589–2566 BCE), the builder of the Great Pyramid. It contained rich grave goods, including gilded furniture; an alabaster canopic box; and a sealed alabaster sarcophagus. Overjoyed, the archaeologists thought they had discovered the first surviving royal mummy from the Pyramid Age.

From the dimensions of the small chamber and conditions of the tomb, archaeologists concluded that this was a reburial after the queen's original tomb, probably near her husband's pyramid in Dashur, north of Giza, had been broken into and robbed soon after her burial. When the sarcophagus was opened, however, it was found to be empty. The robbers had removed the mummy to strip it of its golden jewellery and amulets, but had been disturbed before they could make off with the other precious grave goods. However, the presence of food offerings left by the pharaoh for his mother suggested that officials had not dared tell him that his mother's mummy was missing. The empty coffin had been laboriously carried from Dashur to Giza, reburied in the new burial chamber 30 m (100 ft) underground, without the pharaoh suspecting what had really happened.

BECAUSE YOU'RE WORTH IT

✦

Before glass became widely available, alabaster fulfilled several of its functions. Thin sheets of alabaster were used in windows, but its most common use was to make containers and vases. In ancient Egypt, bulbous bottles modeled on the trunks of palm trees were carved from alabaster to hold cosmetics, scented oils and perfumes. The Greeks called this type of bottle an 'alabastron' after their Egyptian originals, but manufactured them in pottery, glass and metal. Alabastra based on Egyptian and Greek models were made all over the ancient Near East and Europe.

Alum

Alumen

Type: Mineral salts

Origin: Man-made

Chemical formula: AB(SO$_4$)$_2$ 12H$_2$O; Al2(SO$_4$)$_3$

✦ **INDUSTRIAL**
✦ CULTURAL
✦ **COMMERCIAL**
✦ SCIENTIFIC

CRYSTAL CLEAN
Alum crystals, or *tawas*, are marketed as natural deodorants.

The word alum refers to several mineral salts with different industrial, medical, food-technology and cosmetic applications through the ages. Among the most important historically was the use of aluminium sulphate (Al$_2$(SO$_4$)$_3$) as a chemical fixative in the dyeing of yarn and cloth.

COLOUR CONSCIOUS

In the modern world, we take the colour of our manufactured goods for granted, but in Neolithic times, for the most part, human products were the dull grey of stone, the muted browns, ochres and reds of clay, and the off-white, black or brown of untreated animal skins and yarns. The vivid colours found in nature's flowers, insects and birds must have charmed early humans but also made them feel very chromatically inadequate.

Of course, there is no practical reason why pottery should be anything but brown, nor should cloth be any colour but off-white – the addition of colour does not in any way improve their form or function. But being human, especially in the early periods of human history when we lived very close to the natural world, has always been about much more than functionality. In addition to the enjoyment of colour for its own sake, it allowed our ancestors to express differences in social status (imperial purple, for example), in religious belief (such as Islamic green), and national allegiance (the red, white and blue of several national flags).

DYED IN THE WOOL

There are many substances found in nature – in plants, minerals, shellfish and insects – that will yield bright stains in a wide range of hues. The problem, however, is how to ensure that the stain is permanent and does not leach out when the cloth is worn, rained on or washed. Just as there are natural dyes, there are natural fixatives, or 'mordants', that will fix and enhance the colour of yarn and finished cloth (though in the case of stale urine – see quote opposite – one wonders precisely what experiments led to that discovery!). Another natural fixative is one of the many chemicals known as 'alum' (aluminium sulphate), which was used from antiquity in a number of dye processes to obtain colourfast yellows, greens, reds, pinks and purples.

Although the expression 'dyed in the wool' has now taken a slightly negative meaning, describing someone who is politically and socially conservative and who finds it difficult to change his or her views, its original connotations were dependable and firm. The expression came from the textile industry, where it was used to describe woolen yarn that was dyed before it was woven into cloth. The ability to dye yarn increased its value to the producer who might otherwise receive a low price for his raw, uncoloured wool. The export of woolen yarn and cloth was the basis for the economic success of England during the Middle Ages. However, when Henry VIII (1491–1547) declared independence from the Church of Rome to obtain a divorce, he unwittingly cut off England's supply of dyer's alum, the bulk of which came from the papal states. In order to replace it, English dyers turned to native sources of aluminium sulphate by combining shale with human urine.

We shall never know by what chances primitive man discovered that salt, vinegar from fermenting fruit, natural alum, and stale urine helped to fix and enhance the colours of his yarns, but for many centuries these four substances were used as mordants.

A Dyer's Manual *(1982) by Jill Goodwin*

DEODORANT CRYSTAL

✦

Potassium alum $(KAl(SO_4)_2)$, also known as potash alum or *tawas*, is a natural astringent and antiseptic. In recent years it has been marketed in the West as a natural alternative to chemical spray-on and roll-on deodorants. Used in this form for centuries in Southeast Asia, tawas kills the bacteria that cause body odour. Alum is prescribed both externally and internally in Indian Ayurvedic medicine, where it is known as *saurashtri*, and in Traditional Chinese Medicine, where it is known as *ming fan*.

Aluminium
Aluminum

Type: Metal

Origin: Extremely rare as a native metal, it is usually extracted from bauxite

Chemical formula: Al

A luminum, or aluminium, depending on which side of the pond you reside, is the most common metallic element found on Earth. Despite its ubiquity, it was not isolated and produced as a pure metal until the nineteenth century, and only came into widespread use in the twentieth. In the modern world, aluminium is everywhere in our homes and workplaces. If we had to choose a name for the industrial–consumer society that emerged in the mid-twentieth century, we could call it the 'Aluminium Age'.

+ *INDUSTRIAL*
+ CULTURAL
+ *COMMERCIAL*
+ SCIENTIFIC

THE PINNACLE OF THE ALUMINIUM AGE

Casting around for a single object that would encapsulate all the achievements – technological, commercial, social, artistic and economic – of the period, I considered various products. Should it be the aeroplane, many of whose components are made of the metal? Or maybe the computer, which likewise makes extensive use of aluminium? However, after some thought, there was one product that seemed to stand out above all others as a worthy representative of our consumer society and way of life: the aluminium beverage can, used to package beers and sodas.

The choice of the beverage can might strike the reader as a bit of a joke, but the more I thought about it, the more I decided that it was indeed the right artifact to go for. First, the beverage can is made of almost pure aluminium alloyed with small quantities of other metals; second, the can is one of the most common mass-produced items currently manufactured in the metal industry, with 100 billion cans produced yearly in the U.S. alone (that's about one per day per American citizen); third, the manufacturing process is a marvel of modern automation; and fourth, the can's contents (beers and sodas) function, design and marketing make it perfectly representative of our consumer lifestyles. If Earth were suddenly destroyed by an asteroid and the only thing that survived were a single beverage can, the crew of a passing alien ship coming across it floating in the interstellar void could use it to reconstruct much of our technology and culture, our physical

PRECIOUS
Because initially aluminium was so difficult to make, it was more expensive than gold.

appearance, physiology and biochemistry. The can, which was once the ultimate symbol of our throwaway culture, now leads the way in recycling – a symbol of the new concern for the environmental wellbeing of our planet and the preservation of its diminishing resources.

MORE PRECIOUS THAN GOLD

Although aluminium is the most common metallic element in Earth's crust, it is very rarely found as a native metal. It was only identified as an element in the early nineteenth century by the British chemist and inventor Humphry Davy (1778–1829), who discovered that it was the metallic base of alum, which is why he decided to call it aluminium. The Danish chemist Hans Christian Oersted (1777–1851) was one of the first scientists to succeed in producing the first aluminium metal in the first quarter of the nineteenth century, but the various extraction processes were time-consuming, expensive and yielded tiny quantities of the metal. During the first half of the nineteenth century, aluminium was regarded as an expensive novelty with few practical applications.

THE THIRTEENTH ELEMENT

✦

The Russian love affair with the metal is celebrated in *Aluminum: the Thirteenth Element*, a 240–page tribute to the element published by the world's largest aluminium company, United Company RUSAL, headquartered in Moscow. Although unlikely to ever make the *New York Times* bestseller list, the book covers the history of the element from antiquity to the modern period, with special reference to the aluminium industry in the former Soviet Union and modern-day Russia. Once the world's leading aluminium producer, Russia has since been overtaken by the People's Republic of China.

CROWNING GLORY
The Washington Monument was capped with the largest aluminium block produced at that time.

For a time, aluminium was more rare and costly than gold, and it was displayed with pride at international exhibitions worldwide. The builders of the Washington Monument decided to cap the giant obelisk with the largest block of aluminium cast at that time, weighing 2.85 kg (just over 4 lb), to act as the monument's lightning rod. The French emperor Napoleon III (1808–73) was fascinated by the new lightweight metal because of its possible military applications and also because of its rarity. At an imperial banquet, the ordinary guests had to make do with gold cutlery, but the guests of honour were furnished with aluminium cutlery. Considering that the cheapest pots, pans and utensils are now made out of aluminium, today that gesture would be considered quite an insult.

In 1886 two inventors, the American Charles Hall (1863–1914) and the Frenchman Paul Héroult (1863–1914), working independently, discovered a commercially viable means of producing aluminium by electrolysing alumina salts in a solution of molten cryolite. Their method, which became known as the Hall–Héroult process, was soon used to produce thousands of tons of the metal, reducing its cost by a factor of 200 and making aluminium available for a wide range of industrial and domestic uses. Aluminium is easy to work and durable, has good resistance to corrosion, and is lighter than iron or steel. One of its earliest practical applications was in construction, where its weight-to-strength ratio made it a particularly attractive material. The timing of Hall and Héroult's discovery and its commercial development are not coincidental. The process requires large amounts of electricity, and its development and commercialization coincided with large-scale electrification in Europe and North America.

FOILED AGAIN

✦

One of the most familiar domestic applications of aluminium is aluminium foil, which is sometimes mistakenly called 'tin' foil in the UK because of the earlier product made of that metal that it superseded. Aluminium foil was first produced in Switzerland in 1910 and in the U.S. in 1913. Aluminium packaging protects food and beverages from light, oxygen, bacteria and bad smells, with the added advantage of being non-toxic itself, vastly increasing a product's shelf life.

Planes, trains and automobiles

Aluminium has a huge range of applications in the modern world. In the home, most kitchens are equipped with a roll of aluminium foil for cooking and wrapping leftovers. The metal is also widely used in construction, so if you live in a modern house or apartment block, your door and window frames are probably made of aluminium. The metal's lightness makes it a natural choice for constructs where weight is critical to the composition, such as aircraft design. Although the first cars with aluminium bodies date back to the mid-twentieth century, the higher production cost of the metal meant that most cars were made of steel. However, with the inexorable rise in crude oil prices in the late twentieth century, the weight reduction allowed by the use of aluminium car bodies and components has now made the use of the metal economically viable in the automobile industry. The first all-aluminium model rolled off the Audi assembly line in Germany in 1999. Although science has given us many new materials, the versatility of aluminium means that we shall continue to live in the Aluminium Age for decades to come.

> **And soon the earth was covered with plastic bags and aluminum cans and paper plates and disposable bottles and there was nowhere to sit down or walk, and Man shook his head and cried: Look at this Godawful mess.**
>
> *Art Buchwald (1925–2007)*

LIGHT VEHICLE
With ever-increasing oil prices, the light all-aluminium car has become cost-effective.

Asbestos

Amiantos

Type: Silicate mineral

Origin: Extracted from six serpentine and amphibole minerals

Chemical formula:
$Mg_3(Si_2O_5)(OH)_4$;
$Fe_7Si_8O_{22}(OH)_2$

✦ **INDUSTRIAL**

✦ CULTURAL

✦ COMMERCIAL

✦ SCIENTIFIC

Although it might appear that divine providence has provided humans with a range of minerals, each one suited to a stage of their technological development, in a few instances, a material once thought to be a boon to humanity turned out to be a curse. Such is the case of asbestos, whose use triggered the most complex, costly and long-lasting industrial illness and injury litigation in history.

THE MIRACLE FABRIC

The ancient Greeks and Romans knew that cloth woven from asbestos (or more correctly *amiantos*) was not damaged by fire, and they considered it to be a magical material that warded off evil influences (see box, p.33). They also had practical uses for the mineral: to make everlasting wicks for funerary lamps and shrouds for cremations that allowed bodies to be burnt and the mortal remains kept separate from the ashes of the funeral pyre. The first-century Roman writer and naturalist Pliny the Elder, although he made many errors in his description of the mineral, was among the first to note that asbestos weavers suffered from respiratory diseases. Despite this early awareness of the health hazards of asbestos, it would take another two millennia and countless deaths for its use to be controlled in the developed world.

During the Middle Ages, there are a few references to asbestos cloth. The Emperor Charlemagne (747–814), the first 'emperor of the Romans' in Western Europe since the fifth century CE (although he himself was a Frank, a descendant of the barbarians who had brought the Western Roman Empire to an end), had a tablecloth made of asbestos. After meals, he liked to amaze his dinner guests by throwing the cloth into the fire to clean it and pulling it from the flames unscathed. Pope Alexander III and the mythical Prester John, believed to be the ruler of a Christian kingdom in Central Asia, were both said to have robes woven from asbestos.

The rarity of asbestos in pre-industrial times combined with the much shorter life spans of average humans meant that deaths caused by exposure to the mineral would have been minimal. Its widespread industrial use in the developed world dates back only to the nineteenth century. At first, it was woven into fabric to be

APPLICATIONS
Although asbestos was known in antiquity, its large-scale industrial use dates back to the nineteenth century.

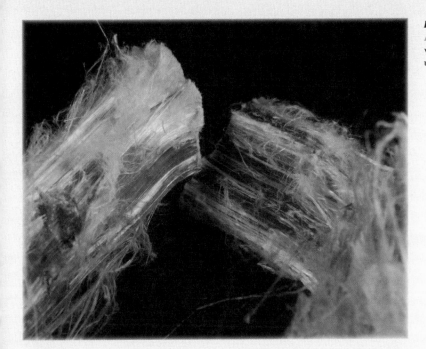

used as insulation. By the twentieth century, asbestos was widely used in building: in fire-retardant coatings, concrete bricks, pipes and pipe insulation, flooring, ceiling, roofing, garden furniture and fireproof drywall. In the 1950s, the American cigarette brand Kent introduced the first filter-tipped cigarette, which used asbestos in its patented 'Micronite' filters. Another major source of asbestos particles in the environment was due to its use to make the break pads and shoes of automobiles until the 1990s.

Asbestos is not one mineral, but is made up of six different fibrous minerals: chrysotile, amosite, anthophyllite, actinolite, crocidolite and tremolite. The fibres of chrysotile are serpentine (curly) and those of the other five are amphibole (needle-shaped). Chrysotile, also known as 'white' asbestos, is the most commonly found asbestos mineral in Earth's crust and accounts for 95 percent of asbestos products. The remaining 5 percent are made up of amosite, or 'brown' asbestos, which is mined in South Africa, and crocidolite, or 'blue' asbestos, mined in South Africa and Australia, which is also the most dangerous to humans. The world's current leading producers of asbestos are Canada and Russia.

> **In the home build with DURASBESTOS, the imperishable building material. Better than wood because it requires no paint, is fire resisting and white ant proof. More economical because it is easily and quickly fixed without waste.** *Australian press advertisement for an asbestos product, 1929*

THE INVISIBLE KILLER

Asbestos is not a poison that kills quickly by attacking and breaking down the body's tissues and organs as arsenic and mercury are known to do. Typically, illness and death from asbestos-related diseases are caused by exposure to the mineral over a long period of time. Most victims are men and women who have worked in asbestos mining or manufacture, as well as family members, who have been exposed to dust brought home on the clothes and bodies of asbestos workers. Another group at risk are construction workers who regularly handle or remove asbestos materials when renovating buildings, unless they wear respirators and protective clothing. However, to reassure those readers who may have been exposed to asbestos while carrying out their own home improvements, they are very unlikely to fall ill from a single exposure.

The fibres of asbestos are composed of extremely fine, fragile molecular lattices. Even carrying finished asbestos products will disturb and break the fibres into microscopic pieces that are invisible to the naked eye, and cause them to be released into the environment where humans will inhale them. Long-term exposure to asbestos fibres is associated with two diseases: asbestosis and mesothelioma. The former is a chronic inflammation of the lungs caused by scarring by asbestos fibres. In the

SLOW BUT DEADLY
Asbestos-related diseases are caused by long-term exposure to the mineral's microscopic fibres.

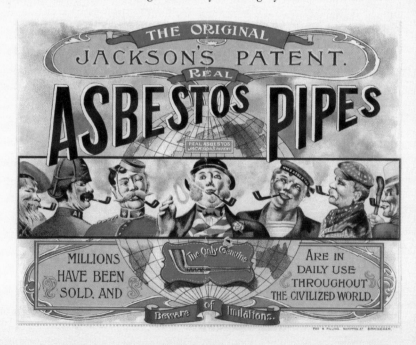

KILLER SMOKES
Asbestos was once used to make smoking-related goods, including pipes and cigarette filters.

most advanced and severe cases, the reduction of lung capacity may induce respiratory or heart failure and lead to death. Mesothelioma is an asbestos-related cancer of the mesothelium, the protective lining that covers the body's internal organs. Symptoms of mesothelioma may not appear until 20–50 years after exposure to asbestos.

Pliny's warnings about the dangers of asbestos went unheeded until the late nineteenth century. In 1899, the British pathologist Montague Murray conducted a post-mortem on the body of an asbestos factory worker, and testified that he had found asbestos fibres in the man's lungs, which he believed had contributed to his death. Subsequent cases in the U.S. and UK provided mounting evidence of a link between the disease and the material, but the first diagnosis of asbestosis was not made in the UK until 1924. A firm link between asbestos and mesothelioma was established in the 1940s. By then the major U.S. asbestos manufacturers had realized the dangers to their workers, and they sponsored their own medical research into asbestos-related diseases, but on the condition that the findings would be kept secret. Between the 1940s and 1980s, U.S. asbestos corporations managed to suppress the medical evidence and successfully lobbied against legislation protecting both asbestos workers and the public.

In the 1980s, governments across the developed world finally began to act to control the importation and use of asbestos products. The European Union, Japan, Australia and New Zealand instituted total bans on the use of asbestos and instituted asbestos-removal legislation from schools, hospitals, other public buildings, and later from private homes. Sadly, asbestos continues in widespread use in many countries in the developing world. In 1989, the Environmental Protection Agency in the U.S. issued the Asbestos Ban and Phase Out Rule. The rule was challenged and overturned in the courts in 1991, which means that asbestos can still be used in consumer products in the U.S. The first lawsuits filed by asbestos workers began in the 1920s; class action suits continue to this day, being the most complex and lengthy litigations in history, with an estimated cost of $200 billion in the U.S. alone.

Amber

Anbar

Type: Organic mineral

Origin: Fossilized tree resin

Chemical formula: $C_{10}H_{16}O$

The fossilized sap of prehistoric trees, amber is a semi-precious gemstone of organic origin. Traded along the 'Amber Road' that linked the Baltic Sea with the Mediterranean world, amber has been a prized commodity since Neolithic times. Although much imitated and faked in the modern period, genuine amber is still popular as a decorative stone used in personal adornment, especially in Russia and the Baltic region.

✦ INDUSTRIAL

✦ **CULTURAL**

✦ **COMMERCIAL**

✦ **SCIENTIFIC**

NATURE'S PLASTIC

Before the invention of coloured glass and plastics, amber would have appeared to be a miraculous, semi-magical material. Once polished, the most prized pieces have an attractive, translucent golden-brown hue – as rich and smooth as honey. Less desirable pieces are an opaque brownish-yellow. Amber is soft enough to be carved, and it can be reheated so that it can be worked into different shapes. The fossilized sap of trees and ferns tens of millions of years old, amber sometimes has 'inclusions' – organic matter trapped in the sap as it is set. The most sought after are animal inclusions (see quote) of insects and invertebrates, some long extinct. These not only have curiosity value, but are also of enormous scientific interest, as they preserve specimens in their entirety, rather than the 2D of usual stone fossils (unfortunately, they will not provide us with a means of restoring life to long-extinct species of mammals and reptiles; see the box opposite).

> **Whence we see spiders, flies, or ants entombed and preserved forever in amber, a more than royal tomb.**
>
> *Sir Francis Bacon (1561–1626)*

When amber is exposed to UV light, it fluoresces in different colours, including blue, yellow, green and red, depending on its place of origin. A characteristic of amber from the Dominican Republic is that when it is viewed under direct sunlight, it is an iridescent blue – hence its name 'blue amber' – but when viewed against direct sunlight, it is golden brown like Baltic amber. The colour is not caused by pigmentation in the amber itself but is literally a trick of the light as it passes through the material in different directions.

Unfortunately, it is amber's similarity to artificial plastics and polymer
resins that has proved to be its downfall in the modern period. Amber
has not only lost its unique appearance, but it is also very easy to fake
with modern materials. The fakers have developed many tricks to fool
the careless and the gullible. In addition to out-and-out fakes made of
plastics and synthetic polymers, they pass off imma-
ture amber, known as copal, as the genuine article.
Although copal is also solidified tree resin, it is of much
more recent origin – sometimes only a few hundred
years old – and its structure has not stabilized
completely, meaning that it is not as dense or strong as
the genuine article. In addition, real amber can be
heated, reworked and several small fragments can be
amalgamated into a larger piece; it can also be combined
with copal to make a composite material. The fakers
add plant and animal inclusions, passing off modern
insects as their prehistoric ancestors, in order to increase
the value of their fakes. The easiest and least destructive test to tell amber from plastic is to illuminate it
with UV light to check whether it fluoresces.

THE LORDS OF AMBER

We owe the name amber to the Arabic *anbar*. The
Arabs, however, confused amber with ambergris, a
substance secreted by sperm whales and used in the
perfume industry. Archaeologists estimate that the
trade in amber, along what is now known as the 'Amber
Road' from the Baltic to the Mediterranean, began in
the Neolithic period (10,000–7000 years BP). Like the

DINOSAUR AMBER

✦

In the *Jurassic Park* novels
and films, scientists resurrect
dinosaurs by extracting their DNA
from blood taken from mosqui-
toes preserved in amber.
Although theoretically possible,
sadly, with our present technology, this is not practically
achievable. The oldest mosquito-
like insect found in amber dates
back to around 100 million years
BP, when Earth was populated
by the dinosaurs. BUT (and it is
indeed a very big but), even
sealed within amber, DNA
degrades, and the sampled
dino-DNA would be incomplete,
out of sequence, and mixed up
with the mosquito's own genetic
material, hence extremely difficult
or impossible to reconstruct.

more famous 'Silk Road' that links China with the Mediterranean world, the Amber Road was not one road but a network of overland and river routes from Northern Europe southwards. Like the commodities traded on the Silk Road, amber was not carried by merchants all the way from the Baltic to Egypt, for example, where amber was found in the tomb of Tutankhamun (c. 1341–1323 BCE). It would have been traded between neighbors, both as a natural stone and as finished objects, and gradually made its way south in a complex web of commercial exchanges that brought the products of the Baltic to southern Europe and the Near East, and goods from Egypt and the Levant to Scandinavia and Russia.

In 1099, the forces of the First Crusade recaptured Jerusalem, the historical Holy Land and its Christian sites, and much of what is now southern Turkey, Armenia, Lebanon, Syria and Israel, from a divided Islamic world empire more concerned with its own internal power struggles than with stopping a small Western invading army. The shock of the fall of Jerusalem, which is the third holiest site in Islam after Mecca and Medina, galvanized the Muslim states to mount a counteroffensive. The Kingdoms of Outremer,

RESTORATION
Looted by the Germans, Russia's Amber Chamber has been painstakingly reconstructed.

NORTHERN TREASURE
Baltic amber was one of
the main sources of wealth
for the Teutonic Knights.

however, managed to survive until the late thirteenth century. One of
the legacies of the crusades was the creation of several orders of knights,
including the Knights Templar, the Knights Hospitaller and the Teutonic
Knights, who had taken up the Cross to recapture and defend the
holy places.

Once they had been expelled from the Near East, the orders found
new roles in Europe. Some retained their mission to fight the westwards
spread of Islam, but others, such as the Teutonic Knights, established
themselves in northern Europe, parts of which were still pagan. Like the
Knights Templar, the well-disciplined and well-organized Teutonic
Knights became so powerful that they were able to challenge the
authority of local rulers to establish their own empire. After the conversion of the last north European pagans in 1387, the knights turned to
expanding their political power and developing their commercial empire.
Until the early fifteenth century, they controlled the lucrative trade
between the Baltic and southern and western Europe,
and called themselves, the 'Lords of Amber', after
one of the most valuable commodities that
they traded. As the developing national
states of Poland and Lithuania became
more established, they challenged the
supremacy of the Teutonic Knights. The
Poles and Lithuanians broke the power of the
knights in the Battle of Grunwald in 1410.
The order survived until the early nineteenth
century, however, when Emperor Napoleon I
(1769–1821) finally disbanded it.

REAL OR FAKE?
A popular gemstone used
to make jewellery, amber
is easy to fake with modern
polymer resins.

Silver

Argentum

Type: Precious metal

Origin: Rarely found as native silver, and usually extracted from mineral ores

Chemical formula: Ag

+ INDUSTRIAL
+ *CULTURAL*
+ *COMMERCIAL*
+ SCIENTIFIC

THE IMPURE METAL
Unlike gold, which is found in nuggets, silver is found in ores associated with other metals, especially lead.

S ilver has been minted into coins since antiquity. It remained a major medium of exchange until the introduction of banknotes. In the fifth century BCE, the fortuitous discovery of a rich deposit of silver ore in Greece changed the course of history, and helped preserve Western European civilisation. Today silver, though far less valuable than gold or platinum, remains a favourite metal for the manufacture of jewellery, household ornaments, tableware, sporting trophies, medals and commemorative coins.

THE EMPIRE STRIKES

Were it not for the fortuitous discovery of silver deposits in Attica, eastern Greece, in the fifth century BCE, the world might be a very different place. When we think of the historical threats to Europe from the Near East and Asia, we might recall the invasions of the Roman Empire by Attila the Hun (d. 453 CE) in the fifth century, of Europe by militant Islam in the seventh century, and by the Mongols in the thirteenth century. However, one of the greatest threats to the Western world dates back to the fifth century BCE, when the Persian Empire twice attempted to conquer the 'cradle' of Western civilisation, the ancient Greek city-state of Athens. In 480 BCE, the city fell and was razed to the ground by the Persians, who gleefully smashed the Acropolis, burning its archaic temples and statues.

Athens's population and army, however, had wisely abandoned the city, and the Athenians and their allies went on to score two extraordinary, and as it turned out for the future of European civilisation, crucial victories: the first at sea in the Straits of Salamis (480 BCE) and the second on land at Platea (479 BCE). The battles halted the Persian Empire's relentless westwards expansion, and fatally weakened it, opening the way in the fourth century for Alexander the Great of Macedon (356–323 BCE) to topple the Persian King of kings Darius III (c. 380–330 BCE) and conquer a Hellenistic empire that stretched from Greece to modern-day Pakistan.

But let's wind back the clock to the year 499 BCE, to the time when Greece stood alone against the might of the

GREECE TRIUMPHANT
The defeat of the Persian
invasions allowed
Alexander the Great to
conquer the Persian
Empire.

greatest empire the world had ever seen: Persia. Greece was then not a unified country, but a patchwork of city and island states, covering mainland Greece, the Aegean islands and the coastal region of Asia Minor (now Turkey) – Asian Ionia. For centuries, the Greeks had been more likely to fight one another than an external enemy, but the threat of conquest or annihilation managed to unite them temporarily. Asian Ionia succumbed to Persian pressure and submitted to Darius's rule, though its allegiance was temporary and always subject to Persian victory. At the beginning of the Greco-Persian Wars (499–449 BCE), things seemed to be going Persia's way. The empire easily crushed a revolt in Asian Ionia, supported by Athens and other Greek cities, and moved to punish the Greeks for their presumption. The empire had untold wealth through its control of the Near East and Egypt, and considerable military manpower, including an Indian elephant corps, the first to see action against European troops.

The vast army mobilised by Darius I (550–486 BCE) appeared to be unstoppable, and the fall of Greece imminent. The growing Western European world that stood behind Greece – then consisting of Greek colonies in southern Italy, Sicily and southern France; the Phoenician kingdom of Carthage in North Africa and its colonies in southern Spain; the Etruscans and still partially civilised Latins of central Italy; and the Celtic peoples of northern Italy, Gaul, Iberia and Britain – would have been no match for Persia had she managed to overcome Athens and Sparta.

SILVER TWENTY-FIFTH

✦

The value of silver is underscored by its use in the Western world to mark the achievement of twenty-five years of marriage. The earliest reference to silver wedding anniversaries dates back to medieval Germany, when friends and family of a couple married for twenty-five years presented the wife with a silver wreath. To have been married that long was probably a rare occurrence during the Middle Ages, when the average life expectancy was less than 40 years.

PAX PERSIANA?

A Persian victory under Darius or his successor Xerxes I (519–465 BCE) presents us with a fascinating alternative world history; one in which the Old World would not have been Hellenised by Alexander the Great, but 'Persianised' by Darius and his heirs. The Persians – despite their bizarre portrayal in the film *300* (2007) – were not bloodthirsty monsters dressed in outlandish clothes and wearing heavy makeup with multiple tattoos and face piercings. To the Greek victors (who wrote the history of the war), they represented all that was worst in Asiatic despotism, decadence and corruption, but Alexander, who succeeded Darius III as ruler of the known world, turned out to be just as despotic, violent and corrupt: he brought an end to Greek independence and Athenian democracy, just as Darius and Xerxes had threatened to, and his conquests laid the groundwork for the even more despotic, violent and culturally monolithic Roman Empire.

The Persians, like many ancient empire builders, did not seek to create a culturally unified empire, imposing their own language, religion and institutions on conquered peoples. When they occupied a country, they appointed a Persian administrator, or *satrap*, to replace the former ruler, but they ruled through the local institutions and elites. In a very real sense, this was a fatal miscalculation. While later empires, such as those of the Macedonians and Romans, forcefully imposed their culture on conquered peoples, the Persians did not. However, that is not to say that a later, more farsighted Persian ruler might not have seen Persianisation as the only way for the empire to survive.

Although the Greeks called the Persians 'barbarians', it was the Greeks who were the true barbarians. Persia had an ancient predecessor culture, Elam, which dated back to the fourth millennium BCE, and the empire included the first civilisations of the Near East: Babylonia, Egypt and Phoenicia, compared to which, the Greeks, for all their vaunted achievements in mathematics, philosophy and democracy, were uncivilised newcomers. The Persians were Zoroastrians, a sophisticated religion based not on a multitude of

MINTED
The silver *denarius* was the main denomination used in the Western Roman Empire.

gods in human or animal form but on a dualistic theology based on the conflict between good and light; darkness and evil. Zoroastrianism, although not a monotheistic faith, played an important foundational role in the history of the three 'Religions of the Book': Judaism, Christianity and Islam. In other fields, such as architecture, the arts and literature, Persia was a worthy match for classical Greece. Hence a world dominated by Persia would have been very different but not necessarily less civilised or accomplished.

SILVER-PLATED
In regions of the world where gold was scarce, currencies were backed by silver bullion.

TRUST IN ATHENS' 'WOODEN WALLS'

Around 483 BCE, the Athenians struck not gold, which is extremely rare in Greece, but a rich deposit of silver-bearing ores at Laureion (Laurium) on the east coast of Attica. Athens was famously the inventor of 'democracy', but this assertion has to be qualified: the city denied the vote to foreigners, women, minors, slaves and the insane, meaning that out of an estimated population of half a million, the 'electorate' of Attica was around 43,000 – probably far smaller because the *ekklesia*, or popular assembly, met in the city of Athens at the Pnyx on the Hill of the Nymphs, and those living outside the city would have found it difficult to attend on a regular basis. The quorum of the ekklesia was 6,000 citizens, and it was probably something around that number that met for its fateful meeting in 483.

LUCKY STRIKE
The wealth of Athens was based on the Laureion silver mines in eastern Attica.

The ekklesia, guided by its elected magistrates and generals, had to decide what to do with the silver windfall. They could have voted to split the proceeds amongst themselves (which, let's admit it, is probably what many of us would have done), but swayed by the oratory of Themistocles (c. 524–459 BCE; see quote below), the ekklesia voted, to its undying credit, to use the cash to build a navy of 200 warships, of which 100 had

SOUND INVESTMENT
Athens owed its victory over Persia to its investment in a fleet of new warships.

ПРИРОДА и ЛЮДИ.　　467

Θемистоклъ передъ Саламинской битвой приноситъ въ жертву трехъ персидскихъ дѣвушекъ

been built by 480. When the Persians prepared to invade for the second time, the Greeks asked the Oracle of Apollo at Delphi what they should do. The oracle answered that the Athenians should abandon the city of Athena to its fate and put their trust in their 'wooden walls'.

A few die-hards interpreted this to mean the wooden palisades that protected the rock of the Acropolis and its sanctuaries, where they prepared to resist the siege. But the majority accepted that the wooden walls referred to Athens's newly built navy, and they withdrew across the sea to the relative safety of the Island of Salamis. The Athenian fleet, although outnumbered by about two to one by the Persians, consisted of faster, better armed and more manoeuvrable trireme galleys. In the ensuing battle, the Greeks lured the Persians into the narrow Straits of Salamis, where their superior numbers were more of a hindrance than an advantage. Unable to manoeuvre, disorganised and attacked by a determined enemy who had nothing to lose, the Persians suffered a catastrophic defeat, losing up to 300 ships. Xerxes, who had witnessed the battle seated on a golden throne on land, was forced to withdraw his undefeated army to Asia. Without naval superiority, he realised that he would never have been able to overcome Greek resistance.

And, first of all, the Athenians being accustomed to divide amongst themselves the revenue proceeding from the silver mines at Laurium, [Themistocles] was the only man that dared propose to the people that this distribution should cease, and that with the money ships should be built [....] So that with this money a hundred ships were built, with which they afterwards fought against Xerxes. *'Themistocles' from the* Lives of the Noble Grecians and Romans *by Plutarch (c. 46–120 CE)*

The silver legacy of Laureion

Although the city of Athens itself had been destroyed, the Athenians and their allies had won the war, and Persian power had been broken forever. Athens, the senior partner in the alliance, with its largest navy, went on to dominate the whole Aegean region, creating its own empire. By its victory, Athenian democracy was hailed as superior to other forms of government, and it was to classical Athens that the founding fathers and democratic reformers of eighteenth-century France, Britain and America turned to for inspiration.

Artistically, the Athenian victory was just as far-reaching. Pericles (c. 495–429 BC), who dominated the Athenian political scene for four decades, oversaw the city's 'Golden Age', when the temples of the ruined Acropolis were rebuilt, giving the world the glories of the Parthenon and Erechtheion, which became the models for classical architecture from Rome to the neo-classical revival of the eighteenth and nineteenth centuries (see Marble, pp.106–109). In every field of the arts, drama and literature, Western European culture is indebted to classical Athens. Although the city and its glories were all but extinguished after the Islamic conquest of Greece in 1456, thanks to the silver of Laureion, the ideals and achievements of Athenian democracy and culture survived and blossomed for long enough to become the basis for Western culture in the modern era.

WEALTH OF ATHENA
Athens' military victories against Persia brought vast wealth flooding into the city.

SILVER CENTURIES
The silver mines of Laureion continued to be exploited until the nineteenth century.

Clay
Argilla

Type: Phyllosilicates

Origin: Slow mineral deposition and erosion

Chemical formula: $Al_2(SiO_3)_3$

+ **INDUSTRIAL**
+ **CULTURAL**
+ **COMMERCIAL**
+ SCIENTIFIC

GOOD EARTH
Clay deposits are found worldwide and are easily accessible.

The archetype of a god or goddess creating the first humans from clay is not unique to Christianity but is found in the religious traditions of Asia, the Americas, Africa and the Near East. The choice of clay is evidence of its importance to early humans, who used it to make containers and cooking pots, statuary and musical instruments. Clay in the shape of sun-dried and fired bricks and roofing tiles is one of the most common and versatile building materials used by humans from prehistoric times to the present day.

SWEET AND SOUR MAMMOTH

According to the archaeological record, the human relationship with clay began, not with a functional object such as a container for food or water or a cooking pot, but with figurines of humans and animals, baked at low temperatures in an open fire. The thousands of small clay statuettes and clay balls unearthed at Dolní Vestonice in the Czech Republic (see the box opposite) were found smashed, suggesting that they might have been intentionally destroyed in magical rituals. A similar ritual purpose has been suggested for the slightly later animal paintings found in the caves of Lascaux, France (c. 17,300 BP). The Czech figurines date

> **And the Lord God formed man of the dust of the ground, and breathed into his nostrils the breath of life; and man became a living soul.**
>
> *Genesis 2:7, King James Bible*

from a period before our ancestors founded permanent settlements. They lived as hunter-gatherers, used stone, wood and bone weapons and tools, and followed the game herds that they depended on for survival.

The earliest pottery utensils that archaeologists have uncovered come from the Yuchanyan Cave in Hunan Province, China, and have been dated to c. 18,000 years BP. The cave was used as a hunters' camp during the late Upper Paleolithic (40,000–10,000 years BP). In 2009, archaeologists found the remains of two pottery 'cauldrons' – deep beaker-shaped vessels associated with stone tools, charcoal and ashes from an open hearth,

and animal bones, meaning that they were probably used to cook the Paleolithic equivalent of sweet and sour pork. A rival claim for the world's oldest pottery comes from the Jomon ('cord marking') period (16,000–2300 years BP) in Japan. It is likely, as with many other human inventions, that pottery making was discovered in several regions independently. It would be fitting, however, if the first pottery had originated in East Asia, which went on to produce some of the world's finest ceramics and porcelain wares.

Pottery developed independently in the Americas, Africa and the Near East. Humans made pots by shaping the clay by hand or coiling, until the invention of the potter's wheel in Mesopotamia between 8,000 and 6000 years BP. Because early pottery was fired at relatively low temperatures in bonfires or simple pit kilns, it had to be made in simple, rounded shapes to avoid cracking. The development of the purpose-built kiln, which allowed pottery to be fired at much higher temperatures, permitted much greater variety in shapes and designs. Pottery remains the preferred material for many items of tableware, coffee and tea wares, cooking and serving dishes, vases and decorative objects.

HOUSES OF THE GODS

Once humans had begun to build permanent settlements, in areas poor in stone and wood, they turned to clay as their building material of choice. One of the world's most famous early buildings was made of fired clay bricks:

And they said one to another, Go to, let us make brick, and burn them thoroughly. And they had brick for stone, and slime had they for mortar. And they said, Go to, let us build us a city and a tower, whose top may reach unto heaven.

FIGURATIVE
The first sculptures, such as this *dogu*, were human and animal figurines.

VENUS IN CLAY

✦

The oldest ceramic object made by humans that has been found is not a cooking pot or drinking bowl, but a statuette dating back to the Gravettian culture (c. 28,000–22,000 BP), unearthed at Dolní Vestonice in the Czech Republic. Although called a 'Venus', the buxom female figurine has no relationship with the much later Greco-Roman goddess of that name. The small statuette is 11 cm (4.4 in) high, and has large breasts, a full stomach and childbearing hips – the kind of woman you'd likely see pushing a shopping cart around the local superstore, though probably with a few more clothes. Her facial features are sketched with a couple of rough strokes, so it is unlikely that she is a portrait of a living person. Found alongside the smashed figurines of animals and clay balls, she may have been used in magical rituals.

Such is the description of the Tower of Babel in Genesis 11:3–4 (King James Bible, 1611). In the subsequent verse, a rather touchy Jehovah punishes the presumption of the tower builders by confounding their languages and scattering them across the face of the earth. Although there is no archaeological evidence for the biblical confusion and scattering, many massive pyramid-like structures, known as ziggurats (literally 'raised buildings') made from sun-dried and fired bricks have been excavated in Mesopotamia (now Iraq) and Elam (now Iran). The precursors of the ziggurat were the temples and shrines of Mesopotamia's Ubaid period (c. 8,500–5800 years BP): large rectangular buildings built of sun-dried mud bricks raised on platforms.

Sun-dried mud brick quickly degrades, even in the relatively dry conditions of Iraq, and instead of demolishing buildings and starting anew from ground level, the ancient Sumerians and Babylonians filled old buildings with mud bricks and built on top, producing higher and higher constructions. The resulting architectural layer-cake, once abandoned and degraded by the elements, is known as a 'tell'. In the nineteenth century, European archaeologists trying to find the cities mentioned in the Old Testament such as Babel and Erech, excavated the tells and unearthed the ancient cities of Uruk, Ur and Babylon. At the centre of these cities was a ziggurat, which served as the main place of worship, and the 'house' of the city's patron deity, where the god was believed physically to reside. Unlike the stone pyramids of Egypt, which were built as tombs with subterranean or internal burial chambers, a ziggurat was a solid step pyramid that served as a platform for a shrine accessed by ramps and external staircases. They were built of a core of sun-dried bricks, faced with fired bricks that were glazed in different colours. The glazed bricks served both as decoration and to protect the sun-dried core.

The most famous ziggurat, and probably the model for the biblical Tower of Babel, was Etemenanki ('The Foundation of Heaven and Earth'), the ziggurat of Marduk, the patron deity of Babylon. Although little of the ziggurat remains in the present day, an ancient account of the building by the Greek historian Herodotus (c. 484–425 BCE) describes it as being 91 m (300 ft) high and 90 m^2 at the base. It rose in seven tiers faced with coloured glazed bricks, accessed by three linked staircases, with a large shrine on its summit, which served as the residence of the god. According to Herodotus, the shrine did not house the cult image of Marduk, but was furnished with a large couch and a golden table and was the home of the god's human 'bride'. In the fourth century BCE, Etemenanki was demolished on the orders of Alexander the Great, who intended to rebuild it on an even grander scale. His early death, however, halted the project, and all that was found of the building when Babylon was excavated in the nineteenth century was its massive foundations.

SUPERLATIVE
The world's largest mud-brick building in the world: Mali's Djenné Mosque.

Arsenic

Arsenicum

Type: Metalloid

Origin: Native arsenic and arsenic-bearing minerals

Chemical formula: As

✦ **INDUSTRIAL**

✦ CULTURAL

✦ COMMERCIAL

✦ SCIENTIFIC

To the modern reader, the mention of the word 'arsenic' suggests the foul murders of the Victorian period, when it was the poison of choice for those wishing to dispose of an inconvenient parent, child or spouse. Arsenic, however, has a much longer history, dating back to prehistoric times and antiquity when it had medical, artistic, cosmetic and industrial applications.

THE UNDECIDED ELEMENT

Chemists do not consider arsenic to be a true metal, though it has enough of the properties of a metal to be classed as a 'metalloid', along with silicon (Si) and antimony (Sb). Despite its fearsome reputation as a poison, native arsenic and various organic and non-organic arsenical compounds are relatively common in the environment: in the soil, plants, animals (especially in fish and shellfish) and in the human body, where it plays a part in metabolism. The ancient Chinese, Indians, Greeks and Romans used arsenic in their medical remedies, and although the exact formulations of ancient poisons are not known, it is probable that they also used arsenical compounds for this purpose.

ARSENIC, n. A kind of cosmetic greatly affected by the ladies, whom it greatly affects in turn. 'Eat arsenic? Yes, all you get,' Consenting, he did speak up; 'Tis better you should eat it, pet, Than put it in my teacup'. – *'Joel Huck.'* The Devil's Dictionary *(1911) by Ambrose Bierce*

The Arab alchemist Abu Musa Jabir ibn Hayyan (c. 721–c. 815), known in the West simply as Geber, was the first to prepare what became known as 'inheritance powder' – the white, tasteless, odourless and highly toxic arsenic trioxide (As_2O_3) – favoured by murderers wishing to dispose of an inconvenient relative so that they could inherit his or her property. This form of arsenic had the great advantage that it was impossible for the victim to identify it by taste or smell, and also because the symptoms of poisoning were similar to those of food poisoning, intestinal diseases and cholera, which were common killers before the twentieth century.

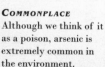

COMMONPLACE
Although we think of it as a poison, arsenic is extremely common in the environment.

POISONED PAPER
It is likely that green
wallpaper caused
Napoleon's death.

MURDER BY TRIAL AND ERROR

Although arsenic can be administered in gaseous
form, topically on the skin or added to food or drink,
the latter method is the only realistic way of commit-
ting murder. A fatal dose of arsenic varies between
125 mg (0.000044 oz) and 250 mg (0.000088 oz),
depending on the age and health of the individual.
Given a sufficiently high dose, a victim will develop a
headache, followed by vomiting and diarrhea as the
body attempts to expel the poison. But once the
arsenic has penetrated the major organs, the victim
experiences sweating, dehydration, difficulties with
speech, stomach cramps, burning pains in the urinary
tract and anus, convulsions and delirium, followed
within 24 to 48 hours by coma and death from heart
and respiratory failure.

A victim can recover from a non-fatal dose because, unlike other
poisons such as mercury that accumulate in the body, arsenic is expelled,
allowing the victim to make a full recovery. However, in many cases,
because the would-be murderer was often a trusted spouse or relation,
and the symptoms similar to those of food poisoning, he or she was able
to experiment with dosages without fear of detection. It is unknown
exactly how many people were murdered with arsenic over the ages, but
the numbers must run into the tens of thousands. As there was no reliable test to detect arsenic until the nineteenth century, many murders

DEATH BY DESIGN

✦

Was the Emperor Napoleon I
(1769–1821) murdered by the
British while he was prisoner on
Saint Helena? When a sample of
Napoleon's hair was analysed, it
was found to contain unusually
high levels of arsenic, raising the
possibility of poisoning. A more
likely explanation is that the
emperor's well-appointed living
quarters were decorated with
wallpaper coloured in Imperial
green and gold with the arsenical
pigment known as Scheele's Green.
In the island's damp climate, a
fungus growing on the wallpaper
could have converted the arsenic
pigment into arsine gas that would
have slowly poisoned the great
man. A rather more mundane
explanation is that the high levels
of arsenic were due to efforts to
preserve the body for its long sea
journey back to France.

would have remained undiscovered or would have been misdiagnosed as deaths caused by common diseases that had similar symptoms.

In the chronicles of poisoning, the *primus inter pares*, the Borgias, were the world's 'first criminal family'. This Italian clan that included the corrupt Pope Alexander VI (1431–1503), who fathered a number of children while he was a cardinal. The Borgias earned their fearsome reputation for their liberal use of 'La Cantarella' – a poison thought to contain arsenic trioxide. Two of Alexander's children, Cesare (1476–1507) and Lucrezia (1480–1519), were notorious for their use of La Cantarella – the beautiful Lucrezia administering the poison into her victims' wine with the aid of a hollowed-out ring. A couple of centuries later, another Italian, Giulia Tofana (d. 1659), made her own branded potion, 'Aqua Tofana' ('Tofana water'), probably of arsenic and belladonna, which she sold to wives who wished to dispose of their husbands. She was executed after confessing under torture to have provided the means for around 600 wives to murder husbands who had outlived their usefulness.

FAMILY FIRM
The Borgias are said to be the world's first criminal family.

INDUSTRIAL ACCIDENTS

We have already come across arsenic in the entry on bronze. During the early Bronze Age (5300–3200 years BP), arsenic was alloyed with copper to make 'arsenical bronze'. Ores containing both arsenic and copper are fairly common on Earth, and humans probably first made the alloy by accident. The addition of arsenic makes the resulting alloy stronger, easier to cast and more ductile than pure copper, and it can also be used to give a silvery sheen to the metal. Arsenical bronze was not entirely phased out after the introduction of tin bronze, as in some cultures it was used to make thin sheets of bronze for ritual or decorative purposes.

During the Industrial Revolution, the most common uses for arsenical compounds were as pigments and colourants. One of the most sought-after was 'Scheele's Green' (copper arsenite; $CuHAsO_3$), first formulated by the German-Swedish chemist Carl Scheele (1742–86) in 1775. The rich emerald green colour was used to colour wallpaper (see box, p.49) and wall hangings, furnishing fabrics and clothing. Despite its toxicity, it was also used as a food colouring for sweets and beverages. There were several major incidents of arsenic poisoning during the nineteenth and early twentieth centuries. In 1858, a batch of sweets contaminated with arsenic trioxide killed 22 people in Bradford, England; in Manchester, England, in 1900, 6,000 people were poisoned by beer containing arsenic; and as late as 1932, wine containing the residue of arsenical pesticides poisoned the entire crew of a French battleship.

Some cases of arsenic poisoning were neither murders nor industrial accidents, but cases of self-inflicted poisoning. Small amounts of arsenic trioxide act as a stimulant to the metabolism (see box, opposite), a fact known to traditional Chinese and Indian medical practitioners who prescribe remedies containing traces of arsenic.

In the late eighteenth century, a snake-oil salesman calling himself 'Doctor' Fowler sold a patent remedy called 'Fowler's Solution', which contained the toxic potassium arsenite ($KAsO_2$). Marketed as a cure-all and general tonic, the solution is suspected to have caused liver disease, hypertension and cancer. One possible high-profile victim of the remedy was Charles Darwin (1809–82), whose mysterious bouts of ill health throughout his adult life have been attributed to his addiction to Fowler's Solution.

PIGMENTED
Arsenic comes in a range of colours made into artists' pigments.

COLOUR ME DEAD
Copper arsenite, the main ingredient used to make Scheele's green.

Asphalt

Asphaltos

Type: Pitch

Origin: Compressed dead micro-organisms and algae

Chemical formula: CS_2

+ **INDUSTRIAL**
+ CULTURAL
+ COMMERCIAL
+ **SCIENTIFIC**

I n the modern world, asphalt is a component of asphalt concrete, which we use to surface our roads, motorways, pavements and sidewalks. But historically, asphalt was an ingredient of one of the most important weapons of the early Middle Ages: 'Greek Fire'.

THE BULWARK OF CHRISTENDOM

For many Western Europeans, classical history ends with the barbarian invasions of the fifth century CE, and the abdication of the last Roman emperor based in Italy, the grandly named Romulus Augustus (c. 460–c. 490) who conjoined in his name those of the founder of Rome and of its first emperor, but whose reign lasted just one year (475–76 CE). The Eastern Roman, or Byzantine, Empire, however, endured for another 1,000 years, finally coming to an end with the fall of Constantinople (present-day Istanbul) to the Ottoman Turks in 1453. The fiction that the emperors of the East ruled the whole of the former Roman Empire endured for centuries, until the coronation of the first Holy Roman Emperor in the West in the year 800.

In the early centuries of the Byzantine period, the empire was plagued by many enemies: barbarians from northern Europe and Central Asia, and its greatest foe and rival as the first millennium's world superpower, the Sassanid Empire of Persia (205–651 CE; a much later incarnation of the empire that had threatened the ancient Greeks). The war between the Persians and Byzantines continued for centuries, with notable victories and defeats on both sides, but in 627 CE, the Emperor Heraclius (c. 574–641 CE) annihilated the Sassanid army and broke Persian power once and for all. He returned to Constantinople exultant, believing that the glory days of the Romans were about to be reborn. It is one of the great ironies of history that his victory coincided with the emergence of a new power that was about to change the world forever: Islam.

Before his death, the Prophet Muhammad (570–632 CE) succeeded in uniting the warring tribes of Arabia, creating one of the most formidable fighting machines the world had yet seen. With the Persians and Byzantines exhausted by their long conflict, they were no match

WATERPROOF
One of the first uses of asphalt was to waterproof boats and buildings.

for the Arab jihadists, or 'holy warriors'. Within a few years, Arab Islamic armies led by the heirs of Muhammad engulfed the Persian Empire, Afghanistan and parts of modern-day Pakistan, and extended north from Arabia across the Near East as far as southern Turkey, and West across North Africa to the Iberian Peninsula. Instead of saving the empire, Heraclius witnessed its near-total destruction, with the loss of its richest provinces of Syria, Palestine, Mesopotamia (now Iraq) and Egypt. The reader might wonder what this lengthy historical preamble has to do with asphalt, a type of pitch we know as a constituent of the asphalt-concrete that covers our roads and motorways, which isn't one of the world's most exciting substances, when compared to, say, gold or uranium. But at this critical juncture in history, asphalt became one of the most important minerals on the planet.

Asphalt is found in natural deposits worldwide. One of the most famous modern examples is the La Brea tar pits in Los Angeles, CA (see box, right). Asphalt, like other hydrocarbons, including petroleum, is made of organic matter compressed under high pressure. In antiquity, asphalt was used as an adhesive and mortar, as well as to waterproof ships, containers and buildings threatened by floods.

LA BREA TAR PITS
✦

One of the attractions of LA, after you've taken in Rodeo Drive, the Hollywood sign and the studio tours, are the La Brea tar pits in Hancock Park in the downtown Miracle Mile district. Originally a natural formation created as asphalt seeped up through faults in the rocks, the tar pits now visible were excavated as asphalt mines. In prehistoric times, animals became trapped in the tar pits and died, and the pits are full of the bones of long-extinct species, including mammoths, giant sloths and American horses and camelids.

BURNING WATERS

Like other hydrocarbons, asphalt is an inflammable semi-liquid substance, though not to the same degree as refined gasoline, which ignites on contact with a naked flame. But it was these properties of asphalt that the Byzantines used to create one of the most feared and effective weapons before the introduction of gunpowder to the West: Greek Fire. Many Greek philosophers and scientists were also practical inventors. They had the kind of minds that, while they wrote treatises on higher morals, ancient dramatic art or astronomy, might come up with a giant crane that would grab enemy ships out of the water and drop them onto the rocks, killing the crew, or giant magnifying glasses that could be used to focus sunlight to set fire to enemy ships.

> At that time Kallinikos, an artificer from Heliopolis, fled to the Romans. He had devised a sea fire that ignited the Arab ships and burned them with all hands. Thus it was that the Romans returned with victory and discovered the sea fire.
>
> Chronicle *of Theophanes (c. 760–c. 818)*

According to one chronicler of the period (see quote, left), in the last quarter of the seventh century, as Arab armies overran the empire, a scientist from Heliopolis (now Baalbek, Lebanon) called Kallinikos fled to Constantinople, bringing with him the formula for the new weapon. Later historians have questioned the existence of Kallinikos, or that he was the inventor of Greek Fire. The ancient Romans and Greeks had always used incendiaries in warfare, and it is more likely that Kallinikos improved an existing formula, or maybe that he devised the siphon (a kind of pump and spray mechanism) used to deliver it in battle. Greek Fire was principally a naval weapon, though it was also used in land warfare. Because warships were made of wood, it was particularly effective in sea battles, as the inextinguishable fire would engulf enemy ships and their crews.

LOST SECRET
The recipe for Greek Fire was lost when the crusaders took Constantinople in 1204.

Constantinople is built on a peninsula surrounded on two sides by water. A double line of walls and moats protects the city's landward side. They were so formidable and well built that they protected the city from capture until they were breached by cannon in the fifteenth century. In the seventh and eighth centuries, the Arabs

FLAMETHROWER
Greek Fire was sprayed
onto enemy ships with a
siphon much like a modern
flamethrower.

realised that to capture the city, they would need to control the sea so
that they could either starve it into submission or launch assaults on the
weaker sea walls. In 674, the Arabs besieged the city, blockading it by
land, and assembled a large fleet to mount a sea blockade and launch
assaults. The Byzantine navy armed special ships with Greek Fire
siphons, and in 677 they destroyed the Arab fleet that was massed for an
assault in the Sea of Marmara. Unable to prevent the re-supply of the
city by sea or to breach its walls, the Arabs withdrew. The same sequence
of events repeated itself in the siege of 717–18, when again
the Byzantines used Greek Fire to foil Arab landings and attacks on the
sea walls.

The A-bomb of its day, Greek Fire was a closely guarded secret, and
its exact composition remains unknown. In 1204, the Fourth Crusade
organised to re-take Jerusalem from the Muslims ended in the capture by
deceit of Constantinople, and the establishment of the crusader Latin
Empire of Constantinople. In the chaos that ensued the change of
regime, the secret of Greek Fire was lost. Historians have reconstructed
the most likely formula from descriptions of its effects and the materials
available at the time: Greek Fire was projected from a siphon, hence it
had to be liquid; it ignited readily, floated and remained alight on
the surface of the water; and it was only possible to extinguish
with vinegar, sand or human urine. The most likely formula
given the characteristics described above is a
mixture of quicklime, sulphur, naphtha and
asphalt. Despite its unremarkable appearance,
and its current rather mundane use in road building,
for five centuries, asphalt ensured the survival of
the Byzantine Empire, and preserved Christendom
from almost certain annihilation.

SMOOTH OPERATOR
Today, asphalt provides
the smooth, waterproof
surface for motorways
and pavements.

Gold

Aurum

Type: Precious (transition) metal

Origin: Native gold; mineral ores; seawater

Chemical formula: Au

+ *INDUSTRIAL*
+ *CULTURAL*
+ *COMMERCIAL*
+ SCIENTIFIC

Pre-eminent among the minerals found on Earth, gold symbolises the idea of wealth, and at the same time, physically embodies it in the form of bullion, coin and jewellery. For the love of gold men have crossed oceans, explored continents and slaughtered millions, yet, compared to iron or copper, coal or clay, gold is of little practical use. The value humans have placed on the metal is a kind of shared dream and hope that its untarnished glitter might somehow rub off on our all-too-tarnished souls.

GO WEST, YOUNG MAN

'In fourteen hundred and ninety two,/Columbus sailed the ocean blue' begins the poem, as everyone knows, but how many remember the later couplet 'Columbus sailed on to find some gold/To bring back home, as he'd been told'? As is equally well-known, the Italian-born navigator Christopher Columbus (1451–1506) sailed west from Spain across the Atlantic in the hope of reaching East Asia, and, thus, opening a new trade route to the spices, treasure and manufactures of the East for his Spanish masters. In four voyages between 1492 and 1503, he discovered the West Indies and Central and South America, though he himself remained convinced that he had reached the East Indies, Japan and China. He benefited little from his great discovery, suffering disgrace and imprisonment. His achievements, however, transformed the world, shifting its axis westwards, where it has remained until the present day.

The East, from the perspective of Western Europeans in the late fifteenth century, started at the fabled city of Constantinople (now Istanbul), and extended to the mysterious realms of Cathay (China) and Xipangu (Japan), where, it was said, gold was as common as base metal. While the Byzantine Empire (395–1453) minted the gold solidus, which it used as its main unit of currency, the West was on the silver standard. Gold was rare and therefore valuable, with the added attraction of being one of the few metals that does not tarnish or oxidise (rust), and with copper, the only other metal that was not a dull, functional, silvery grey. In terms of its practical usefulness,

MANIA
Gold has an attraction that far outweighs its practical uses.

GO WEST
Columbus set sail in search
of the gold of the Indies.

however, gold, until its modern usage in electronics and dentistry, is
about as useful as a glass hammer. It is too soft to be made into tools,
weapons or machinery, and anyone depending for his life on gold
armour would quickly discover to his cost that it was not only crip-
plingly heavy, but also rather bad at stopping steel blades and arrows.
When minted into coins and made into jewellery it is usually alloyed
with silver or another metal to harden it.

FLEECED
Jason returning with the
stolen Golden Fleece.

Legends about the fabled wealth of the East
began long before Columbus's time. In the ancient
Greek myth of the Golden Fleece, Jason and his
hardy band of heroes (though pirates might be a
better description) sail to the kingdom of Colchis
on the east coast of the Black Sea in search of the
magical artifact. Slaughtering and seducing his
way across the known world, Jason steals the
fleece, gets the girl and returns triumphant to
Greece. The modern interpretation of the story is
that the natives of the region used fleeces to sieve
gold dust from rivers. Hence the myth is really
about a piratical raid for treasure. In the succeeding
millennia, expeditions to find both real and imagined gold – usually already belonging to other
people – became a common fictional idea and
historical event.

FOR THE LOVE OF GOLD

The love of gold seems to be almost universal among human cultures, with the exception of the Plains Indians and other hunter-gathers, who found the metal useless and therefore without value. But among the so-called civilised, settled peoples, gold has always had an extraordinary and, some would say, a mystifying attraction. Until the twentieth century, gold was the basis of the world economic system and under-wrote its currencies once most governments had abandoned coins for banknotes. However, quite early on, it was realised that while the supply of gold in the world grew at a very slow rate, the world economy was growing exponentially – in other words, gold would never keep up with the growth of the money supply. In the end, the whole system broke down after World War II, when governments had to print more money than they had in gold reserves to rebuild their shattered economies. Once, a banknote was a promise to pay the bearer its equivalent in gold, but thereafter this was a fiction. Try to go to the Federal Reserve or the Bank of England with your dollar bills and pound coins and ask for gold and you'll get a rather curt reply.

But in the fifteenth century, the wealth of an individual or state was measured by how much gold they owned. As the Spaniards were going to find to their detriment a couple of hundred years later, this fostered a dangerous confusion between the product of economic activity – gold earned from trade and industry – with gold itself. By one of those acci-dents of history, Catholic Spain found itself in possession of the greater part of the New World, with the exception of Brazil, grabbed by the

GOLD STANDARD
Gold was the basis of
world currencies until the
twentieth century.

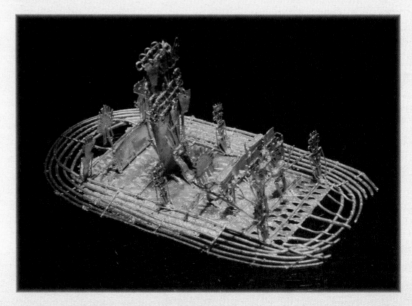

FOOL'S GOLD
The legend of El Dorado
led countless men to their
deaths in the jungles of
South America.

Portuguese, and Canada and the eastern seaboard of the United States, colonised by Britain, Holland and France. But these did not matter to Spain because they had no gold. Columbus did come home with gold from his journeys to the West Indies and the mainland, but not enough to satisfy his royal employers, which landed him in trouble. But soon the Spaniards heard stories of fabulous kingdoms, rich beyond the wildest dreams of avarice, in the interior of Central and then South America – the Aztec and Inca empires.

SPOILS OF WAR
Aztec ear ornaments looted by the conquistadors.

THE CROSS AND THE SWORD

Spain, recently liberated from Muslim rule, was a deeply Catholic and intolerant society. Its Holy Inquisition pursued heretics, Muslims and Jews with fundamentalist vigour, and while maybe not as murderous in reality as in Hollywood folklore, was as brutal and effective a tool of state oppression as the Gestapo and the KGB. It was Spain and not Protestant England or Holland that made first contact with the most advanced cultures of the Americas. An intriguing historical alternative presents itself if the Pilgrim Fathers had landed in Mexico and not Massachusetts. The result might have been the same, however, as the Pilgrims were probably just as intolerant as the Spanish Catholics.

The Aztec Empire – though confederation might be a better description – occupied most of modern Mexico with its capital at Tenochtitlan (now Mexico City). The empire was fairly recent, the Aztecs having only achieved dominance in the Valley of Mexico in the fifteenth century. Like several empires of the ancient Near East, they ruled from a distance, extracting tribute from conquered peoples but leaving their rulers and elites in place. Their rule was constantly challenged by rebellions, and there were important independent enclaves within the empire – all of which was exploited by the astute Hernán Cortés (1485–1547). Cortés was ostensibly bringing the one true faith to the pagan Native Americans, but what he was really in search of was gold. He found it in huge quantities.

GOLDEN DREAMS

✦

After the Spanish conquistadors had plundered the gold of the Incas and Aztecs, they were still not satisfied. They heard tales (embellished, one hopes, by the Native Americans to lure them to their deaths), about the golden man, El Dorado, the ruler of a fabulous city of gold, which was to be found hidden within the dense jungles of South America. The origin of the story was a ritual of the Musica people of Colombia; they rowed their new chief covered in gold dust into the centre of a sacred lake where he made offerings to the gods as part of his coronation. The legend prompted several expeditions to the interior of the continent, the first setting out in 1541; although it discovered the full extent of the Amazon River, it also led to the deaths of most of the gold-hungry explorers.

The pre-Columbian peoples of Mesoamerica present us with an interesting series of contrasts. The Aztec and Maya had developed the plastic arts, and the sciences of

HOLOCAUST?
The Spanish conquest of the Americas has been compared to genocide.

mathematics and astronomy to a surprising degree, yet they subsisted with Stone Age technology. Although the Aztecs could make exquisite golden jewellery and objects, their warriors still fought with obsidian-bladed weapons that had been phased out in the rest of the world at the end of the Stone Age. The Incas had developed metallurgy beyond the working of gold, but were still very far behind the technology of the late Middle Ages in Europe. The Aztec and Maya had a complex hieroglyphic writing system, used by the elites, but the Inca made do with the quipu knot system, which they used for recording trade, production and taxation. The Incas had the llama as a pack animal, but the Mesoamericans, with no large mammals to domesticate, made do with manpower.

THE BLACK LEGEND

Much has been made of the dreadful fate of Native Americans at the hands of the conquistadors. At various points in history, the historical view was so negative that it became known as the 'Black Legend'. The arrival of Spanish colonists in Central and South America, so the legend goes, not only led to the destruction of native cultures, but the elimination through imported European diseases of up to 95 percent of the population. Beyond dispute are the violent ends of the Aztec and Inca empires and the suppression of their cultures and religious beliefs, and the deaths of millions from smallpox, influenza and cholera. But were the Spaniards worse than other European powers of the day? Some point to the much less damaging conquest of India by the British, but that occurred in the eighteenth century, at a time when Christianity had lost much of its fundamentalist fire, and, more importantly, when the technologies of India and Britain were not so unevenly matched.

POWDERED GOLD
Gold exists in many forms, like this pure gold precipitate.

When they arrived in Mexico in 1519 and in Peru a decade later, the Spaniards found not cities of gold, but gold jewellery and artifacts amassed over centuries by the ruling elites who used it to decorate their temples, palaces, tombs and persons. Gold was never a currency or medium of exchange as it was in the Old World. Economically, pre-Columbian societies were very different from fifteenth-century Europe: the Aztecs operated a tribute system that ensured the flow of foodstuffs, raw materials and luxuries to the capital, and the everyday economy was based on barter. The Inca

Metallic elements are heavy. In planetary terms, this would mean that when Earth was forming, iron, gold and other precious metals sank to the centre of the planet to form a solid core, around which flows a vast layer of liquefied rock known as magma. What scientists have now realised is that there is about one thousand times more gold in Earth's crust than there should be. It should all be a few thousand miles down under our feet around a literally gold-plated iron core. The explanation that scientists have come up with is that most of the surface gold on Earth is of extraterrestrial origin. No, not little green men, but a series of massive meteorite impacts 3.9 billion years ago, which is known as the 'terminal bombardment', that deposited about 20 billion tons of material – including gold and platinum – on Earth's surface.

NOBLE METAL
Gold is the metal of choice for the manufacture of royal regalia.

have been described as a primitive communist state, though communitarian might be a better label, where communities held property rights under the aegis of a centralised state. The Incas associated gold with their principal deity, Inti, the sun. His main temple, the Coricancha in the capital Cuzco, was covered in gold sheets both inside and out. For Native Americans, gold had a symbolic significance, and they were mystified by the Spaniards' obsessive desire to acquire it; all the Spaniards did with the precious objects and jewellery they obtained was to melt them down into ugly blocks that they sent back to Spain.

THE COSTS OF EMPIRE

The Spaniards stripped Mexico and Peru of its gold only to discover that the supply of the metal in the New World was just as limited as in the Old. They took their treasure back to Spain, which in the sixteenth century became the richest country on Earth in terms of bullion. But by the eighteenth century, Spain discovered the true price that they had paid for Aztec and Inca gold. The British, French and Dutch, who had been denied the easy pickings of Central and South America, had made do with less promising lands in North America. What they had developed were economies based not on the exploitation of a finite resource but on the exploitation of natural resources, trade and manufacture.

Once one of the most advanced regions in Europe, Spain became an economic backwater, with an increasingly fractious and costly empire. Spain, which had once threatened England with its giant armada (1588), was constantly defeated by the British and Dutch, and was dependent on its ally France during its conflicts with Northern Europeans. In the end, it was France, once it had rid itself of its king, and swapped him for an emperor (Napoleon I; 1769–1821) that brought an end to the Spanish American Empire. After the conquest of Spain by Napoleon, the empire disintegrated, and one by one the countries of Latin America declared their independence.

On a desert island gold is worthless. Food gets you through times of no gold much better than gold gets you through times of no food. If it comes to that, gold is worthless in a goldmine, too. The medium of exchange in a goldmine is the pickaxe.

Moist von Lipwig's musings on gold in Terry Pratchett's Making Money *(2007)*

While the Spanish had used their empire as a kind of piggy bank, raiding its precious metals – gold, and then when that became scarce, silver – the British, French and Dutch developed commercial networks, sending raw materials to the home country to be manufactured into goods that were re-exported worldwide. The Spanish economy would not emerge from the morass of empire until it had lost all of its overseas possessions, and even then it remained socially, politically and economically disadvantaged until the end of the Francoist dictatorship in 1975. Much is made of the post-imperial problems of Britain in the twentieth century and of the United States in the twenty-first, but compared to the leaden legacy of the Spanish Empire, the British and Americans have had it easy.

In the modern world, gold, although stripped of its official role in the economic system, retains a primacy as the preferred investment in times of economic crisis. When land and property prices collapse and equity prices crash and burn, the safe refuge for the investor is gold. At the time of writing in summer 2011, the gold price hit a record high of $1,800/oz ($64/g) (compared to $40/oz [$1.40/g] for silver). As the supply of newly discovered gold is falling, the price can only increase, so the dream of gold's worth will continue, until we find a way of extracting the millions of tons of the metal that lie at Earth's core.

SOLID-GOLD INVESTMENT
In 2011, gold hit the record price of $1,800/oz ($64/g).

HEAVENLY WEALTH
Although they preach poverty, churches are vast consumers of gold.

Chalk

Calx

Type: Sedimentary rock

Origin: Remains of micro-organisms, marine animals and algae

Chemical formula: $CaCO_3$

✦ **INDUSTRIAL**

✦ **CULTURAL**

✦ COMMERCIAL

✦ SCIENTIFIC

The soft sedimentary rock known as chalk has played an important symbolic role in the culture of southern England since prehistoric times. Chalk was also the raw material for lime mortar that was used from the Roman period until the nineteenth century.

ENGLAND'S WHITE BATTLEMENTS

To any Englishman or woman of a certain generation, the mention of chalk will probably suggest two images: the chalks and chalkboards of his or her school days, and the chalk of the white cliffs of Dover. The former, although commonly referred to as 'chalks', are in fact gypsum (calcium sulphate). The white cliffs, made of true chalk, calcium carbonate, streaked with flint, stand like battlements defending the English coastline where it faces France, which can be seen on the other side of the narrow Strait of Dover. Celebrated in song during the World War II, the cliffs symbolised British resistance against the threat of Nazi invasion, and the hope of victory and peace to come.

The cliffs were never more than a symbolic defensive formation, as they do not form a continuous barrier along the coast, and successful invaders, such as the Romans in the first century CE and the Normans in the eleventh, had no problems in finding safe anchorages and level beaches on which to land. In the days of sail and steam, the white cliffs of Dover were the first sight of the mother country that

FOSSILISED
Chalk is made up of the fossilised remains of microscopic organisms.

WHITE WALLS
The cliffs of southern England are a symbolic line of defence.

greeted returning Britons, akin to the sighting of the Statue of Liberty for those arriving by ship in New York. The cliffs are part of the geological formation known as the Downs (incorrectly, as these are hills), of which there are two in the Southeast: North and South; these are bands of chalk deposits formed during the Cretaceous period around 60 million years BP from the skeletal remains of microscopic marine animals and plants.

RUDE GIANTS AND WHITE HORSES

Perhaps some of the most mysterious and intriguing chalk creations are the giant human and animal figures that are carved into chalk hillsides all over the British Isles. The most famous of these are found in southern England: the Long Man of Wilmington in East Sussex, who stands 69.2 m (227 ft) tall; the 55-m (180-ft) Cerne Abbas Giant, also known as the 'Rude Man', in Dorset; and the 110-m (374-ft) Uffington White Horse in Oxfordshire. The origins and functions of the carvings remain a mystery. Among the more farfetched explanations is that they, like the figures in the South American Nazca Desert of Peru, were carved to be seen by the crews of passing UFOs.

Of the three carvings, the highly stylised Uffington Horse is thought to be the most ancient, dating back to the Bronze Age, as it is associated with the nearby Bronze- and Iron-Age hill fort now called Uffington Castle. It is possible that the horse was the symbol of the fort builders or a representation of the Celtic horse goddess Epona. The dating of the two giants at Wilmington and Cerne Abbas is a much more contentious issue. The Rude Giant, thus known because of his obvious virility and lack of trousers, could be a representation of the Greco-Roman hero Hercules. But because the earliest accounts of the giant date back to the eighteenth century, historians have concluded that it is only 200 years old. There are several legends associated with the Rude Giant. One old wives' tale is that sleeping on the giant's impressive manhood can cure couples of infertility. This has led to considerable congestion in the area on warm summer nights.

TALL GUY
England's chalk carvings include the Long Man of Wilmington.

ELEMENTARY MY DEAR FAULDS

✦

Powdered chalk is still used by CSI teams to collect fingerprints from crime scenes. The Scottish physician Henry Faulds (1843–1930) discovered that fingerprints could be used as a means of identification while he was working in a hospital in Tokyo in the late nineteenth century. When a man was wrongly accused of theft from the hospital, Faulds cleared him by showing that his fingerprints did not match those found at the crime scene.

Coal

Carbo carbonis

Type: Sedimentary rock

Origin: Plant matter in water protected from oxygen

Chemical formula: C with other elements

+ **INDUSTRIAL**
+ CULTURAL
+ **COMMERCIAL**
+ **SCIENTIFIC**

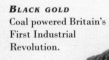

BLACK GOLD
Coal powered Britain's First Industrial Revolution.

Coal is the most important mineral of the past two centuries. As the fuel of the factories and railways of the First Industrial Revolution, it made possible the urbanisation and industrialisation of the developed world in the nineteenth century, beginning with Britain. Its generalised use in the past two centuries, however, may have disastrous consequences for the future of human civilisation. If the worst predictions about man-made climate change are correct, coal may bring about the end of the industrial civilisation it helped to create, and possibly of the human race itself.

SATANIC MILLS

I want you to imagine a landscape from which all the noises, sights and scents of industry are absent, save for the churning of the waterwheel and the creak of the windmill. Outside the larger market towns, the air is pure, the rivers unpolluted, and the vistas unscarred by power lines, motorways or railways. Movement follows the slow, plodding pace of the ox-drawn cart, and does not exceed the gallop of the horse. 'A rural idyll that never really existed', you might exclaim. But this was probably the scene that would have greeted the visitor to the British Isles before 1700, when the economy was primarily agrarian, and manufacture still at the pre-industrial scale. Although the environment was in much better shape than it is today, life was far from perfect. War, disease and famine ensured that life expectancy was much shorter than it would be in the succeeding centuries.

A visitor coming to Britain in the mid-nineteenth century would have surveyed a very different scene. In a century and a half, Britain's Industrial Revolution had transformed many parts of the country: woodland, fields and pastureland had made way for mines, textile mills, foundries and potteries, and towns and villages had grown into new industrial conurbations, linked to one another by a network of railways. England's 'green and pleasant land' to quote William Blake's (1757–1827) poem 'Jerusalem', had been taken over by 'dark satanic mills'. Blake and others deplored the new industrial landscape of Britain, not just because of the environmental degradation it

LOST CHILDHOOD
Children were employed
in mines because they
could get into restricted
spaces.

had wrought, but also because of the terrible social conditions it imposed on the newly formed industrial working class.

The miners, and factory and mill workers, detached from the agrarian communities that had provided a basic level of social and economic support during periods of crisis, as well as regulating their conditions of employment through custom and law, had no legal protections from the worst forms of exploitation of early capitalism, and were without the safety nets of public assistance and healthcare. Children as young as four were sent to work in the mines and mills, where many would die in accidents or from industrial diseases in their teens and twenties. Miners and mill workers worked long hours in dangerous, backbreaking jobs, for low wages, and they were always at the mercy of employers who could dismiss them in periods of economic downturn. It took decades of reform and social struggle to improve the conditions of the working classes in the developed world.

What had caused this radical physical and social transformation? Historians have come up with polit-

My name's Polly Parker, I come o'er from Worsley
My mother and father work down the coal mine
Our family is large, we have got seven children
So I am obliged to work down that same mine
And as this is my fortune I know you'll feel sorry
That in such employment my days I must pass
But I keep up my spirits, I sing and look cheerful
Although I am but a poor collier lass.

Traditional miner's song, 'Collier Lass'

BLACK TIDE

✦

The environmental damage done by coal is not limited to atmospheric pollution and climate change. In 2008, 300 acres of a quiet corner of Tennessee were covered by toxic black sludge that escaped from the ruptured containment area of the Tennessee Valley Authority's coal-fired Kingston Fossil Plant. The sludge, known as 'fly-ash slurry', is a byproduct of the burning of coal to produce energy. As it flooded from the plant, the black tide demolished the buildings in its path, covered agricultural land in a thick layer of ash, and flowed into the area's river system, causing millions of dollars of damage.

ical, economic, social and even religious theories to explain why the First Industrial Revolution began in Britain. And while many socioeconomic factors contributed to the event, it would have been impossible without one particular mineral that is readily found throughout the British Isles: coal. Coal, extracted from deep pits or strip-mined from the surface, fed the steam engines that powered Britain's mills, foundries, trains and ships, and, once converted into gas, lit its cities. Without it, Britain might have become a mercantilist power much like Holland (which had no coal of its own) and not the industrial and imperial superpower that dominated the world during the nineteenth century.

AN ACCIDENT OF GEOLOGY

Through an accident of geology, as fortuitous and random as the discovery of the largest reserves of petroleum under the countries of the Near East, major deposits of coal formed under the British Isles, in particular Wales, northern England and Scotland. Coal, like other hydrocarbons, was originally organic matter – the remains of the vast forests that covered Earth until 305 million years ago during the Carboniferous Period. Under normal circumstances, dead vegetation will rot and return its carbon into the atmosphere, but when plant matter accumulates in acidic water with little oxygen, it does not decompose but turns into peat that acts as a natural carbon store. Over millions of years, the peat bogs are covered by sediments and compressed into coal.

Of course, Britain is not the only country in the world with major coal deposits. Coal is found on every continent, and the current leader in terms of world production is the People's Republic of China. However, as historians have pointed out, while plentiful supplies of coal, and of other raw materials such as copper and iron, were crucial to industrialisation in the UK, of themselves they are not sufficient to explain it. Several historians point to technology as the principal driver of the Industrial Revolution, in particular the development of the first commercial steam engines in the early eighteenth century, and their

PUFFING DEVILS
The first steam
locomotives were built
to haul coal in collieries.

evolution from large static engines, like the low-pressure Watt engine (1774), into much smaller high-pressure steam engines that powered the first locomotives and steamships in the early nineteenth century.

Other historians focus on the loss of surplus labour, which was no longer needed on the land, leaving people free to migrate to new industrial cities, or to the culture of mercantilist capitalism fostered by Protestantism. But without coal to smelt stronger iron to make high-pressure boilers and to fire the furnaces to turn water into steam, there would have been no viable steam engines, no deep mines, mills or railways, no working class, no industrial cities and no mercantilist capitalism.

HOT COALS

Where Britain had shown the way, others followed, beginning with Belgium, Germany, France, Japan and the eastern seaboard of the U.S. in the nineteenth century, and Russia in the early twentieth century. In the mid- and late twentieth century, the leading economies of the developing world, led by the countries of Southeast Asia, South Korea, China, India and Brazil, all invested heavily in developing their industrial infrastructures. In most instances, this meant generating energy with coal, which remains today the cheapest power-generating technology available, although in terms of its carbon emissions is also one of the most damaging for the global environment.

FULL STEAM AHEAD
Coal-powered steam
quickly overtook
wind-dependent sail.

And did the Countenance Divine,/Shine forth upon our clouded hills?/And was Jerusalem builded here,/Among these dark Satanic Mills?

'Jerusalem' *by William Blake*

I realise that the mention of climate change and global warming brought on in part by the burning of fossil fuels for the past two hundred years, releasing billions of tons of the greenhouse gas carbon dioxide (CO_2) into the atmosphere, will annoy some of my readers who prefer to believe that climate change remains unproven, or is a perfectly natural cyclical phenomenon. However, considering the steady rise in CO_2 emissions, which shows no sign of slowing as China and India build new coal-fired power plants and continue to industrialise, many of us will be given the opportunity to find out – by 2050, if not earlier – whether the climate scientists are right or merely crying wolf.

I will not repeat here the many arguments and facts and figures given by both sides of the climate change debate. But I will take you back to where we began this entry: the British landscape, which despite two and a half centuries of industrialisation is still a remarkably green and pleasant land of rolling hills, hedgerows, picturesque villages and small market towns. Britain, however, is a low-lying island, and the southeast

of the country that is home to the capital city, London, and holds a large percentage of the population, its business and commercial hub, and most of its new high-tech industries, is gradually sinking into the North Sea. Combine this sinking effect with a possible two-metre sea-level rise caused by global warming by the end of the century, and most of historic England will disappear underwater. The remaining high ground would form an extended island archipelago that would enjoy a balmy Mediterranean or even sub-tropical climate – a bonus for the surviving English and overseas tourists.

Coal is the one mineral whose removal from the earth would completely change our social, political, economic and technological development in the past two hundred years. Without coal, we would not have had the First Industrial Revolution – the Age of Steam – and hence, it would have been unlikely that we would have had the Second Industrial Revolution – the age of electricity and of the internal combustion engine. Also gone would be the social transformations of society that coal made possible: the creation of the working class with all its political implications, the growth of large cities, and the vast improvements in living standards, education and life expectancy that were the payoff for a century of misery, dislocation and social unrest.

CENTRAL HOT AIR

✦

The use of coal as a fuel was well known during classical antiquity. In Britain, the Romans exploited the island's extensive coal deposits to heat public buildings and private homes between the first and fifth centuries CE. They invented the world's first central-heating system, known as a hypocaust, in which air heated by a coal-fired furnace was circulated under raised floors to heat the rooms above. After the collapse of the empire in the West in the fifth century, the technologies that used coal were lost, and records of its use in Britain only resume in the twelfth century. Despite the cold and dampness of the climate, central heating was not reintroduced into Britain until the nineteenth century.

Coral

Corallium

Type: Organic mineral

Origin: Exoskeleton of several species of coral

Chemical formula: $CaCO_3$

Gemstone coral, the exoskeletons of several species of marine polyps, was once believed to be a magical substance that could ward off illness and misfortune. In modern times, coral reefs are valued not only for their biodiversity and intrinsic beauty but also because they are major earners of tourist dollars.

+ INDUSTRIAL

+ *CULTURAL*

+ *COMMERCIAL*

+ SCIENTIFIC

LIVING GEM
Coral is the hard exoskeleton of marine organisms.

HEALING TOUCH
In India, red coral is still believed to have healing powers.

PRODUCTS OF THE MYSTERIOUS WEST

Gemstone coral, like other precious and semi-precious minerals, have been traded since prehistoric times. Like the trading of amber and pearls, the trade in coral linked distant parts of the globe in the first international commercial networks. Coral is found in shallow waters of Earth's warmer seas and oceans, and some of the best gemstone-quality coral, the tree-like, red *Corallium rubrum*, comes from the coastal waters of the Mediterranean. Historically, its principal market, however, was not in Europe but in India. While many exotic products were imported from the East to the West in antiquity and the Middle Ages, coral travelled in the opposite direction.

The popularity of coral in India was due to folktales of its magical and healing powers. One of the minerals associated with the nine planets in Indian Vedic astrology, coral was linked to the red planet Mangal (Mars), whose attributes are courage, strength, aggression and vitality. The colour red also associated it with blood, and it was thought to cure diseases of the blood and circulatory system. Coral jewellery was worn as a form of talisman to ward off misfortune in several cultures. In south India, married women still wear coral jewellery to preserve the harmony of their unions.

> Syria was thy merchant by reason of the multitude of the wares of thy making: they occupied in thy fairs with emeralds, purple and broidered work, and fine linen, and coral and agate.
>
> *Ezekiel 27:16, King James Bible*

CORAL RIVALRIES

In antiquity, the Greek colony of Massalia (now Marseilles in southern France) exported Mediterranean coral to the Celtic peoples of Gaul (France) and Germania (Germany), who used it as an inlay decoration for bronze jewellery and weapons. The ancient Romans, like the Indians, believed that coral had the power to ward off illness and danger, and they gave coral necklaces to their children. In later centuries, the shifting control of the Mediterranean coral trade highlighted the rise and fall of national powers in the region. During the medieval period, the republics of northern Italy, such as Venice and Florence, exploited the rich coral beds off the North African coast.

In the sixteenth century, Spain held the rights to the area but relinquished these to France in the seventeenth century. The French have held them until the modern period, with a brief British interregnum during the Napoleonic Wars (1803–15). In the modern period, the working of Mediterranean coral has become an Italian monopoly, centred in the cities of Naples, Rome and Genoa. However, coral, like other organic gemstones that can easily be faked with materials such as plastics, has suffered a loss of popularity in the modern period.

REEF WRECKS

✦

The decommissioned aircraft carrier USS *Oriskany*, now nicknamed the 'Great Carrier Reef' by divers as a reference to Australia's Great Barrier Reef, is the largest artificial reef created by humans. The 30,800–ton, 904-foot (276-m)-long *Oriskany* was sunk off the Florida coast in May 2006 to serve the dual functions of providing a solid substrate for the growth of new corals and a home for many marine species, and a new diving attraction take pressure off natural reefs that are degrading because of overuse. The *Oriskany* is just one of many man-made objects that have been used to create artificial reefs in recent years, including cremated human remains mixed with concrete and formed into pillars and sculptures, and old New York City subway cars.

UNDER THREAT
Corals are threatened by overexploitation and environmental degradation.

Ivory
Eburneus

Type: Organic mineral

Origin: Elephant tusks (dentine)

Chemical formula:
$Ca_5(PO_4)_3(OH)$ with organic matter and water

✦ INDUSTRIAL

✦ **CULTURAL**

✦ **COMMERCIAL**

✦ SCIENTIFIC

Although 'ivory' can come from a range of different animals, the term is commonly understood to mean the material taken from the tusks of African and Asian elephants. In ancient times, elephants had a much greater range than they have today, extending to North Africa and the Near East. Due to hunting and now poaching of elephants for ivory, the species has been on the retreat for millennia and is now threatened with extinction in the wild.

TINKLING THE IVORIES

Who should we blame for the sad plight of the African and Asian elephant? We could start with Wolfgang Amadeus Mozart (1756–91), along with the many other European composers and soloists of the eighteenth and nineteenth centuries, who made the piano one of the world's most popular and versatile musical instruments. A primitive version of the piano – with fewer keys – first made its appearance in Italy in the late sixteenth century, but when Johann Sebastian Bach (1685–1750) first heard it around 1730, he was so unimpressed that he continued composing for the organ and harpsichord. By Mozart's day, however, the piano had displaced its rivals as the main performance keyboard instrument, and when Ludwig van Beethoven (1770–1827) was composing, the piano had entered its golden age, having increased from five to just over seven octaves, with a total of 52 white keys.

Until the invention of plastic ivory simulants in the twentieth century, the white keys of a piano were made of wood covered with a thin slice of the finest soft white African-elephant ivory, which had to come from a freshly killed animal. An average 31-kg (70-lb) elephant tusk could be diced and sliced to make the keys for 45 piano keyboards. Although the process was fairly efficient and little of the tusk was wasted, this was of little comfort to the elephant that had given its life so that little Molly or Freddie could laboriously pick their way through 'Für Elise' to the delight of their parents but probably of few others. And

MASS PRODUCER
The demand for ivory has led to the decline of the elephant since antiquity.

that was the problem: had the demand for ivory been limited for the instruments of composers, soloists and professional musicians, the elephant might be in much better shape today.

During the Stone Age of home entertainment – we're not just talking before the iPhone and PlayStation, but before TV, radio and even the wind-up gramophone – the piano was the flatscreen TV and Nintendo Wii of its day. Throughout the nineteenth century, middle-class families gathered around the upright piano in their parlours and drawing rooms for a wholesome sing-along or impromptu concert, and every bar, saloon, club and restaurant had a piano for entertainment. The popularity of pianos in the developed world in the nineteenth and early twentieth centuries led to a massive cull of sub-Saharan African elephants. Between 1905 and 1912 alone, an estimated 30,000 African elephants were slaughtered to meet the demand for piano keys.

TONE DEATH
The piano threatened the survival of the African elephant in the nineteenth century.

THE PRESIDENT'S TEETH

The elephant once had an extensive native range in the Old World, with populations as far west as Syria in the Near East and across North Africa. The elephants that Hannibal (247–182 BCE) took across the Alps to attack Rome, for example, were representatives of an extinct sub-species of small North African forest elephant. The Mediterranean elephant, however, was hunted to extinction for its ivory in antiquity. As the biblical quote on p.79 shows, even in ancient times, ivory had to be imported to the Near East from the fabled land of Ophir, which scholars have placed in either sub-Saharan Africa or western Asia. The story of the elephant's long decline continues to the present day with poaching for ivory for the East Asian market (see box, p.76, and below).

In pre-industrial times, ivory provided an attractive, versatile material that was soft

Quinquireme of Nineveh from distant Ophir
Rowing home to haven in sunny Palestine,
With a cargo of ivory,
And apes and peacocks,
Sandalwood, cedarwood and sweet white wine.
'Cargoes' by John Masefield (1878–1967)

FORCED MUTATION
Poaching is leading to
the evolution of a
tuskless elephant.

enough to carve into exquisite figurines, bas-reliefs and jewellery, as well as into small decorative objects, such as boxes, pipes, seals and netsuke. The ancient Greeks created extraordinary giant chryselephantine statues of the gods by combining ivory and gold over a wooden framework (see box, p.79), and the Romans buried their dead in caskets decorated with ivory carvings. However, because it is an organic material, ivory degrades quickly when buried in the earth, and few of the many artifacts made of ivory in antiquity have survived into the modern period.

As we have seen above, elephant ivory had a more functional use as piano keys, and it was also used to make buttons, shirt stays, fan ribs and billiard balls until the discovery of plastics in the last quarter of the nineteenth century. Another early use of ivory was to make sets of false teeth. Until the eighteenth century, when ceramic dentures were invented, false teeth were carved from ivory and set into gold supports. One notable wearer was George Washington, who owned several sets of false teeth made of human and animal teeth and ivory.

Elephants were not the only animal sources of ivory for consumer and luxury goods. It was harvested from other land animals with large teeth and tusks, including hippos and wild boars, and sea

SURVIVAL
OF THE TOOTHLESS
✦

Twentieth-century poaching has physically altered the morphology of the African elephant. In the early twentieth century, only one percent of African elephants were born without tusks, while at the beginning of the twenty-first, the figure is closer to 30 percent. Although, in the short term, the loss of tusks may help preserve the elephant, in the long term, the forced evolution of the species may prove disastrous for its survival in its native sub-Saharan habitats. African elephants evolved with tusks, which they use in a wide range of behaviours, including feeding and mating.

mammals, including sperm whales, narwhals and walruses. However, in terms of the quantity of ivory obtained per animal killed, and the relative ease of hunting them when compared to a narwhal or hippo, the elephant was the obvious choice. There remains one legal, unregulated source of ivory from a member of the elephantid family: the tusks of the long-extinct mammoth, which have been unearthed in large numbers in Russia.

CELLULOID SAVED THE ELEPHANT

The sad plight of the African elephant had already become a concern in the mid-nineteenth century. Alarmed by a steady decline in ivory supplies, Phelan & Collander, an American firm that manufactured billiard balls, offered a $10,000 prize to anyone who could come up with a synthetic alternative. In the late 1860s, two American brothers, John and Isaiah Hyatt, took up the challenge and began their experiments with 'Parkesine', the first man-made plastic invented by British inventor Alexander Parkes in 1862. In 1870, the pair developed their own version of Parkesine, consisting of a mixture of nitrocellulose and camphor, which they called 'Celluloid'. Although their invention is now forever associated with

EXTINCTIONS
North African and Near Eastern elephants became extinct in antiquity.

the film industry, in the nineteenth century, celluloid was the world's first commercially successful plastic, with a wide range of manufacturing applications.

Instead of claiming the $10,000 prize, the Hyatts wisely decided to exploit the new material themselves. In 1872, they patented their unfortunately named 'Stuffing Machine', which is the ancestor of modern plastic injection-moulding technology. The Stuffing Machine produced blocks and sheets of celluloid that could be worked into finished products. They began with the manufacture of billiard balls and went on to produce many other products formerly made of ivory, such as buttons, combs and spectacle frames, which they could produce at a much more competitive cost. Although saving the African elephant was probably very low on their list of priorities, the Hyatts made an important contribution to the animal's survival.

'LAUNDERING' ILLEGAL IVORY

With elephant populations in serious decline around the world at the end of the twentieth century, the United Nations imposed a first moratorium on ivory sales in 1989. The ban was partially lifted in 2002 to allow several countries in southern Africa to sell their stockpiles of confiscated poached ivory. According to many conservationists, however, the net result allowed criminal gangs to launder their illegally acquired supplies of African ivory through legitimate channels and worsened the plight of the already endangered species.

Plastics have now replaced elephant ivory for all practical applications. In the twentieth century, the Japanese piano manufacturer Yamaha pioneered the use of 'ivorite' to replace ivory keyboards, a move imitated by all other major manufacturers. Unfortunately, the demand for illegally poached ivory continues to be a serious threat to the survival of both Asian and African elephants. The bulk of poached ivory is destined for markets in East Asia. In Japan and China (and other countries with important Chinese communities), individuals use signature seals that were traditionally carved out of ivory (though

POACHERS' CHARTER
Poachers have exploited the partial lifting of the moratorium on ivory sales.

IVORY GIANTS

✦

The ancient Greek sculptor Phidias (c. 480–430 BCE) created two of the largest indoor statues ever made: the Athena Parthenos (447 BCE) and the seated Zeus of Olympia (432 BCE). Both stood over 12 m (40 ft) high, and were made of chryselephantine – ivory and gold plates over a wood and bronze armature. The cult statue of Athena that stood in the Parthenon in Athens 'wore' 1,100 kg (2,500 lb) of gold as her dress and accessories – representing a greater part of the treasury of Athens. Although lost in antiquity, the full glory of Phidias's creation can be appreciated in the life-size gilded replica that stands in the Nashville Parthenon in Tennessee.

historically not necessarily from elephant ivory). Poached ivory is also made into jewellery, fine-art carvings and tourist souvenirs.

The history of the human exploitation of organic minerals is not a particularly happy one for the animal producer, merchant or buyer. Species producing minerals such as pearls (see Nacre), ivory and coral have been hunted to near extinction to satisfy humanity's desire for luxury goods. Perversely, even after a synthetic material has been invented to replace and improve on nature's original, humans still hanker after the 'real thing'. However, the elephants will probably have the last laugh at humanity's expense, as smooth, translucent elephant ivory – another of nature's plastics – is, like amber and coral, very easy to fake with modern plastics and polymers. To fool even the most wary customers, the fakers create their artifacts from ground-up bone and ivory combined with polymer resins. Therefore, as with the faking of other increasingly rare organic minerals, human dishonesty may succeed, where conservation has failed, in overcoming human ignorance and greed.

His hands are as gold rings set with the beryl: his belly is as bright ivory overlaid with sapphires. His legs are as pillars of marble, set upon sockets of fine gold: his countenance is as Lebanon, excellent as the cedars. *Song of Solomon, 5:14*

Slate

Esclate

Type: Metamorphic rock

Origin: Recrystallised sedimentary rocks

Chemical formula: SiO_2 with other minerals

✦ **INDUSTRIAL**
✦ CULTURAL
✦ COMMERCIAL
✦ SCIENTIFIC

Typically known as one of the principal natural materials for the manufacture of roof tiles, slate also played an important role in education as a reusable resource to students when paper was scarce or expensive.

SCHOLASTIC SLATE

The word 'tablet' has recently taken on a new meaning and now refers to the latest breakthrough in portable, handheld, touch-screen computer technology, which are coincidentally roughly the same size, shape and thickness as the small slate writing tablet that I remember owning as a child. Encased in its plain wooden frame, the black piece of slate seemed to be full of possibilities – though these would have to be created with the help of white and coloured chalks that had also been provided. To a child of a different age, a simple piece of polished rock was a wonderful present that kept him amused for hours. Today's children, however, would probably stare at it, and after a few seconds, ask where the on switch was. But enough of this maudlin, melancholy nostalgia! I am not writing this book on a slate with chalk, thank the gods, but on a laptop.

> **I do come home at Christmas. We all do, or we all should. We all come home, or ought to come home, for a short holiday – the longer, the better – from the great boarding school where we are forever working at our arithmetical slates, to take, and give a rest.** *Christmas greeting written by Charles Dickens (1812–70)*

Paper has not always been as available or as cheap as it is today, so slate, as an inexpensive, endlessly reusable alternative, presented many advantages for the medieval classroom. England in the late Middle Ages is thought to have been one of the most literate societies in the world thanks to a network of village schools, where the parish priest taught the children of tenant farmers their ABCs and 123s. A twelfth-century tablet from Hastings, East Sussex, has engraved on it the letters of the alphabet and the opening lines of the Lord's Prayer in Latin to be used as a model.

WATERTIGHT
Slate is now mainly
used as flooring and
roofing material.

LEAF-LIKE ROCK

Slate is metamorphic rock, which means that it began
life as one form of rock – in the case of slate, shale –
which is metamorphosed (changed) into a new type
of rock. Structurally, slate is foliated; that is, it has a
leaf-life structure that allows it to be cleaved into flat
sheets. This explains its principal contemporary use,
now that tablet computers have replaced writing
slates, as a material for roof and floor tiles. Slate is
quarried extensively in the Galicia region of northern
Spain and in Wales, western Britain, to provide tiles
for the world market. Slate is non-permeable to water,
and therefore makes an excellent, durable tile or
shingle roof; its water resistance also means that it
will resist frost damage that can damage more absor-
bent materials in freezing conditions.

Although not as 'flashy' as gold or silver, or as
'explosive' as saltpetre or uranium, slate is a
mineral that has played a valuable supporting
role in the history of humanity, providing both a
reusable, eco-friendly writing resource to
scholars, and ensuring that they would be dry
during their lessons.

SLATE ART

✦

For thousands of years before the
arrival of the Europeans, Native
Americans made 'gorgets' that they
wore either sewn onto clothes or as
pendants. About 6.35 cm (2.5 in)
long, and made of polished slate,
gorgets were decorated with
patterns of engraved line. They are
thought to have indicated tribal or
clan allegiance, or to have been
badges of social rank and status.
Another Native American use for
slate is to make blades for the ulu,
the traditional Inuit knife of the
metal-poor Arctic.

STYLISH SLATE
Slate was an important
artistic medium in the
Americas.

Iron
Ferreus

Type: Metal

Origin: Meteorite iron, native iron and iron ores

Chemical formula: Fe

+ **INDUSTRIAL**
+ **CULTURAL**
+ **COMMERCIAL**
+ SCIENTIFIC

LATE BLOOMER
Iron production is far more complex than bronze smelting.

The fourth most common element in Earth's crust, iron, is relatively difficult to extract from iron ores so that it can be made into useful metal. Hence, the Iron Age was one of the great technological achievements of humanity in antiquity, succeeding the discovery of copper and bronze metallurgy. The widespread dissemination of iron technology, however, had a strange birth, at a time when a large part of humanity was plunged into the first and darkest of its Dark Ages. Once iron had become established, it replaced other metals for most practical and industrial uses.

THE FIRST 'DARK AGES'

In earlier entries, we chronicled the emergence of copper and bronze metallurgy in the Old World, and we described how its manufacture and trade spurred an initial development of human civilisation, with sophisticated commercial, technological, cultural, intellectual and artistic achievements. This period came to an abrupt and brutal end in what is now called the Bronze Age Collapse (c. 1200–1150 BCE), which was followed by centuries of darkness, with the destruction and abandonment of many urban centres, and the disappearance of civilisation in many areas. As in the later period we know as the Dark Ages, after the collapse of the Western Roman Empire in the fifth century, urban living, writing and technology were lost in certain regions but survived in others. Even in the areas most affected, however, a few centres survived – though much diminished – and other parts of the globe, such as China, were not affected by the collapse.

The plight of those who did suffer, however, was terrible and often terminal. The city-state of Ugarit on the Syrian coast was an important trading centre during the Bronze Age, which maintained links with Egypt, Greece, Cyprus and Mesopotamia. It had its own alphabet of 31 letters, which is thought to have played an important role in the development of later scripts, including our own. In the early eleventh century, Ugarit came under attack from the mysterious

and yet unidentified 'Sea Peoples', who were piratical raiders much more terrible than the Vikings that attacked Europe between the eighth and eleventh centuries. Around 1190 BCE, the last king of Ugarit sent desperate letters to his neighbours and allies for help against the Sea Peoples, saying, 'The enemy's ships came; my [cities] were burned, and they did evil things in my country'. No help came, as his allies were beset by their own problems, and soon after, the city was attacked and completely destroyed, never to be rebuilt. A similar fate awaited countries and cities in the regions, including the Empire of Hatti (now Anatolia, Turkey) a decade later, which also disappeared from the annals of history. Pharaonic Egypt managed to repulse the Sea Peoples, but in the following century succumbed to Nubian invaders from the south.

IRON WARRIORS?

An earlier generation of archaeologists and historians proposed that the Sea Peoples and other invaders who destroyed the Bronze Age civilisations of Greece, the Near East and Egypt were armed with superior weapons made from iron that outmatched the bronze weapons of their settled enemies. The transition of one group of cultures for another could thus be explained neatly in terms of technological progress – maybe as sad as the extinction of pre-Columbian cultures in the Americas, but ultimately an unavoidable (and positive) result of technological change.

IRON PILLAR

✦

The iron pillar of Delhi is such an extraordinary artifact that ufologist Erich von Däniken (b. 1935) claimed that it could only have been made by extraterrestrials. His assertion rests on the fact that, although made of almost pure wrought iron, the massive pillar, which stands 7 m (23 ft) and weighs six tons, has not rusted since it was erected during the reign of the Hindu king Chandragupta Vikramaditya (375–414 CE) sixteen centuries ago. The pillar, which used to stand in a Hindu-Jain temple, was incorporated into a mosque after the Muslim conquest of northern India. The 'miraculous' pillar, which is an impressive piece of ironwork for any period, does not rust because it contains high levels of sulphur, which has formed a rust-resistant layer over its surface.

This neat historical progression, however, is not confirmed by a growing number of archaeological finds that have moved the discovery of iron metallurgy hundreds of years into the past.

Although it was once thought that the Hittites discovered how to work iron between the fourteenth and twelfth centuries BCE, and that the Sea Peoples acquired their knowledge and disseminated it across the Mediterranean world, this is not borne out by the archaeological record, which reveals that Hatti was no richer in iron artifacts than other settled cultures of the day. In 2005, a discovery in Turkey near the site of Kaman-Kalehöyük put back the manufacture of iron and steel artifacts in the region to 4,000 years BP. A Japanese team working in the area discovered two small iron fragments that are not meteorite iron and are thought to have formed part of a knife blade. This suggests that iron technology developed in southwest or south-central Asia, possibly in the Caucasus region.

Iron objects are known from second- and third-millennium Egypt and Mesopotamia, although many of the earlier artifacts were made from unsmelted meteorite iron (see box, p.86). Iron metallurgy developed around 4,000 years BP in India, where a sophisticated iron industry had developed by the first

PRIZE EXHIBIT
The iron Eiffel Tower was built as the gateway for an international exhibition.

millennium BCE that was capable of producing large forged pieces by the early centuries CE. China also had an early iron industry, though the Bronze Age in China lasted until the third century BCE.

LET'S HIT IT AND SEE!

If Bronze-Age cultures did know about iron, why did the metal not supplant bronze earlier? Despite its unfortunate habit of corroding when exposed to air and humidity, iron is lighter, stronger and keeps an edge better than copper or bronze, making it superior for armour and edged weapons. Steel, which we shall deal with in a later entry, is much better for the manufacture of weapons than either wrought or cast iron, which are either too soft or brittle. The answer to this archaeological puzzle, which is yet to be resolved, probably comes in several parts: technological, aesthetic and commercial.

STRIKING DIFFERENCE
Early iron swords were often inferior to bronze ones.

To begin with technology, iron is far more complex to produce and fashion into tools and weapons than either copper or bronze. When copper ores are smelted in a furnace, liquid copper flows to the bottom, with the waste material, or slag, at the top. The metal can then be poured out of the furnace into moulds with relative ease. When iron ores were placed into the low-temperature furnaces of the Bronze Age, instead of becoming a liquid, they would have remained solid as a dense spongy mass consisting of metal and slag. Any iron produced as a byproduct of copper smelting would probably have been discarded as worthless. At some point in history, a smith must have become curious about this unattractive semi-molten lump and decided to do what so many humans have done in the intervening millennia: hit it and see what happens.

CUTTING EDGE
Once perfected, iron was far superior to other metals.

If the iron 'bloom', as this stage is known, is hammered on an anvil while still molten, the slag will be forced out, leaving, after several reheatings and hammerings, a residue of wrought iron. Not only is the process time-consuming, it is also counterintuitive, when compared with the production of bronze. The wrought iron thus produced was suitable for the manufacture of small pieces, but making larger pieces, such as swords, would have demanded a high degree of skill and expertise, and an added investment in terms of fuel, time and energy. The wrought iron thus produced was often inferior to the tried-and-tested bronze, and early iron swords had the distressing habit of shattering in battle.

BENDY SWORDS

When the Romans invaded Britain in the first century CE, they reported that their British adversaries sometimes had to withdraw from battle to straighten their bent iron swords. The Romans themselves did not entirely phase out bronze swords until the Imperial period, reserving their use for officers while legionaries had to make do with iron. Iron technology improved slowly, and a full understanding of its chemistry was not achieved until the Industrial Revolution. Hence, in the early Iron Age, the quality of an iron weapon was dependent on the skills and experience of individual smiths, who thus earned the reputation of holding secret, magical knowledge. The extra investment in skill, time and energy in making iron implements, so the theory goes, would have delayed its widespread adoption in many areas.

Two further factors probably played a role in delaying or speeding up the transition from bronze to iron. The first, which may have slowed its adoption, is aesthetics — a force not to be underestimated in human cultures in which a relatively useless metal — gold — is prized over all others. Copper and bronze have an attractive golden-yellow hue, and when corroded, they have an equally prized green patina. Iron, on the other hand, is a dull silver-grey, and corrodes to an ugly, flaking reddish-brown. The Egyptians disliked iron, which they considered to be an impure, ugly substance. They rarely used iron as an offering to the gods, though they, too, ultimately admitted its superi-

IRON FROM THE SKIES

✦

In the nineteenth century, Europeans discovered that the Inuit peoples of Savissivik, Greenland, made iron tools and weapons, although they had no known source of the metal in the region, and no knowledge of the complex technologies to extract and smelt iron. The mystery was finally solved in 1894, when the American explorer Robert Peary (1826–1920) found the source of the iron to be taken from chunks of the largest iron meteorite ever found on Earth. The meteorite, which landed near Cape York around 10,000 years BP, broke into several large fragments known to the Inuit as the Tent (31 metric tonnes (34 tons)); the Man (20 metric tonnes (22 tons)); the Woman (3 tonnes (3.3 tons)); and the Dog (400 kg (800 lb)). In a typical act of cultural vandalism, Perry carried off the meteorites and sold the fragments to an American museum for $40,000.

ARCTIC MYSTERY
The Inuit made iron utensils without any iron technology.

MYSTERY SOLVED
Seen here, part of the
ferrous meteorite that was
the source of Inuit iron.

ority for weaponry. The second factor, which may have speeded up its adoption, is commercial.

The Bronze Age collapse, so one theory goes, disrupted the long-distance trading networks that linked northern Europe to the Mediterranean, and therefore starved the bronze industry of one of its key ingredients: tin. Copper and bronze smiths would have had no choice but to find an alternative to replace diminishing supplies of tin bronze. While it is true that trade decreased, or ceased altogether in the most affected areas, bronze continued to be produced in large quantities in the Near East and Mediterranean. Iron metallurgy became fully established in the Old World between 1100 and 800 BCE, but it did not fully displace bronze for many practical applications until the first centuries CE. In the Americas, the Iron Age began with the arrival of the Spanish in the fifteenth century. Of the leading cultures of the Mesoamerica, the Aztecs and Maya, although superb

GREEN REVOLUTION
Iron implements revolu-
tionised agricultural
production.

gold- and silversmiths, subsisted with Stone and Bronze Age technologies, and the Inca and other Andean cultures of South America knew how to work copper and bronze but not iron (other than meteorite iron). The technological disparity between the metallurgical technologies of the Old and New Worlds is one factor that explains the rapid conquest of the Americas.

SLOW COOKERS
Cast-iron cooking utensils have been made since ancient times.

CASTING IRON

Iron technology evolved from wrought iron, which did not require high-temperature furnaces, to cast iron, which does. The first cast iron was made in China in the first millennium BCE. For once, the Chinese, who have given the world so many inventions, were behind when it came to iron metallurgy. Archaeologists believe that the secret of making wrought iron was introduced to China from Central Asia. At this time, the Chinese had extremely sophisticated bronze-casting technology, and very efficient furnaces that could reach much higher temperatures than European or Near Eastern furnaces. It is conjectured that the furnace of a Chinese smith making wrought iron must have reached the magic temperature of 1,150°C (2,010°F). At that point, instead of forming a bloom that could be hammered into wrought iron, *shu thieh* ('ripe iron'), the metal combined with the carbon in the furnace to make an iron-carbon alloy with more than two percent of carbon, became molten, and solidified into cast iron, *sheng thieh* ('raw iron'). This new type of iron could be poured into moulds like bronze. By the middle of the millennium, the Chinese were casting large iron objects such as cauldrons. They developed blast furnaces before

BRIDGING THE GAP
Improvements in iron technology led to the metal's use in civil engineering.

the first century BCE, and were powering them with waterwheels by the first century CE. Similar developments did not take place in the West until the medieval and early-modern periods.

Iron and steel technology not only enabled the Chinese to develop their agriculture and other industries, but also to dominate their less advanced neighbours. In the second century CE, the Han dynasty (206 BCE–220 CE) imposed a monopoly on the production and sale of iron, and forbade the export of iron tools and weapons to maintain its advantage over their 'barbarian' neighbours. Another Chinese discovery that improved the quality of iron was 'puddling', literally stirring the molten iron to change its carbon content. Again, this technique was not discovered in the West for centuries. From the seventeenth century onwards, however, all the innovations in iron and steel technology took place in the West. In Europe, certain areas with access to high-quality coal and iron ores, such as the UK, Belgium and the Ruhr region in Germany, had an advantage when it came to developing new industrial technologies such as steam power. Britain took the lead in the development of fixed steam engines in the 1780s, and of the railways in the 1830s. These two advances required matching developments in metallurgy, to provide iron strong enough for boilers, rails and architectural members.

For the LORD thy God bringeth thee into a good land, a land of brooks of water, of fountains and depths that spring out of valleys and hills; /A land of wheat, and barley, and vines, and fig trees, and pomegranates; a land of oil olive, and honey; /A land wherein thou shalt eat bread without scarceness, thou shalt not lack any thing in it; a land whose stones are iron, and out of whose hills thou mayest dig brass. *Deuteronomy 8:7–9, King James Bible*

Kaolin
Gaoling

Type: Silicate mineral

Origin: Kaolinite

Chemical formula:
$Al_2Si_2O_5(OH)_4$

✦ **INDUSTRIAL**

✦ CULTURAL

✦ **COMMERCIAL**

✦ SCIENTIFIC

SECRET RECIPE
Kaolin is the basic material
used by the Chinese to
make porcelain.

Kaolin is one of the main ingredients for the production of high-fired Chinese ceramic wares known in the West as porcelain. Much admired since their first import to Europe during the Middle Ages, Chinese porcelain wares were finally reproduced in Germany at the beginning of the eighteenth century.

DARK DEEDS AND 'WHITE GOLD'

Despite earlier, unfounded claims, the first high-fired ceramic porcelain wares to be made in Europe were produced in Saxony, Germany, in the early eighteenth century. The credit for the discovery, traditionally given to the alchemist Johann Böttger (1682–1719), probably belongs to the German polymath Ehrenfried von Tschirnhaus (1651–1708). Mathematician, doctor and physicist, von Tschirnhaus became interested in reproducing porcelain, which had until then been imported at high cost from China and Japan. An empirical scientist, he experimented with different types of clay and firing temperatures until, around 1704, he succeeded in making a small porcelain cup.

At this point, von Tschirnhaus was entrusted with the care of a 19-year-old maverick alchemist, Johann Böttger, who was on the run from the king of Prussia's court after he had claimed to be able to transmute base metal into gold. The Elector of Saxony, Augustus II the Strong (1670–1733), who 'rescued' Böttger, was also eager to discover his secret, and he placed the young man in the protective custody of von Tschirnhaus. At first, Böttger showed no interest in von Tschirnhaus's work on porcelain, but harassed by the king to make gold, in 1707, he reluctantly agreed to help the older man. It is unknown how much Böttger contributed to von Tschirnhaus's discovery, but three days after the latter suddenly died of dysentery in 1708, the porcelain cup he had made was stolen from his house – it is now thought that Böttger himself was the thief. The following year, Böttger announced to Augustus that he had discovered how to make porcelain. In 1710, a grateful Augustus appointed Böttger as the head of the new porcelain factory that he established in Saxony, which would later become the world-famous Meissen factory. Although Böttger never succeeded in making gold, the fine porcelain of Meissen became known as 'white gold'.

STOP THIEF!
Böttger (above), the man who stole Tschirnhaus's discovery.

FLATTERY
A Meissen copy of a Chinese original.

THE CHINA CONNECTION

Historically, the Chinese would not have understood the term 'porcelain' as it was used in Europe. The word is derived from the Latin/Italian *porcellana*, which is given to certain species of crustaceans and shell-fish, with delicate, coloured shells that were thought to resemble Chinese ceramic wares. Another name given to porcelain in the UK is 'china', from its country of origin. The Chinese themselves classified their ceramics in different ways, including high-fired and low-fired wares; southern or northern wares, with the demarcation line formed by the Yellow and Yangtze rivers; by decoration, colour or style; or by their date of manufacture.

Chinese porcelain is made from kaolin, named from a European rendering of the place name Gaoling ('High Hill') in the city of Jingdezhen, Jiangxi Province, which is still known as China's 'Porcelain Capital'. Porcelain is made of kaolin, which is extracted from kaolinite clay, and combined with feldspar rock, known as pottery stone or petuntse, feldspar and quartz. The secret of porcelain that so long eluded Europeans was not just the materials used in its manufacture, which are common all over the planet, but the high firing temperature of around 1,300°C (2,380°F). This ensures that the clay vitrifies into an extremely hard, translucent material that can be made much

CHINESE GIFT

✦

The earliest recorded piece of Chinese porcelain to reach Western Europe is a Qingbai vase dated to the beginning of the fourteenth century, which was made in the potteries of Jingdezhen. A Chinese embassy travelling to Rome to see the pope in 1338 presented the vase to the king of Hungary. Soon after its acquisition, the king had a silver base, handle, lid and spout added to the vase so it could be used as a wine ewer. After being owned by several crowned heads of Europe, it found its way to the British Isles into the collection of Fonthill Abbey, where it was restored to its original form.

The material of porcelain is composed of two kinds of clay, one called Pe-tun-tse and the other Kao-lin. The latter is disseminated with corpuscles, which have some shimmer, the former is simply white and very fine to the touch. *From the Letter of Father Xavier d'Entrecolles (1664–1741); published in 1712*

thinner than earthenware, and into complex, sculptural forms such as Meissen figurines.

The exact date when the Chinese first made porcelain is still a matter of scholarly debate. The question is made more confusing because the difference between proto-porcelain and true porcelain wares remains blurred, as there is no universally accepted definition of porcelain. According to some specialists, the first true porcelain was made during the Han Dynasty (206 BCE–220 CE), but ceramics made from kaolin fired at high temperatures have been found dating back to around 3,000 years BP. The Chinese wares that the layman would immediately recognise as porcelain were made during the Song (960–1279), Yuan (1279–1368) and Ming (1368–1644) dynasties – especially the blue-and-white wares of the Ming period, which were later much imitated in Europe.

An interesting aside in the history of ceramics is that the Chinese, having reached extraordinary heights in the manufacture of porcelain that was as fine as eggshell and as translucent as alabaster, never developed a glass industry. Although they made glass beads and discs in antiquity, they did not make glass for bottles and windows until the modern period.

FRAGILE TREASURES
Masterpieces of the potter's art from a factory in China.

THE BEAUTIFUL BONE

Starting in 1712, Father Xavier d'Entrecolles, a Jesuit missionary in Jingdezhen, published a series of letters describing the manufacture of porcelain (see quote, opposite). Although von Tschirnhaus and Böttger had already made their breakthrough in Saxony several years earlier, the letters encouraged other European manufacturers in France and England to experiment with porcelain wares of their own. The eighteenth century saw the emergence of different types of soft- and hard-paste porcelains. Soft-paste wares were manufactured in the royal factory established in Sèvres in 1756 to meet the needs of the French court at Versailles.

The British version of soft-paste porcelain is 'bone china', first made in London in 1748, and perfected by Josiah Spode (1733–97) in his factory in Stoke-on-Trent around 1790. Bone china consists of 25 percent kaolin, mixed with 25 percent Cornish stone and 50 percent bone ash. Pieces are fired at 1,200°C (2,200°F), a slightly lower temperature than hard-paste porcelain. One of the most enduring decorative schemes for bone china is the 'willow pattern', which was modelled on Chinese blue-and-white wares. The Chinese garden scene was first handpainted onto dishes, but later applied with printed transfers. A fanciful story of the love of a lowly servant for the daughter of a Mandarin was made up to popularise the pattern. The style became so popular that Chinese manufacturers copied it for their export wares to Europe.

LIKE A HOUSE ON FIRE

✦

Every French schoolboy and girl is taught that Bernard Palissy (c. 1510–89) was the first man to succeed in making porcelain-like ceramics in Europe. After seeing a piece of Chinese porcelain, he worked obsessively for 20 years to try to recreate it. At times, he was so short of funds that he had to burn his furniture and floorboards to feed his kiln, much to the annoyance and despair of Madame Palissy. Although Palissy never succeeded in reproducing porcelain, he did create a type of tin-glazed, decorated pottery that was later known as 'Palissy ware'.

Graphite

Graphit

Type: Native element mineral

Origin: Found in metamorphic rocks, igneous rocks and meteorites

Chemical formula: C

+ **INDUSTRIAL**
+ **CULTURAL**
+ COMMERCIAL
+ SCIENTIFIC

MAGIC MARKER
Natural graphite can be cut into pencils without further processing.

Although graphite has a range of important industrial applications, the best-known use of the mineral to the layperson is as the 'lead' in pencils. Graphite pencils first appeared in the sixteenth century, and went on to revolutionise both writing and drawing.

THIS ISLAND NATION

England (and the British Isles more generally) owes much of its uniqueness and independence of spirit to the fact that it is an island nation on the edge of the European continent. Although the Strait of Dover is only 34 km (21 miles) across, it has furnished England with a formidable barrier against continental aggression. The strait has only failed on two occasions: in the first century, when the Romans invaded several times before establishing themselves permanently, and in the eleventh, when the Normans overcame English resistance at the Battle of Hastings in 1066. There have been more recent threats, of course, such as the 1803 invasion dreamed up by Emperor Napoleon I (1769–1821), and a similar plan by Adolf Hitler (1889–1945) in 1940. One of the greatest threats to English independence, however, came in 1588, when King Philip II (1527–98) of Spain launched the *Grande y Felicísima Armada* ('Great and Most Fortunate Fleet'), popularly known as the Spanish Armada, in an attempt to conquer England, depose its Protestant queen, Elizabeth I (1533–1603), and return the country to the Catholic fold.

The invasion, masterminded by Philip and entrusted to the dual command of the Dukes of Parma (1545–92) and Medina Sidonia (1550–1615), the former the governor of the Spanish Netherlands (now Belgium, Luxemburg and parts of Holland), and the latter the admiral of the fleet, would see the armada sail from its bases in Spain and Portugal and rendezvous with the invasion force off the Flemish coast. The Spanish sailed into the Channel and engaged the English fleet which, through a combination of superior naval technology and the judicious use of 'fire ships' filled with gunpowder and pitch, managed to hold off the armada and prevent it from linking up with the invasion force. The fleet was forced to sail home, taking a route around Scotland and Ireland, and suffered heavy losses.

CANNONBALL RUN

One of the technological and tactical advantages that the English had over the Spanish was in naval gunnery. In the naval engagements of the preceding centuries, the main tactic was to get close enough to the enemy vessel to immobilise it with grappling irons to enable marines to board. The aim was to capture the ship rather than sink it, because it was a valuable prize in itself. But during the engagements against large and heavily armed Spanish galleons, smaller English warships had to make best use of their advantages: greater manoeuvrability and speed, and improved gunnery, with which they could sink enemy ships while remaining out of range. Part of this advantage was due to graphite.

MAKING THEIR MARK
Graphite helped English gunners defeat the Spanish Armada.

The best-known use of graphite is in the manufacture of writing and drawing pencils. Although the core of a pencil is usually called 'lead', it is in fact black graphite-carbon or powdered graphite mixed with clay. Graphite also had early industrial applications, including its use as a 'refractory' to improve the casting of iron. In the first half of the sixteenth century, the English struck 'black gold' at Grey Notts Fell in the Lake District – not petroleum, but one of the purest graphite deposits on Earth. The locals found the graphite useful to mark their sheep, and it was made into pencils until the late nineteenth century. During the Elizabethan period, however, it was used as a refractory to line the moulds for iron cannonballs. The resulting shot was rounder, smoother and could be fired further and with greater accuracy, giving the English navy an advantage over its continental rivals. Hence, English graphite played its part in preserving an independent, Protestant England, and in giving her a naval advantage that she kept until the twentieth century.

In spite of everything I shall rise again: I will take up my pencil, which I have forsaken in my great discouragement, and I will go on with my drawing.

Vincent van Gogh (1853–90)

TO THE POINT
The core of a modern pencil is made of clay and graphite.

Gypsum

Gypsatus

Type: Sulphate mineral

Origin: Sedimentary rocks, as sand, and as deposits in hot springs

Chemical formula: $CaSO_4 \cdot 2H_2O$

+ **INDUSTRIAL**
+ CULTURAL
+ **COMMERCIAL**
+ SCIENTIFIC

Gypsum occurs in several forms: as sand and crystals, as alabaster, and as chalky deposits in sedimentary rocks. It is the main ingredient of plaster of Paris, a substance that has played an important role in architecture, the fine arts and medicine.

GETTING PLASTERED

While on a cycling holiday in Italy in 2002, I came off my bike in a descent in the picturesque Lazio hills north of Rome. It was not a particularly bad fall – more shocking than initially painful. I dusted myself off and checked the bike for damage. It was only after we had stopped for the night, and I had spent several sleepless agonising hours that I realised that I had probably broken something in the fall. The diagnosis, once I'd made it to a local hospital and had my hand x-rayed, was a fracture of the small, but annoyingly important, scaphoid bone, which is one of the carpal bones linking the hand to the arm. The treatment prescribed was to set the hand below the fingers and the arm below the elbow in a plaster cast that would immobilise the wrist and allow the bone to heal.

The cast was made of the traditional material used for this purpose since the nineteenth century: bandages impregnated with plaster of Paris that dried in minutes and formed a hardened shell around the forearm in under an hour. The joint had to be completely immobilised, the doctor explained in broken English, so that the bone would knit properly. He advised rest and the least possible exertion, which, as I was on a cycling holiday, I took with a certain amount of advisement (i.e., ignored).

The immobilisation of limbs after a fracture is not a new idea. In pre-industrial times, doctors knew that people with broken arms and legs could lose the full functionality of their limbs if they were treated incorrectly. The fifth-century BCE Greek doctor Hippocrates (he of the oath) recommended that broken bones be set with the help of a bench complete with a rope-and-pulley system that immobilised the patient and ensured that the bone would heal in the correct position. Doctors during antiquity and the

PLASTERED
Gypsum is the main ingredient of household plaster.

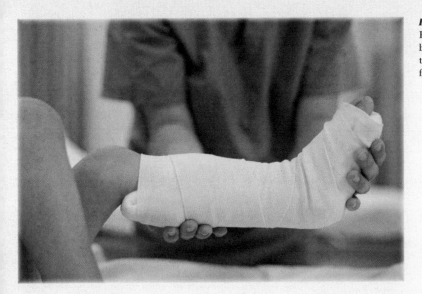

medieval period understood the use of splints held in place with stiffened
bandages to keep bones in the correct alignment. Until the nineteenth
century, a variety of substances were used to stiffen bandages. In ancient
Egypt, for example, doctors used materials and techniques employed
during the embalming of mummies. Even today, with x-rays and other
high-tech imaging techniques, an incorrectly set bone can leave a person
disabled and in pain and requiring surgery and the
rebreaking of the limb.

The problem facing patients and doctors when
treating a fracture meant a long period of immobility,
which was not practical for people who had to work to
survive, or for soldiers on the battlefield, who required
immediate, emergency treatment. In the nineteenth
century, doctors, working in civilian and military
settings, began to experiment with different ways of
stiffening bandages. The most suitable material that
doctors found, from its use as a fast-drying plaster in
art and design, was plaster of Paris (named after a
large gypsum deposit found in the Montmartre

**A deal box or trough was prepared, six inches in
depth, and of sufficient length to take the whole of
the limb [....] The plaster of Paris, in a liquid state,
was then poured into the box, until it covered the limb
to the depth of an inch.** *'Plaster of Paris in the treatment
of fractures' from* The Lancet, *1834*

CALCIUM TREAT

✦

The traditional East Asian diet,
which is low in dairy products,
includes few natural sources of
calcium, which is important for
healthy bone and teeth formation
and maintenance. Tofu, coagulated
soymilk made into blocks, which
resembles certain unpasteurised
cheeses from Europe, such as
mozzarella and ricotta, is a rich
source of dietary calcium, not from
the soybeans themselves but
because of the use of gypsum as a
coagulant that makes the oily
soybean paste into a tofu that is
soft with a grainy texture.

COOL SANDS

✦

Under very special circumstances, gypsum can become eroded into fine white sand. Unlike the yellow sand we are used to on the beach that is made of silica crystals, gypsum sand crystals are soluble in water. In areas with regular rainfall and rivers, the gypsum crystals would dissolve and be carried by rivers to the ocean. In a high, dry, mountain-ringed valley in New Mexico, however, the conditions are just right for large amounts of gypsum crystals to accumulate, drift and form sand dunes, creating the White Sands National Monument. Unlike other types of sand, white gypsum does not absorb the sun's heat and is comfortable to walk and sled on even in the hot summer.

HEATPROOF
Unlike beach sand, gypsum sand does not heat up in the sun.

quarter of the French capital). In early experiments, the entire limb was encased in a massive plaster cast, which although it ensured that the break would heal correctly, meant the patient was incapable of moving for several weeks.

Plaster of Paris bandages were first introduced in the mid-nineteenth century by a Dutch military surgeon, who used linen strips impregnated with dry plaster that were moistened as they were applied to a broken limb. A few years later, a Russian surgeon devised a similar method to treat casualties during the Crimean War (1853–56). By the end of the century, the technique had become the standard treatment for breaks and fractures in both civilian and military hospitals. Although still cumbersome, a cast around a lower or upper extremity allowed some movement, as I can testify from my own Italian experience. Undeterred by my rather cumbersome new plaster accessory, and getting rather strange looks from other cyclists and drivers, I completed the remaining 100 or so miles (160 km) of my cycling holiday to reach Rome, happy but plastered. After six weeks, I can assure the reader, the cast had done its job, and the bone had healed.

THE CARVER'S CHOICE

One of the first uses of gypsum, in the form of gypsum alabaster, was as a soft, translucent material ideal for carving intricate shapes for ornaments and statuary. Along with items made from true, or calcite, alabaster, gypsum alabaster carvings have been found from all the major ancient cultures of the Old World. The stone was used during the medieval period to carve fine altarpieces and funerary monuments in Britain. Because it is water-soluble, however, gypsum cannot be used as an external building or ornamental material. Other artistic uses of gypsum in the form of plaster of Paris are to make moulds for cast-metal sculptures or copies of existing works of art to be displayed as museum exhibits or used as models for art students.

MODEL CASTING
Major works of art were reproduced in plaster for exhibition in museums.

One of the world's most famous collections of plaster casts can be seen in the Cast Courts of the Victoria and Albert Museum in London. The works of art reproduced include full-size statues, such as Michelangelo's *David*; parts of historic buildings, such as the Portico de la Gloria from the Cathedral of Santiago de Compostela; and, most impressively, a complete cast of Trajan's Column, erected in Rome in 113 CE, which has to be displayed in two halves because of the height of the original.

Mercury
Hydrargyrum

Type: Transition metal

Origin: Native mercury and minerals, particularly cinnabar

Chemical formula: Hg

I f gold is symbolic of wealth, and iron of industry, mercury represents humanity's long occult tradition of magic and pseudo-science. Before the full understanding of the chemistry of the elements, mercury was regarded as a quasi-magical substance, intimately related to the twin chimeras of alchemy: the Elixir of Life and the Philosopher's Stone – the former said to grant immortality and the latter to turn base metal into gold. Mercury was used as a medication, but today we know that it is highly toxic, and is one of the most dangerous pollutants of the industrial age.

+ **INDUSTRIAL**

+ **CULTURAL**

+ COMMERCIAL

+ **SCIENTIFIC**

THE BIRTH OF AN EMPIRE

In the third century BCE, the most powerful person on the planet was not a descendant of Alexander the Great (356–323 BCE) or a Roman consul, but the first emperor of China, Qin Shi Huang (259–210 BCE). As we have touched upon in the entries on bronze and iron, southern Europe and the Near East experienced a disastrous breakdown of civilisation during the Bronze Age Collapse (c. 1200–1150 BCE), which initiated a first Dark Ages and prompted the emergence of new cultures in the region and encouraged the transition from bronze to iron technologies.

Cinnabar became a favourite ingredient in life-prolonging elixirs by virtue of its producing, when heated, the 'living' metal, mercury. It was claimed to be capable of converting other metals into gold, as well as of being able to prolong life for an indefinite period. Alchemy and the Alchemists *by R. Swinburne Clymer*

China, in contrast, experienced a very different cultural and technological trajectory. According to China's own traditional histories, civilisation began with the Xia Dynasty (around 4,100–3,600 years BP). Archaeologists are yet to identify physical evidence of the Xia, but by the Shang Dynasty (c. 2,700–2,056 years BP), we have evidence for a sophisticated urban culture that produced particularly fine bronze artifacts. From its heartland in modern Henan and Shaanxi provinces, Chinese civilisation gradually expanded to occupy the whole of central and northern China. Although the region was united in terms of its culture, politically it remained divided into several kingdoms until the end of the Warring States Period (c. 475–221 BCE). The king of the

TOXIC ORE
The high mercury content of cinnabar ores makes them toxic.

state of Qin, Qin Shi Huang, achieved the first unification of China by a programme of ruthless conquest and the creation of an imperial ideology that survived until the overthrow of the monarchy in 1912.

THE GREAT LEVELLER

Despite his immense power and wealth, the First Emperor of China was a deeply troubled man. He was, like so many powerful men after him, afraid of the one certain fact of human existence that could not be changed by all the world's power and riches: death. This, however, did not stop the emperor from trying to find a way to cheat the Grim Reaper. In an age long before humans developed a scientific understanding of the world, the Chinese developed a system of beliefs that combined magic with a number of surprisingly accurate observations of the natural world. Although the Chinese had an advanced medical system, it was not based on an understanding of human anatomy and germ theory, but on a belief in *qi* ('vital energy') and the balance of *yin* (the negative) and *yang* (the positive) within the body.

Chinese physicians and alchemists thought that

UNDER PRESSURE
Torricelli replaced water with mercury to make the first practical barometer.

AS HEAVY AS AIR
◆
Until the Scientific Revolution, the accepted wisdom was that the atmosphere, the gaseous layer that surrounds Earth, did not exert any force on the surface of the planet. Air, after all, does not appear to have weight. But because we do not live in a vacuum, it must have mass and therefore an effect on the surface and the things on it. Several Italian scientists, including Gasparo Berti (c. 1600–43), Galileo Galilei (1564–1642) and Evangelista Torricelli (1608–47), conducted a series of practical experiments to investigate what we now call 'atmospheric pressure'. Berti designed an apparatus consisting of a 10.5-m (34-ft) high open-ended tube filled with water, standing in a basin of water. Instead of flowing out of the bottom, the water was maintained at a certain level by the air pressure. Although Berti's device worked well to measure atmospheric pressure, it was far too large to be practical for any day-to-day use. Berti's experiments gave Torricelli the idea of using a liquid heavier than water to measure air pressure. When he hit on mercury, he was able to reduce the height of the column to 80 cm (31 in), and thus created the first working mercury barometer.

FLOWING METAL
Mercury is unique among metals in being liquid at room temperature.

TRANSMUTATION
Alchemists claimed they were able to turn mercury into gold.

matter was created by the interaction of five 'elements': earth, air, fire, metal and wood (compared to the West's earth, air, water and fire, with an optional fifth, ether). Like their European, Near Eastern and Indian counterparts, Chinese alchemists believed in the existence of a substance that would grant immortality: the Elixir of Life. To make it, they turned to materials that resisted the decay wrought by time, such as jade, gold and the 'living metal' extracted from cinnabar ores, quicksilver or mercury. Qin Shi Huang devoted considerable time, energy, and money in trying to discover the secret of immortality. He sent several naval expeditions to discover the elixir, and had his alchemists prepare their own versions of the substance. Later recipes reveal that these probably contained such life-enhancing ingredients as arsenic, sulphur and mercury.

Mercury is now known to be an extremely dangerous pollutant that accumulates in the food chain, particularly shellfish and fish, which are then eaten by humans. One of the most destructive outbreaks of mercury poisoning was Minamata disease, which affected tens of thousand of people in Japan during the 1950s and 60s. The symptoms of the disease included muscle weakness, neuropathy, insanity, paralysis and death. Although the First Emperor was probably fairly paranoid to begin with, his regular intake of mercury to prolong his own life probably contributed to his descent into madness, as well as his early death at the age of 49.

As befitted the sovereign of the world's greatest empire, Qin Shi Huang was buried in a tomb of unparalleled magnificence near the city of Xi'an in Shaanxi province. His tomb was constructed within a vast earth mound, but the most spectacular part of the funerary complex discovered in 1974 is the 8,000–strong Terracotta Army made of life-sized warriors, who

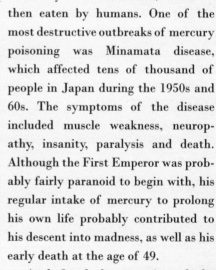

FATAL METAL
Mercury is one of the
most lethal industrial
pollutants.

stand guard around the emperor's tomb. According to period descriptions, the burial chamber contained further wonders, including a huge map of the empire, with the rivers reproduced in mercury. Whether this is true, and whether the tomb remains intact or was plundered in antiquity, is unknown, as the mound has never been opened in the modern period. Even the atheistic and iconoclastic Communist dictatorship of Mao Zedong (1893–1976) did not dare disturb the sleep of the country's founder. Remote soundings, however, have revealed the existence of a large chamber inside the mound, as well as very high levels of mercury in the soil.

The alchemical obsession with the discovery of the entirely mythical Elixir of Life and the Philosopher's Stone, which could transmute base metals into gold, continued to occupy the minds of alchemists until the Scientific Revolution of the seventeenth century. As many of the men considered to be the fathers of modern science, such as the discoverer of gravitation, Isaac Newton (1642–1727), were also alchemists, the search for immortality played an important role in the foundations of the modern sciences of physics and chemistry.

MEMORIAL FOUNTAIN

✦

The city of Almadén in Spain is historically one of the largest producers of mercury from cinnabar ores in the world. During the Spanish Civil War (1936–39), the city underwent a brutal siege by the troops of General Franco (1892–1975). The American sculptor Alexander Calder (1898–1976) created a mercury fountain for the 1937 Paris World's Fair as a memorial of the atrocity. The circular fountain is now on permanent display in Barcelona.

Potassium

Kalium

Type: Alkali metal

Origin: Mineral ores and organic deposits in caves

Chemical formula: K

+ **INDUSTRIAL**
+ **CULTURAL**
+ **COMMERCIAL**
+ **SCIENTIFIC**

Although metallic potassium was not isolated until the early nineteenth century, potassium compounds have had several important uses since antiquity, notably as a fertiliser, to replace the depletion of potassium in soils, and as one of the alkalis employed in the manufacture of soap.

CLEANING UP

There are two rival explanations for the origins of soap in Europe, the first claiming that the Romans discovered how to make it, and the second that it was the invention of the barbarian Gauls and Germans. The Roman story goes that on top of Mount Sapo, which overlooks the River Tiber in Rome, there stood a temple, where, as was the Roman custom, animals were sacrificed and their flesh was burnt on a pyre so that the sacrifice could reach the gods. The resulting wood ash mixed with animal remains – potash (potassium carbonate, K_2CO_3) and animal fat, the two constituents of soap – would have become combined on their way down the hill and reached the Tiber, where they would have given the water an unusual cleansing power much appreciated by the ladies of the area.

Although charming, the story is now thought to be complete fiction. When animals were sacrificed, archaeologists point out, the tastier morsels – the flesh and fat – would be eaten by the priests and devotees, while the gods had to make do with the skin, entrails and bones, which would not have contained enough animal fat to make soap in the manner described in the story. The ancient Greeks and Romans, though both fastidious about personal hygiene, and famous for their public baths, did not use soap to clean themselves. Greek athletes, after a hard day's workout at the gymnasium, covered their bodies with a mixture of olive oil and sand, which was scraped off with a metal instrument called a strigil, before they entered the bath for a leisurely soak.

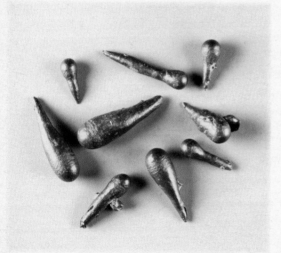

UNDIFFERENTIATED
Potassium is an alkali metal that was long confused with sodium.

You need only one soap

IVORY SOAP

Pure—First quality,
Not expensive
Will wash anything
No chapping **IT FLOATS**

The simplest and rudest preparation of potash is called ash balls in England, and weed ash in Ireland. It cannot be said to be properly an article of commerce, although a considerable quantity is annually made by the peasantry of both countries, and disposed of among the neighbouring farmers and bleachers. *From the 'Economy of the Laundry' (1852)*

SOFT SOAPING

According to Roman sources, it was the uncouth barbarian tribesmen of Gaul and Germania who first made soap from wood ash and animal fat, and used it daily to clean themselves. The combination of potash with animal fat makes 'soft' soap, which remains semi-liquid, and would have been like the shower gels of our own day (without the exciting range of colours and scents). The addition of salt causes the mixture to harden and makes 'hard' soap that could be cut into cakes and blocks. In periods when salt was scarce or expensive, however, and in much of domestic soap manufacture, soft soap would have been the preferred option.

In the early eighteenth century, just as soap technology was improving, and soap was becoming a widespread commodity, the English crown imposed a tax on it that artificially inflated its price, discouraging its use among the general population. The tax increased to three pennies per pound in 1816, effectively making soap a luxury item. In 1853, the British government, finally realising the health benefits of making soap more generally available, abolished the tax, although it had raised the not inconsiderable sum of £1 million annually.

DIETARY POTASSIUM

+

Potassium is an essential dietary supplement that helps maintain the fluid balance within our cells and plays an important role in the proper functioning of the nerves and brain. Fortunately, potassium is present in most fruits, vegetables, meat and fish, but particularly rich sources include parsley, chocolate, pistachio nuts, avocados and bran. According to recent studies, many Americans, Germans and Italians have diets that are deficient in potassium, increasing their risks of hypertension, stroke and heart disease.

OVERTAXED
The British government taxed soap until 1853.

Marble

Marmor

Type: Metamorphic rock

Origin: Metamorphism of limestone

Chemical formula: $CaCO_3$

During classical antiquity, marble was the stone of choice for statuary, temples, palaces and major public buildings. The fine white translucent marble from Mount Penteliko outside Athens was used to build the monuments on the city's Acropolis, which remained models for world art and architecture for millennia after their construction.

LOSING HER MARBLES

The former actress and signer Melina Mercouri (1920–94) during her eight-year tenure as Minister of Culture of Greece (1981–89) made repeated, passionate attacks on the British government for its refusal to return the Parthenon, or Elgin, Marbles to Greece, prompting an overjoyed British tabloid press to run headlines as comical as 'Melina loses her marbles'. Thomas Bruce, seventh Earl of Elgin (1766–1841), illegally looted (according to the Greeks) or legally acquired (according to the British) the sculptures along with architectural members from the already ruined buildings of Athens's Acropolis between 1801 and 1812, when Greece was a province of the Ottoman Empire. Elgin claimed that he acted to save the marbles from destruction – a claim accepted by the British government, which purchased the collection for the British Museum in 1816.

For an earlier book, I imagined the Acropolis of Athens as it would have appeared in 415 BCE. In 480 BCE, during the Greco-Persian Wars (499–449 BCE), the Persians took the city and reduced the Acropolis to rubble, smashing and burning its ancient temples, votive altars and statues. Until the ascendancy of Pericles (495–429 BCE), who dominated the Athenian political scene during her Golden Age, the Acropolis remained in ruins. He persuaded the popular assembly of Athens to use the considerable revenues of the Athenian Empire to rebuild the Acropolis and to create a stage of unparalleled magnificence for the city's religious and civic festivals. Although the great scheme was not completed in Pericles's lifetime, it was added to and embellished throughout antiquity, by the Athenians themselves, the Macedonians and the Romans.

INNER LIGHT
In sunlight the Pentelic marble of Athens glows with a soft radiance.

PAST GLORIES
The ruins of the Acropolis
of Athens as they appeared
in 1821.

A JOURNEY BACK IN TIME

Anyone who has been to Athens can testify to the
beauty of its site, which is still dominated by the huge
rock of the Acropolis at its centre, despite the rather
ugly modern constructions that now surround it and
have spread to the foot of the neighbouring mountains.

For the visitor at the end of the fifth century BCE,
Athens is a much smaller walled town. He will climb to
the top of the fortified Acropolis through its one official entrance on the western side, the monumental
gateway known as the Propylaia (437–432 BCE),
which incorporates the small Temple of Athena Nike
(finished c. 410 BCE). Once through the gateway, the
visitor's eye will first be drawn to the 10-m (30-ft)-tall
bronze statue of Athena Promakhos, whose helmet
and spear point can be seen from Cape Sounion, the
promontory on the easternmost coast of Attica. But
the statue will not detain the visitor long, as beyond it,
and two low undistinguished buildings, is the glory of
the Acropolis: the Parthenon (447–432 BCE). This
incorporates two chambers within its beautifully
proportioned colonnaded walls: one housing the huge
cult image of Athena in gold and ivory, and the other,
the treasury of the Athenian empire. Unlike the
churches of later times, the Parthenon does not host
religious services and observances; these which take
place outdoors at open-air altars on the Acropolis. The
Parthenon is more akin to the monuments set along the

TEAR OF GOD
✦

One of the most iconic Islamic
buildings in the world, India's Taj
Mahal, was built by the Mughal
emperor Shah Jahan (1592–1666)
as a mausoleum for his third wife,
Mumtaz Mahal (1593–1631).
Construction of the Taj began in
1632 and took 21 years to
complete. The building stands on
the Yamuna River just outside the
northern Indian city of Agra. It is
built of white marble inlaid with
precious and semi-precious stones.
Shah Jahan was deposed and
imprisoned by his son, and when
he died, he was buried beside his
favourite wife inside the Taj.

National Mall in Washington, D.C., which were built to be seen and impress the visitor with the nation's wealth and power. North of the Parthenon stands the Erechtheion (421–406 BCE), a building that shows none of its larger neighbour's grandeur, proportion and symmetry. The smaller Erechtheion is a composite structure in several parts, built to accommodate much older shrines and altars within a single building.

TECHNICOLOUR
The marble Parthenon frieze was originally painted in vivid colours.

CLASSICAL DISNEYLAND

What ties these diverse buildings together in one grand architectural scheme, which is still visible today even in its ruined state, is their construction in the fine-grained, white, semi-translucent marble from nearby Mount Penteliko. Although now chipped and dulled by the centuries, the Pentelic marble of the Acropolis would have glowed in the bright Athenian sunlight. While the main architectural members – walls and columns – of the building would have been left plain, the statues on the pediments, friezes, metopes and other decorative motifs would have been painted in bright colours, giving the Acropolis the appearance of a rather tasteful classical Disneyland.

The temples of the Acropolis survived the Christianisation of the empire and the proscription of paganism in the fourth century. The Parthenon and Erechtheion, like many other pagan temples in the Roman world, were converted into churches, with the removal of the cult images of the gods, but otherwise little alteration to the fabric of the buildings. The Parthenon remained a church until the Islamic conquest of Athens in 1456, when part of the building was converted into a mosque. Despite the Islamic ban on human images, the marble sculptures of the Parthenon survived Islamic rule.

IMPRISONED
Michelangelo's *David* 'released' from his marble prison.

In every block of marble I see a statue as plain as though it stood before me, shaped and perfect in attitude and action. I have only to hew away the rough walls that imprison the lovely apparition to reveal it to other eyes as mine see it.

Michelangelo (1475–1564)

The wrecking of the Parthenon was not done by ancient Christian or medieval Islamic zealots, but by seventeenth-century Italians. During the Venetian siege of Athens in 1687, Venetian shells rained on the Parthenon, which was being used as a munitions store by the Ottoman garrison. A huge explosion tore the building apart, scattering fragments of the building and its sculptures across the Acropolis. The damage was compounded when the Venetian commander, Francesco Morosini (1619–94), tried to loot some of the surviving sculptures from the west pediment, but his rope tackle broke, and the sculptures smashed on to the rocks below.

When Elgin arrived in Greece a century later, the ruins of the Acropolis were in an extremely poor condition. For the payment of a bribe, the Turkish authorities sold fragments of the sculptures to visiting Western tourists, and parts of the walls and columns had been looted by the locals to use as building material, or ground up to make mortar and plaster. Elgin removed about half of the surviving Parthenon sculptures, including sections of the frieze, many metopes, and parts of the pediments, which are now on display in the British Museum. For two centuries, the British could claim that their ownership of the marbles had preserved them during the Greek War of Independence (1821–32) and later conflicts, as well as damage from pollution and poor restoration attempts made during the nineteenth and twentieth centuries. These arguments have lost much of their power, however, since the opening in 2009 of the new Acropolis Museum in Athens specifically designed to house all the surviving Parthenon sculptures so that the decorative can once more be viewed and appreciated in sequence as its designer, Phidias, intended.

DISPLACED
London's Marble Arch once stood in front of Buckingham Palace.

Nacre
Nakara

Type: Organic mineral

Origin: Molluscs

Chemical formula: $CaCO_3$

+ INDUSTRIAL
+ **CULTURAL**
+ **COMMERCIAL**
+ SCIENTIFIC

In this entry on nacre, we come to one of nature's miracles – mother of pearl – though one achieved with a material that we have already come across in several entries with much more mundane appearance and applications: calcium carbonate. As mother of pearl or nacreous pearls, nacre has a long history in ornamentation and jewellery.

GRECO-ROMAN GUIDEBOOK

In around 60 CE, an anonymous Greco-Roman merchant wrote one of the most extraordinary geographic texts to come to us from the ancient world. Penned in an informative, matter-of-fact, travelogue style, completely devoid of sea serpents, mermaids and one-footed humans, the *Periplus of the Erythraean Sea* describes the trading routes, tidal conditions, climates, ports, products, kingdoms and peoples of the coasts of East Africa, Arabia, the Persian Gulf and India to the Ganges Delta (in modern-day West Bengal and Bangladesh), as well as touching briefly on the overland route from the Near East to China across Central Asia. The *Periplus* reveals the full extent of the trading links that existed in the Old World during classical antiquity and the range of products that were traded across the vast distances that separated the two superpowers of the day: Rome and Han China. Among the commodities described as originating from Africa, the Persian Gulf and in particular south India, the writer mentions the most coveted of natural gemstones: pearls.

Oysters are not the only species of shellfish that produce nacreous pearls, which are made by other sea- and freshwater molluscs. However, the most sought-after are produced by several species of the oyster genus *Pinctada*, which are found in seas and oceans worldwide, but in antiquity were known from the waters of the Persian Gulf, the Red Sea, the Indian Ocean and the South China Sea. After the conquest and settlement of Central and South America in the sixteenth century, Spanish

MOTHER OF PEARL
Nacre is produced by many shellfish, including the pearl oyster.

ILL-FATED
King Charles I's pearl
earring disappeared after
his execution.

settlers discovered rich pearl fisheries in the waters around the islands of Cubagua and Margarita in the Caribbean Sea. Although pearls have been valued for their natural luster and colour as gems to be mounted on reliquaries, altars and thrones, and to be worn as jewels, they have not been esteemed by all cultures. Historically, the Japanese, for example, who did not have the custom of wearing jewellery, used mother of pearl for inlaid lacquer work (see box, p.112), but took on their role as the world's leader in pearl fishing in the modern period.

AN ITCH TO SCRATCH

There is a common misconception that pearls are created when a piece of grit enters an open oyster. As this must be a fairly common occurrence, as an oyster takes in water and nutrients all the time, we should be knee-deep in pearls. However, the real trigger for pearl formation is when a piece of foreign organic matter, such as a parasite, enters the mantle, or a piece of the oyster's tissue is damaged by an attack by a predator. The oyster will create a pearl sack around the injury or irritant, over which it will deposit microscopic layers of aragonite (a form of calcium carbonate) combined with a horn-like compound called conchiolin. The result is not the dull white of gypsum but the gorgeous rainbow iridescence of nacre, a word derived from the Arabic *nakara*. Although perfectly spherical pearls are prized for necklaces, pearls come in a variety of shapes and colours including tear drop, button, blister and baroque pearls. Among the rarest colours, and therefore the most

From Comari towards the south, this region extends to Colchi, where the pearl-fisheries are; (they are worked by condemned criminals); and it belongs to the Pandian Kingdom. Beyond Colchi there follows another district called the Coast Country, which lies on a bay, and has a region inland called Argaru. At this place, and nowhere else, are bought the pearls gathered on the coast thereabouts.

Description of Indian pearl fisheries from the Periplus of the Erythraean Sea *(c. 60 CE)*

JAPANESE BLING

✦

Japanese art is known for its restrained elegance and sobriety, but this has not always been the case. During the Japanese 'Renaissance', the brief but vibrant Azuchi-Momoyama period (1568–1600), Japanese decorative artists produced luxury goods by combining Japanese techniques such as raden (mother-of-pearl inlay) with European designs and motifs to produce extraordinarily luxurious (though some might say gaudy) pieces of Nanban lacquerware for Japan's feudal ruling class, the *daimyo*, and for export to Europe.

valuable, are black pearls from the Pacific Ocean, but pearls can also be cream, yellow, pink, gold, green and blue.

Unlike amber and coral, pearls are not usually faked, but since the nineteenth century, the production of pearls was transformed by a discovery by the British marine biologist William Saville-Kent (1845–1908) that oysters could be artificially induced to produce them. Until then, pearl fishing entailed the laborious process of collecting oysters from the seabed by hand or with dredges, and opening them one by one to check the mantle for pearls. As pearls are extremely rare, this was not only wasteful (as pearl oysters are not considered very palatable), but it led to the near extinction of pearl oysters in certain regions from over-fishing. It was the Japanese and not Saville-Kent who profited from the discovery, as they patented the technique and went on to dominate the production of artificial pearls for much of the twentieth century.

There are several methods used to create pearls artificially. The closest to the natural process involves the grafting of a peace of donor tissue into the oyster, which will stimulate the creation of a pearl sack. However, this will take as long as the natural process. A much faster method involves the introduction of a bead, which will be coated in nacre in around six months and will produce a perfectly round pearl. If a bead has been used to create a cultured pearl, this can be detected by x-ray. Although indistinguishable by the naked eye from natural pearls apart from their unusual regularity, cultured pearls are much cheaper, and therefore have reduced the overall allure of the gem.

IDENTICAL
It is difficult to distinguish real from cultured pearls.

THE TWO PILGRIMS

Two of the world's most famous and expensive pearls have almost the same name – La Peregrina and La Pelegrina (both meaning 'pilgrim' in Spanish) – and both have extraordinary histories, intertwined with the rise and fall of several of Europe's great noble houses. Discovered at the beginning of the sixteenth century in Caribbean waters, La Peregrina was given to Philip II of Spain (1527–98), who in turn presented it to the Catholic Queen Mary I of England (1516–58), who unsuccessfully tried to bring Protestant England back into the Catholic fold. The pearl was returned to Spain upon Mary's death and was stolen by the French during the Napoleonic Wars (1803–15). The deposed Emperor Napoleon III (1808–73), exiled to England, sold it to a British aristocrat, who in turn put it up for sale at Sotheby's in London in the 1960s. The buyer was the actor Richard Burton (1925–84), who purchased it as a gift for Elizabeth Taylor (1932–2011). The actress admitted in an interview that the heavy pearl had once fallen off its chain, and she had had to rescue it from the mouth of one of her pet dogs – almost the most expensive doggy chew toy in history!

PILGRIM I
This famous pearl was owned by Mary I of England and later by Elizabeth Taylor.

The second pearl, La Pelegrina, has had an even more eventful history, surviving not one but two revolutions. It was discovered near the Island of Margarita in the mid-sixteenth century, and it was also acquired by a Spanish monarch. He gave it to his daughter, the Infanta Maria Theresa (1638–83) when she married King Louis XIV of France (1638–1715). It disappeared after Louis XVI (1754–93) met his end on the guillotine, and resurfaced in the possession of the noble house of Yusupov in Czarist Russia. After the Revolution of 1917, Felix Yusupov (1887–1967) escaped to France, where he was forced to sell the pearl to raise funds in the 1950s.

PILGRIM II
This pearl survived both the French and Russian revolutions.

Natron

Natrium

Type: Transpiro-evaporate mineral

Origin: Natural salts from dry lakebeds

Chemical formula: $Na_2CO_3 \cdot 10H_2O$ with $NaHCO_3$ and sodium

+ **INDUSTRIAL**
+ **CULTURAL**
+ COMMERCIAL
+ SCIENTIFIC

Natron is a natural salt that has several industrial and domestic applications, but its main historical use was in the process of mummification in ancient Egypt. Thanks to its antibacterial properties, natron halted the natural processes of bodily decay and preserved mummies for thousands of years, giving us an unparalleled insight into the appearance, lives and deaths of an ancient people.

THE MUMMY'S CURSE

The Hollywood version of the 'mummy's curse' entails the dreadful fate that awaits those who dare enter the tombs of the pharaohs and meet a horrible death at the hands of the outraged mummy lurching back into life to avenge the sacrilege. The sad truth, however, was that the real curse of the mummy was on the mummy itself. From the earliest times in ancient Egypt, when one would have imagined that religious superstition combined with royal authority and severe punishments might have discouraged the robbing of royal tombs, the allure of easy pickings seemed to have overcome any fear of the legal and supernatural sanctions – most royal burials were ransacked, many only a few days after the funeral. Sadly, the mummy itself was usually the principal target of the robbers, as it was covered in golden jewels and amulets in preparation for its journey into the Underworld.

The reason why a rather obscure pharaoh of the Eighteenth Dynasty called Tutankhamun (c. 1341–1323 BCE) is so well known today, is that his tomb is one of the most intact royal Egyptian burials ever found, whose contents were valued in 2010 at around $50 million (at 2010 prices). Archaeologists believe that even his tomb was broken into and robbed in antiquity, and that the robbers got away with about two-thirds of the jewels stored in the treasure chamber, but never reached the king's mummy in its gilded shrine and sarcophagi. Whenever possible, royal mummies were rescued after robberies, patched up and reburied in much less grand but safer, anonymous tombs, without their horde of treasures, where they continued their eternal sleep, until they were disturbed again by archaeologists.

DRIED MEATS
Natron was used to preserve the organs of mummies in canopic parcels.

The luckiest mummies were either left in their tombs or taken to be exhibited in the museums of London, Paris, Berlin and New York, but the least fortunate were ground down to make into artist's pigment, or displayed as exhibits in fairground freak shows. The mummy of Ramesses I (r. 1295–1294 BCE), an obscure pharaoh of the Nineteenth Dynasty, was removed from its tomb in the mid-nineteenth century and found its way to the Niagara Falls Museum in Ontario, Canada. The museum also exhibited stuffed animal specimens, aboriginal artifacts, mummies and other 'freaks of nature'. The collection was sold to the Emory University in Atlanta, GA, in 1999, where the pharaoh was finally identified some 130 years after he had first made the trip across the Atlantic. In 2003, the king was repatriated to Luxor, Egypt, with full military honours.

PICKLED PHARAOHS

Mummies have been found in Europe, Asia and the Americas, where they were preserved by a

GOLDEN BOY
Tutankhamun remains one of the world's most famous mummies.

particularly dry climate, in bogs or by their burial in frozen ground at high altitudes. Early Egyptian mummies, such as the one nicknamed 'Ginger' – a pre-dynastic male burial dating to around 5,400 years BP now on exhibit in the British Museum in London – were preserved by their internment in dry desert sand. However, around 4,600 years BP, the Egyptians began to embalm the bodies of their dead kings and queens, evolving a complex process that would ensure the preservation of the body until the present day. The preservation of the body itself, which was considered by later religions to be unnecessary, was vital to the Egyptians, who believed that without it, the deceased would not continue to exist in the afterlife. They believed that the human body contained several 'souls', including the *akh* and the *ba*, which had to be kept united within the body and provided with food, goods and servants in the afterlife.

GINGER
Before the invention of mummification, humans were sometimes naturally preserved in sand.

The process of Egyptian mummification changed throughout its long history, and when the Greek historian Herodotus described it comparatively late in its history, in the fifth century BCE (see quote, left), it had three different grades (in modern terms: 'budget', 'deluxe' and 'regal'), depending on the status of the person being buried and the cost of the process required. The best-preserved mummies come from the New Kingdom (sixteenth to eleventh centuries BCE), and include the mortal remains of Tutankhamun and Ramesses II (see box, opposite). For an important royal burial, the process of preparation and interment took several months (or years if you include the time it took to build, decorate and furnish the tomb). After death, the body of the dead pharaoh was entrusted to the care of priest-embalmers, who knew the practical techniques and magical rituals that would ensure the survival of both body and soul into the afterlife.

[The body] is filled with pure bruised myrrh, cassia, and every other aromatic substance with the exception of frankincense, and sewn up again, after which the body's placed in natrum, covered entirely over, for seventy days – never longer. When this period, which must not be exceeded, is over, the body is washed and then wrapped from head to foot in linen cut into strips and smeared on the under side with gum. *Herodotus (c. 484–425 BCE) on mummification*

Egyptian embalmers evolved a particularly effective process to preserve the bodies of the deceased, which has been compared (rather unkindly and also inaccurately) to pickling meat or vegetables. According to Herodotus, the mummification of the body took 70 days. The first task of the embalmer-priests was to remove the soft tissues and organs inside the body that might rot and degrade the body quickly, especially in the hot Egyptian climate. As the aim was to preserve the external appearance of the body as much as possible, the removal of the contents had to be done with great care, so as not to damage the skin and musculature. The brain, whose true function as the seat of consciousness was unknown to the Egyptians, was sometimes removed with a metal hook inserted into the skull through the nostrils, or sometimes left in place. The eyes were also removed and discarded.

THE HEART OF THE MATTER

The abdomen was cut open on the left side with a stone knife so that the internal organs and viscera could be removed. As we have seen in the entry on alabaster, the organs that the Egyptians considered to be important were the stomach, lungs, liver and intestines, which were removed, soaked or dried in natron salts, wrapped in bandages and stored in a canopic box or four separate canopic jars, which would be interred with the mummy. The only organ left inside the body cavity was the heart, considered to be the seat of consciousness and personality, which would be judged in the afterlife.

When the deceased travelled into *Duat*, the Underworld, it was believed that he would eventually reach the place of judgement, where his heart would be weighed by the god Thot against the feather of *Ma'at*, or truth. If the person had led a good life according to Egyptian beliefs, he would live forever in the paradise of *Osiris*, but if the judgement went

AN EMBARRASSING CASE OF MUSHROOMS

✦

'Look on my works, ye Mighty, and despair!' is the inscription of the pedestal of the broken statue in Shelley's (1792–1822) poem 'Ozymandias', describing a ruined monument to Egypt's mightiest pharaoh, Ramesses II (r. 1279–1213 BCE). Like many other royal mummies, Ramesses II was reburied after robbers ransacked his tomb in antiquity. In 1974, archaeologists found that the king's mummy was deteriorating because of a fungal infection. He was flown to Paris for immediate treatment, after the Egyptian government had issued him with a passport that listed his occupation as 'king, deceased'. Granted full military honours during his trip to France, the former pharaoh was cured of his embarrassing infection. A close examination of the mummy revealed that one of the longest living pharaohs was a redhead, suffered from crippling arthritis in old age, and had a serious case of gum disease that may have brought about his death.

PHARAOH: INFECTED
Name: Ramesses II
Occupation: 'King, deceased'.

against him, a monster devoured his heart, condemning him to a second and everlasting death. Elaborate 'heart scarab' amulets were placed over the heart to ensure the best outcome in the judgement. Magical spells, known as 'The Book of the Dead', were written inside the coffin and on the tomb walls to instruct the deceased in how to survive the perilous journey through the Underworld.

With all the soft tissues removed, the body was ready for the second stage of preservation. The simplest method involved packing the body inside and out with dry natron that would draw the moisture out of the tissues, while at the same time killing any pests and bacteria. After the required period, the natron was removed. In order to make the body more lifelike, the embalmers packed the sunken areas of the face and body with linen, sawdust or straw. At this stage, false eyes were inserted into the sockets. In the second, more complex, process, thought to have been used on best-preserved royal mummies, the body cavity was filled and sewn up, and the body was immersed into a bath containing natron salts. A solution of natron would halt the process of decay and kill insects and bacteria, but it also preserved the appearance of the deceased much better than the dry method. The body was now ready for the third and final stage of mummification.

THE BRITISH PHARAOH

✦

In 2011, Alan Billis, a British taxi driver who was dying of lung cancer, agreed to take part in an experiment to discover how the Egyptians had managed to preserve the bodies of their kings and queens in antiquity. After his death, Billis underwent the process of mummification, which was filmed for British television. After the removal of his internal organs (but not his brain), Billis was immersed in a bath of concentrated natron salts that stopped the normal process of decay, and transformed him into the first mummy to have been created in over 3,000 years. His body, wrapped in linen bandages, will be preserved to study the ongoing stages of his mummification.

WRAPPED, SEALED AND DATE-STAMPED FOR ETERNITY

The embalmers wound hundreds of yards of linen bandages around the body, carefully wrapping the fingers and toes separately before covering the whole foot and hand in another layer of linen. Amulets in the shape of scarab beetles and keys of life (*ankh*) were placed in the bandages, and spells and prayers were written on the linen strips to ensure the safe passage of the soul through the Underworld and the survival of the body in the tomb. The bandages were stiffened with resin several times, and further bandages were applied on top until the mummy was sealed within a linen cocoon. The funerary mask was then placed over the head – in the case of a royal burial, this would have been made of precious materials, such as Tutankhamun's gold and lapis lazuli mask – but in the Hellenistic and Roman periods, when ordinary citizens were mummified, much more simple but extremely lifelike funerary portraits were painted on papyrus and wood and placed over the mummy's head.

LIFELIKE
Once mummified, the deceased would be placed in a decorated sarcophagus or papier-mâché mummy case.

The deceased was now prepared for whatever eternity had in store for it, which, as it turned out for many Egyptian mummies, was going to be a very active afterlife indeed. Starting in the Renaissance, European collectors acquired mummies for their 'cabinets of curiosities', and alchemists and magicians ground up their body parts for their potions. Nineteenth- and twentieth-century museums in the developed world exhibited hundreds of mummies to educate the masses about the strangeness of ancient civilisations and the superiority of their own; and twenty-first-century archaeologists have exhumed and studied them with the latest computer-imaging techniques to discover the state of their health, teeth and bones, and extracted their DNA to study their origins.

Preserved by natron, Egyptian mummies have achieved a form of immortality not given to the vast majority of humans, whose mortal remains decompose and are devoured by insects. They uniquely managed to preserve their individual, embodied identities to speak to us today as people of flesh and blood who lived thousands of years ago, and who, above all, loved life so much that they never wanted it to end.

Obsidian

Obsidianus

Type: Volcanic glass

Origin: Volcanism

Chemical formula: SiO_2 with MgO, Fe_3O_4

✦ INDUSTRIAL

✦ *CULTURAL*

✦ *COMMERCIAL*

✦ SCIENTIFIC

According to archaeologists, the black volcanic glass obsidian was the first commodity to be commercially traded in the modern sense of the term. In Eurasia, it remained in use for thousands of years until it was phased out by metal for most practical uses. In the Americas, however, obsidian was made into tools and weapons until the Spanish conquest in the sixteenth century.

THE ULTIMATE SACRIFICE

What every school student knows about the pre-Columbian peoples of Mesoamerica – in particular about the Aztecs (or more correctly, the Mexica), whose empire occupied most of modern Mexico, with its capital at Tenochtitlan (now Mexico City) in the middle of Lake Texcoco – is that their religion centred on human sacrifice. The Spanish conquistadors cited the practice as one of their justifications for their invasion and conquest of the region and the destruction of its Native American cultures, conveniently forgetting that their own Celtic ancestors, as well as the ever-so-civilised classical Greeks and Romans, also practised human sacrifice, though admittedly never on the same scale. The exact number and manner of Mexica sacrifices, however, is still debated, as many historians have pointed out that many Spanish accounts were probably not only biased but also exaggerated, and distorted the Mexica rituals for political and ideological ends.

To the modern mind, there is no more horrific or abhorrent practice than human sacrifice (with the possible exception of cannibalism, which was often associated with human sacrifice in pre-Columbian Mesoamerica). Our unshakeable belief in the sanctity and value of the individual – especially if that individual happens to be you, yourself – means that we imagine that sacrificial victims were dragged kicking and screaming to blood-soaked altars on top of temple-pyramids, where their hearts were ripped out of their living bodies. However, the Mesoamerican worldview was very different from our own. Although the following is a huge oversimplification, in a sense, Mesoamerican religion was a mirror image of Judeo-Christian religion. In Christianity, Jesus Christ, the human incarna-

NATURAL GLASS
Obsidian can be fractured to make knives and arrowheads.

SALT LAKE CITY
The Aztec capital as it
would have appeared to
the conquistadors.

tion of God, is tortured, crucified and finally stabbed with a spear, in
order to bring salvation to humanity. In other words, god himself
becomes the sacrificial victim so that humanity can enjoy (eternal) life.
But in Aztec religion, the roles were reversed, and humans gave their
blood and lives in order to preserve both the gods and the world.

A GOOD DEATH

In Mesoamerica, the idea of sacrifice, of the individual's own blood or of
a victim's blood, heart and life, was at the centre of religious beliefs and
practices. Among the medieval Mexica, as well as the Classic Maya before
them, commoners and nobles practised auto-sacrifice by shedding their
own blood as a personal offering to nourish the gods, atone for transgres-
sions and experience supernatural visions (see box, p.122). In the practice
of human sacrifice, though many victims were non-Mexica prisoners of
war who had been captured specifically to be offered to the gods, others
were Mexica volunteers (or children who had been offered for the purpose
by their parents). The noblest death for a Mexica man was to die in battle,
and for a Mexica woman to die in childbirth. Those deaths earned an

automatic place in the Mexica heaven; the worst death was in one's bed at home, which condemned the deceased to a dreadful afterlife.

To be sacrificed to the gods was considered to be a 'good' death that would be rewarded in the next life. An unwilling victim, who showed signs of fear, cried out and lost control of his bowels, was considered unworthy, and was mocked and killed but not sacrificed. Hence, prisoners of war, who were often captured specifically to be sacrificed, must have, to some degree, accepted their fate and gone to their deaths stoically, certain in the knowledge that they would play their part in the preservation of the world, and that the manner of their deaths would be rewarded in the next life.

War and sacrifice were closely linked in Mexica culture, and the material that tied them together was the natural glass, obsidian, known as *itztli* in the Nahuatl language spoken by the Mexica. Obsidian is a byproduct of volcanic eruptions, and the dark brown or black mineral is found in all regions of the world that have active volcanoes. During the Stone Age, obsidian was an important material for the manufacture of tools, weapons, decorative items, jewellery and mirrors, and archaeologists believe that it was the first commodity to be 'traded' in the modern sense of the word. Like flint, obsidian can be shaped by striking off, or 'knapping', flakes, and because it is a type of natural glass, it can be given an extremely sharp cutting edge. The downside is that obsidian blunts easily and will smash when it strikes a harder material.

BARBED TONGUE

✦

In addition to human sacrifice, the pre-Columbian Mesoamericans practised a form of auto-sacrifice in the shape of bloodletting, in the belief that the shedding of their own blood nourished the gods and allowed them to communicate with the supernatural realm.

A bas-relief from the Classic Maya site of Yaxchilan (now in Chiapas, Mexico), representing an event that took place in 709 CE, depicts the ruler's wife, the Lady Xoc, pulling a rope studded with obsidian blades through her tongue to conjure a vision of a deceased ruler.

The victims [of ritual sacrifice] were usually captives from the wars that were fought expressly for this purpose. At dawn each day, a captive, often drugged on hallucinogens like peyote, or at least semi-drunk on 'obsidian wine' (or pulque, a type of fermented beer made from the maguey plant), was dragged up the steps of one of the main temples of Tenochtitlan.... Four priests held the person over a stone block, while another priest ripped out the victim's still-beating heart with a stone or obsidian blade. The World's Bloodiest History *(2009) by Joseph Cummings*

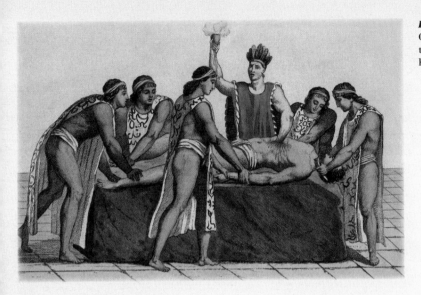

THE FLOWER WARS

The pantheon of Mexica divinities was large and diverse. It included the Mexica tribal god Huitzilopochtli; Tezcatlipoca, the smoking (obsidian) mirror; the feathered serpent, Quetzalcoatl; and the rain god Tlaloc. Each demanded victims and different forms of sacrificial ritual. In the best-known method, the priests stretched the victim over a rounded altar, sliced open his chest with a flint or obsidian knife, and pulled out the heart, which was placed in a stone receptacle in front of the god. Other sacrificial rituals demanded that the victims be burned, buried or flayed alive, or killed in mock gladiatorial combats. Each god required different types of victims: the rain god, Tlaloc, for example, required the sacrifice of children; while for Tezcatlipoca, a Mexica youth volunteered to impersonate the deity and was literally treated like a living god until he, too, was killed.

MEXICA MASK
An obsidian mask on display at the National Anthropology Museum in Mexico City.

As the Mexica became more and more powerful during the fifteenth century, they absorbed most of central and coastal Mexico into their empire. A few states in the Valley of Mexico, however, managed to resist them, including Tlaxcala. One theory holds that the Mexica allowed the Tlaxcalans to keep their independence so that they could go to war with them to obtain the many sacrificial victims that they needed every year. Several scholars have suggested that the arrangement became formalised in what were called 'flower wars', which were fought specifically for the purpose of training young warriors, who needed to capture an enemy to become fully fledged knights, as well as to provide sacrificial victims for the gods of both sides.

STONE AGE WARRIORS
Mexica warriors had to capture an enemy to become knights.

RAZOR SHARP
The *maquahuitl* could decapitate a man or horse with one blow.

THE COMING OF THE IRON MEN

In 1519, Hernán Cortés (1485–1547) led an army of around 630 soldiers and sailors into the Mexica Empire, whose population numbered in the millions. Granted that Cortés had horses, steel and gunpowder weapons, which were all unknown in the Americas, pitted against the Mexica arsenal that consisted of Stone-Age weaponry. However, technology alone cannot explain the destruction of the Mexica Empire, which could call upon vast resources of manpower, in only three years. Mexica warriors, though much less heavily armoured than their Spanish contemporaries, carried spears, bows and arrows, slings and the mace-like *maquahuitl* – a wooden war club whose sides were embedded with obsidian blades. Spanish sources describe the maquahuitl as a formidable weapon that was powerful enough to decapitate a horse in one blow (see quote, below).

Historians have explained the Mexica defeat as being caused by a unique combination of cultural, political, ideological, biological and technological factors. Politically and socially, the Mexica Empire was not a unified entity like the Roman Empire, but a loose confederation of allied, vassal and tributary states. When Cortés arrived, he unwittingly stumbled into a political edifice that had all the internal stability of a poorly built sandcastle. He found willing allies in the Tlaxcalans and other undefeated enemies of the Mexica, who provided him with troop reinforcements and supplies. Ideologically, members of the Mexica elites, including the Mexica ruler Moctezuma II (c. 1466–1520), believed that their world was coming to an end, and that its destruction was inevitable. Hence, initially, they did not prepare a concerted campaign of resistance against the invaders.

> Their weapons were slings, bows and arrows, javelins, and darts [....] These various weapons were pointed with bone, or the mineral *itztli* (obsidian), the hard vitreous substance already noticed as capable of taking an edge like a razor, though easily blunted [....] Instead of swords, they bore a two-handed staff, about three feet and a half long, in which at regular distances, were inserted sharp blades of itztli – a formidable weapon, which, an eyewitness assures us, he had seen fell a horse at a blow.
> History of the Conquest of Mexico *(2004) by William Prescott and John Kirk*

Although their weapons were undoubtedly inferior, the Mexica at first hamstrung themselves by trying to capture their enemies in order to sacrifice them rather than killing them on the spot. They were surprised and no doubt horrified that the Spaniards used completely different tactics in battle, and that in their initial attacks the Europeans used their superior weaponry and cavalry to kill and maim as many of the Native Americans as possible. In the later stages of the conquest, however, the Mexica realised their mistake, and on the evening of June 30, 1520, known to the conquistadors as *La Noche Triste* (the Night of Sorrows), Cortés and his army were forced to flee the Mexica capital, suffering heavy casualties during their retreat to Tlaxcala.

The Mexica had succeeded in expelling the Spaniards from their capital, but it was only a temporary respite. Cortés returned with more Spanish and native troops, more gunpowder and steel weapons, and brigantines to besiege the island-city of Tenochtitlan. In the final assault in 1521, Cortés owed his victory to superior European technology that allowed him to batter and destroy his enemy's defences, and to his allied native troops, but also to a quirk of biology. The Spaniards had brought with them an ally far more deadly than the Tlaxcalans, Castilian steel, gunpowder and horses combined: smallpox. The disease against which the Native Americans had no immunity killed an estimated 40 percent of the city's population, sapping both the strength and morale of the defenders. Those whom the disease spared were starved or beaten into submission. With the fall of the capital and capture of the last independent Mexica ruler, Cuauhtémoc (c. 1495–1525), the Mexica Empire came to an end, and with it, one of the last remnants of the Stone Age.

LAST STAND
The fall of Tenochtitlan meant the end of Mexica culture.

Ochre

Ochra

Type: Clays containing mineral oxides

Origin: Weathering of iron-rich minerals

Chemical formula: Fe_2O_3

✦ INDUSTRIAL

✦ CULTURAL

✦ COMMERCIAL

✦ SCIENTIFIC

By tracing the historical uses of ochre, we revisit a period in human prehistory when archaeologists and anthropologists do not yet agree if the people who employed ochre as a pigment to stain artifacts and human bones can really be called humans at all.

MAKING OUR MARK

The genus *Homo* dates back 2.3 million years, and for 2,250,000 of those years, so one theory goes, archaic humans were not really human in the modern sense of the term. We used tools and lived cooperatively in hunter-gatherer groups, and probably communicated with one another with some form of language, but in that we would not have been that far removed from troupes of modern chimpanzees, which have remarkably similar attributes and abilities.

Then between 80,000 and 50,000 years BP, something extraordinary happened – a genetic mutation, a startling behavioural innovation, or even maybe a visit from ET (you were right, Erich von Däniken, all is forgiven!) – and all of a sudden, we're sitting in the cave around the fire in the evening, cracking open a few beers, chewing over how the day's mammoth hunt went – 'Did you see me? I almost got the big one, but it got away at the last minute!' – while the women are off doing what women do when they don't want to be bored senseless by men's endless boasting and posturing.

ANIMAL CRACKERS
The paintings at Lascaux, France, were made in natural pigments, including ochre.

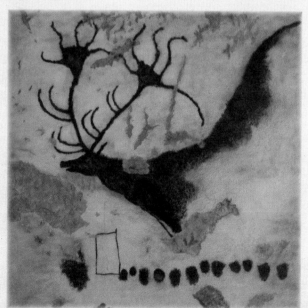

EARTH TONES
Ochre provided humanity with its first pigments.

LITTLE HANDS

At this point in human evolution (or perhaps earlier – see box, below), archaic humans suddenly become behaviourally modern, and they begin to make more complex tools and artifacts, and to develop art, culture and religion – all expressions of their much-improved capacity for symbolic reasoning. Ochre played a central role in these developments all over the planet. The mineral comes in a variety of shades – though admittedly mostly in the yellow, red and brown range

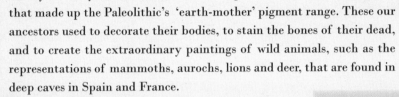

BECAUSE YOU'RE... Ochre is still widely used as body and face paint.

that made up the Paleolithic's 'earth-mother' pigment range. These our ancestors used to decorate their bodies, to stain the bones of their dead, and to create the extraordinary paintings of wild animals, such as the representations of mammoths, aurochs, lions and deer, that are found in deep caves in Spain and France.

Once interpreted as the works of shamans and hunters, who made them to conduct secret magical rituals, possibly performed while under the influence of the Stone Age equivalent of LSD, cave paintings have recently been recast in an entirely new light. The analysis of the many 'flutings' – lines and marks made by fingers on soft surfaces – deep inside the caves reveal that these were made by small children of both sexes as young as five years of age (see quote, below). Whatever our ancestors were up to when they went into the dark places deep under the earth, it was probably not as scary or secret as was once believed. Perhaps, it was a fun family day 'in' on a cold, wet afternoon, when there wasn't anything much to watch from the cave mouth.

The most prolific of the children who made flutings was aged around five – and we are almost certain the child in question was a girl. Interestingly of the four children we know at least two are girls. One cavern is so rich in flutings made by children that it suggests it was a special space for them, but whether for play or ritual is impossible to tell. *Cambridge archaeologist Jess Cooney on the Paleolithic cave art at Rouffignac, France*

BUT IS IT ART?

✦

The objects that archaeologists have identified as humanity's earliest attempts at artistic expression were discovered in the Blombos Cave in Cape Province, South Africa, and have been dated to around 80,000–75,000 years BP, pushing back the horizon of human behavioural modernity by 25,000 to 30,000 years. The finds consist of two small pieces of red ochre, incised with lines creating a cross-hatched geometric design not unlike a doodle you or I might make with a pencil or ballpoint pen during a particularly boring meeting. Found alongside stone and bone tools, and shell beads pierced so that they could be worn as a necklace, were the ochre lumps important artistic or sacred objects, or just something one of our ancestors scratched in an idle moment?

Petroleum

Petroleum

Type: Hydrocarbon

Origin: Fossilised organic material

Chemical formula: C_nH_{2n+2} (general formula for saturated hydrocarbons)

+ *INDUSTRIAL*
+ CULTURAL
+ *COMMERCIAL*
+ SCIENTIFIC

BLACK GOLD
Cheap oil fuelled the twentieth century's car-consumer lifestyles.

In the earlier entry on aluminium, I proposed that the period from the end of World War II to the present could be called the Age of Aluminium, because of the ubiquity of that metal in our homes and workplaces. Another mineral that could just as easily be used to define the industrial–consumer society of the past 60 years is petroleum – crude oil – the primary fuel that drives our automobile culture, and the raw material for our plastics and synthetic fibres. Petroleum was the coal of the Second Industrial Revolution, and without it, our civilisation would never have reached the dizzying heights of present-day affluence and material comfort. The price we, or our children, will have to pay for this orgy of consumerism, is still to be determined.

REARRANGING THE DECK CHAIRS ON THE *TITANIC*

There must be something very special in the mentality of oil-industry executives. They appear to have the same convictions about the intrinsic value of petroleum as a technology and about the right of their industry to survive that are usually associated with the more extreme sectarians of Islam, Judaism and Christianity, who are so certain that they are right (and that they will be proved so at the Rapture or the Last Judgement), that nothing in this life, short of a bullet between the eyes, will change their minds. However, in the light of the history of the past four decades, even the most self-confident oilman must be entertaining a few fleeting moments of doubt.

After the repeated financial earthquakes caused by the oil shocks have shaken the world economy since 1973; after two decades of oil wars in which the U.S. and its allies have been embroiled since the developed world has become dependent for its oil on the reserves that lie under the politically unstable countries of the Near East; after a century of oil spills culminating in the Deepwater Horizon disaster of 2010; and with the mounting evidence of man-made climate change caused by the burning of fossil fuels; you would think that the oil industry might begin to admit that, taking the long view, and within the strict confines of a well-ordered, planned technological realignment, it might be time to get out of the oil business! However, much like the mythical steward aboard the SS *Titanic*, who might have asked the first-class passenger, 'Would Sir prefer to sit on the port or starboard promenade

FIRETRAP
As oil becomes more
difficult to extract,
accidents become
more frequent.

deck? The views of the icebergs are particularly fine at this time of year', oilmen seem to be more anxious to rearrange the metaphorical deck chairs on the good ship Planet Earth, rather than to start pumping out the water and plugging the hole, because with our current space technology, we won't be able to ship out on a space ark to find a new home if we make this one uninhabitable.

To extend the metaphor just a little further, according to years of patient, unexciting research analysing ice cores, fossil pollen and weather-balloon data, we're not just sailing full-steam ahead towards the iceberg, we've already hit it, are holed beneath the waterline, and are taking in water at an alarming rate. And although the crew – the government, scientific establishment and corporate elites – have begun to look longingly at the ship's few lifeboats, on deck, the passengers – i.e., us – are still either ignorant or in wilful denial about the impending fate of the liner. Of course, as

HUMBLE BEGINNINGS
Early U.S. oil production
was measured in thousands
of barrels.

the informed reader will point out, there were survivors in the sinking of the *Titanic*. Out of 2,223 souls aboard, 706 lived to tell the tale. If we used the same calculation for what might happen to humanity because of man-made climate change (and there's no particular reason why not – although, of course, it could be a lot worse), then about two billion of us would survive. Are the oilmen that certain that they and their descendants are going to be among the fortunate third of humanity that makes it to the lifeboats or manages to cling on to the wreckage long enough to be rescued?

IRRESISTIBLE
The power of the oil
lobby ensured the
dominance of the petrol/
automobile combo.

The depressing answer appears to be that because of blind self-interest, based on psychological and ideological motivations, the oil industry and the many economic, industrial and political power elites that depend on it are in wilful denial. Or maybe, they are with Louis XV's (1710–74) mistress Madame de Pompadour (1721–64), who, after encouraging the king to make a series of catastrophic military and financial decisions that brought France to virtual ruin (and would bring about the fall of the French monarchy two decades later), said to her royal lover, '*Au reste, après nous, le Déluge*', which can loosely be translated as 'Who cares what happens after we're gone?'

THE RESISTIBLE RISE OF OIL

In 1941, the German playwright Bertold Brecht (1898–1956) wrote a play titled *The Resistible Rise of Arturo Ui* (1941) as an allegory about the rise of Adolf Hitler (1889–1945) and German fascism in the 1930s. A similar work of fiction could be written about the resistible rise of petroleum and its associated technologies during the past century and a half. Although oil, diesel and petrol, along with the internal combustion engine, may all seem to be part of the very fabric of Western civilisation,

If the world should continue to be dependent upon the fossil fuels as its principal source of industrial energy, then we could expect a culmination in the production of coal within about 200 years. On the basis of the present estimates of the ultimate reserves of petroleum and natural gas, it appears that the culmination of world production of these products should occur within about half a century, while the culmination for petroleum and natural gas in both the United Sates and the state of Texas should occur within the next few decades.

M. King Hubbert (1903–89) in 'Nuclear Energy and the Fossil Fuels' (1956)

and as vital to its survival as liberal democracy, inalienable human rights, and Mom's good old apple pie, they constitute an economic-industrial complex that will be 160 years old when this book is published in 2012.

Many cultures used petroleum and other hydrocarbons during antiquity. The ancient Chinese called petroleum *shi you*, 'rock oil', and used it as fuel for lighting, heating and to boil up seawater to produce salt. The Mesopotamians of modern-day Iraq used their plentiful deposits of petroleum, bitumen and asphalt to waterproof their buildings, and the ancient Persians and Romans used it as fuel for their oil lamps. In the later Roman, or Byzantine, times petroleum was probably a constituent of Greek Fire, a weapon as deadly and effective as our own napalm, which helped preserve the Christian West from barbarian invaders and Islamic conquerors.

In 1852, the Polish chemist Ignacy Łukasiewicz (1822–82) first refined petroleum to produce kerosene, leading to the opening of the first petroleum 'mine' in southeast Poland in 1853. A year later, Professor Benjamin Silliman (1779–1864) of Yale University succeeded in fractionating petroleum by distillation. The initial use of petroleum was as a lighting fuel, as the dominant energy-producing technology of the time was coal-powered steam. In its initial year of operation, the first American oil well, at Oil Creek, PA, produced a rather unimpressive 25 barrels a day.

It is at this point in human history that the planet reached one of its crucial economic, mineralogical and technological turning points: Go down one path in the forest, Little Red Riding Energy Hood, and you will find the mystical, happy land of 'Hydrocarbon Plenty', but go down the other to the 'Land of Alternative Energy Resources', and humanity might have ended up in a completely different geopolitical and ecological position. Humans, of course, went with oil, and have ended up this particular creek, with a paddle – that is, the planet's known

ANCIENT LIGHT
The Romans used petroleum as lighting fuel.

A new source of power [...] called gasoline has been produced by a Boston engineer. Instead of burning the fuel under a boiler, it is exploded inside the cylinder of an engine. The dangers are obvious. Stores of gasoline in the hands of people interested primarily in profit would constitute a fire and explosive hazard of the first rank. Horseless carriages propelled by gasoline might attain speeds of 14 or even 20 miles per hour. The menace to our people of vehicles of this type hurtling through our streets and along our roads and poisoning the atmosphere would call for prompt legislative action even if the military and economic implications were not so overwhelming. *U. S. Congressional Record, 1875*

and estimated oil reserves, including deep-water oil fields and tar sands – though estimates of the exact shape, size and usefulness of the paddle is keeping planners, economists and oil-industry analysts up late at night. But in the early decades of the petroleum boom, U.S. production increased from thousands of barrels in the mid-nineteenth century to hundreds of millions by the beginning of the twentieth century, all of it extracted and distilled to feed the new technological god humanity had forged for itself out of iron and steel: the internal combustion engine.

THE DRAWING POWER OF ICE

The technological–industrial Behemoth that has been driving the world economy since the 1930s is the internal combustion engine (ICE). And depending on your point of view, the resulting cultural shift is either heaven on Earth, if you are a disciple of Henry Ford (1863–1947), the creator of the first mass-market automobile, the Model-T (see box, opposite), or, if you are more concerned with the long-term condition of the planet and the survival of the human species, probably the worst decision our forebears ever made.

In the earliest days of human civilisation, the technological choices were fairly simple and straightforward: I have the choice between an obsidian or flint axe; but as technology becomes more complex, so do the choices, until we get to the point at which we have to choose between VHS and Betamax, or less trivially, between the internal or external combustion engine (ECE) and between petrol and electricity or bio-fuel. In a parallel universe, there is no reason why, given a few different discoveries and investment choices, we would not be driving to work in some kind of super-advanced ECE-driven vehicle rather than

GO CART
The world's first 'automobile' built in 1870.

the current ICE-powered model, or in an automobile powered by batteries or grain alcohol.

The history of ICE technology began in Tuscany, Italy, when a Catholic priest and educator, Eugenio Barsanti (1821–64), hit upon the idea of combusting hydrogen and air in a sealed chamber to drive a simple engine. In 1851, he met the engineer Felice Matteucci (1808–87), with whom he developed the design, finally patenting the first ICE in London in 1854. We are not driving in Italian-made 'Barsantis' or 'Matteuccis' partly because neither of these men quite grasped what they had invented, but mainly because their engine was just about small enough to fit onboard a large steamboat. The first 'automobile' powered by an internal combustion engine powered by petrol was built by the Austrian inventor Siegfried Marcus (1831–98) in 1870. Admittedly it was not much of a looker: it was a vertical ICE mounted on a handcart with nothing in the way of internal or external styling. However it demonstrated the principle, and 20 years later, Mr Benz (1844–1929) and Mr Daimler (1834–1900) were building the first custom automobiles in Germany.

Even then, the petrol ICE had to overcome electric and steam-powered rivals, as well as alternative fuel technologies, as early ICE vehicles could also run on ethanol (grain alcohol) – the original bio-fuel. But with the combined might of the automobile industry,

MODEL CARS

✦

The Model-T Ford (1908–27) was the first automobile to be mass-produced on an assembly line. As such, not only did it revolutionise industrial production, but it was also the first mass-market car to be driven by internal combustion technology. Its huge success ensured that vehicles powered by petrol internal combustion engines would become the industry leaders for decades to come, and realised the dream of its creator, Henry Ford (1863–1947), to 'build a car for the great multitude' that would be large enough for a family but also cheap enough to buy and run, so that every man could 'enjoy with his family the blessing of hours of pleasure in God's great open spaces'.

led by Ford, and the growing oil industry lobby, ICE and petroleum overcame all obstacles and went on to dominate the market until the present day. In the early twenty-first century, despite the development of nuclear and renewable energy sources, oil still accounts for around 30 percent of Europe's energy consumption; 40 percent of North America's; 41 percent of Africa's; 44 percent of Central and South America's; and 53 percent of the Near East's. In 2010, the U.S. guzzled around 19,148,000 barrels of oil a day, of which 51 percent had to be imported, and 72 percent of which was used up by transportation. The U.S. figures are mirrored in most of the developed world. Although lagging far behind the U.S. in absolute numbers, China, Brazil and India are fast catching up.

Oil wars
The West has been involved in oil wars since 1990.

DRIVING MISS DAISY OVER THE OLDUVAI CLIFF

According to systems engineer Richard Duncan's Olduvai Theory, which is a broad-brush application of the Hubbert Curve (see box, opposite) to all human resources, we are about to fall off the Olduvai cliff. The Olduvai Gorge is part of East Africa's Great Rift Valley, which is acknowledged to be the cradle of humanity. As the place where humans first set out to colonise the planet, it is therefore also a suitable name for the economic and technological collapse that might bring about the end of industrial civilisation. The theory proposes that

Driving America
The U.S. consumes over 19 million barrels a day, mostly for transportation.

RUNNING OUT
The Hubbert curve
predicts the end of oil
by the year 2200.

we peaked in terms of production of many non-renewable resources and energy in 1979. The two decades to 1999 constituted a slow but steady decline, in which we lived on borrowed time, money, goods and energy. In the first decade of the 21st century, we experienced an accelerated period of decline and economic disorder, leading us to build up sufficient momentum to launch us over the cliff edge in 2012 (I better make sure the publisher's cheque clears before then) and come crashing back into the Stone Age by about 2030.

If Duncan is correct, then humanity's techno-logical, scientific and industrial age, born in the fires of Britain's Industrial Revolution at the end of the eighteenth century, would have endured for less than three centuries (and our own consumer society for one century from 1930 to 2030) – a very poor show when compared to the 2,000 or so years of the Bronze Age, and the 2.6 million years of the Stone Age. If you are reading this book as you sit around the campfire of your family cave in 2030, then please remember that authors' royalties can be paid in shells, beads and foodstuffs.

HUBBERT'S CURVEBALL

✦

The Hubbert Curve plots the future productivity of the world's oil fields, but it can be applied to any finite natural resource on the planet. M. King Hubbert (1903–89) came up with the idea in the 1950s long before environmentalism was the live-wire issue it is today. A soft-spoken former oilman turned academic, who also worked for the U.S. Geological Survey, Hubbert was no evangelical eco-warrior with a green axe to grind. He studied the production data and made best-guess estimates of remaining oil reserves to predict that the oil would run out by around the year 2200.

Phosphorus
Phosphorus

Type: Chemical element

Origin: Phosphate minerals

Chemical formula: P

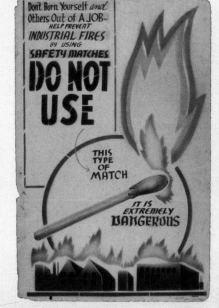

Before the discovery of the inflammable element phosphorus, the act of lighting a fire from scratch involved a time-consuming procedure using a wooden hand drill, two pieces of flint or a tinderbox. Although at first explosively dangerous and toxic to manufacture, the phosphorus match was such a boon to humanity that it quickly superseded all earlier fire-making alternatives.

+ *INDUSTRIAL*

+ *CULTURAL*

+ *COMMERCIAL*

+ *SCIENTIFIC*

FIRESTARTER

The ability to make fire is such an ancient technology that, as we light our candles, stoves and cigarettes with lighters and matches, we don't even think of it as a technological breakthrough. But wind the clock back several million years and fire was a dangerous, unpredictable element in the natural environment – started freakishly by lightning strikes, volcanic eruptions, random sparks from rock falls, and spontaneous combustion, which could kill, injure and choke. Studies of our closest primate relations, the chimpanzee, show that although they have never been observed making or using fire deliberately, they are aware of its existence and dangers, and have been seen performing 'fire dances' in its presence.

Taming fire to use it was one of humanity's greatest early technological achievements and one of its first major manipulations of the environment, as by its control humans could light their caves, warm themselves, ward off dangerous animals, and, of course, make a roast dinner for the family. When humans began to establish permanent settle-

WHITE FOR DANGER
White phosphorus was toxic but much cheaper than red phosphorus.

FIRESTARTER
Friction matches were a major cause of domestic and industrial fires.

Don't Burn Yourself *and* Others Out of A JOB—
HELP PREVENT
INDUSTRIAL FIRES
BY USING
SAFETY MATCHES
DO NOT USE
THIS TYPE OF MATCH
IT IS EXTREMELY
DANGEROUS

Immediately after the discovery of phosphorus, the possibility of utilizing the new element in a technique for generating fire was recognized. Knuckel was working along these lines. He coated a paper with phosphorus and ignited by striking. During the 18th century many imaginative – and dangerous! – variants were presented.

Encyclopedia of the Elements (2004) by Per Enghag

ments and farms, fire would become the basis for 'slash-and-burn' agriculture, which remains an important technique practised by subsistence farmers all over the planet. The transformations of matter that are wrought by fire are many and form the basis of all our subsequent material technologies, beginning with the earliest processes for making ceramics and metals. Yet, considering its enormous importance to human civilisation, fire was not properly tamed until the invention of matches in the eighteenth century. Even then, the material most commonly used, white phosphorus, was extremely unstable, igniting at a touch, and extremely toxic to those working with it (see box, right).

PLAYING SAFE
Fire was finally tamed with the invention of safety matches.

The 'safety match', with its trademark red head, is a Swedish invention. The chemist Gustav Pasch (1788–1862) made the first safety match in 1844, but he was unable to commercialise his invention because of the high cost of red phosphorus compared to the cheaper but toxic white variety. The Lundström brothers, Johan Edvard (1815–88) and Carl Frans (1823–1917), perfected his discovery and went on to dominate the world match industry in the late nineteenth and early twentieth centuries. The secret of their success was to separate the active ingredients between the match head, which contains a mixture of potassium chlorate and sulphur, and the striking surface, which is made of red phosphorus with the grittiness provided by powdered glass. The simple act of striking a match is an unregarded marvel of chemical engineering.

FIRE IN THE BLOOD

✦

On the one hand, the element phosphorus is highly toxic and inflammable, but on the other, without it organic life would be impossible. It is so inextricably involved at the molecular level with the most basic processes of metabolism that without it our biochemistry would just break down. It is part of the structural framework of our genetic material (both RNA and DNA), and it is an integral component of ATP (adenosine triphosphate), which is the fuel that powers our cells. At a higher physiological level, phosphorus is an important component making up bones and teeth.

GROWING PAINS

Phosphorus is so important to all biological systems, including our own, that it plays a leading role in the agricultural technologies that sustain our civilisation, both as a constituent of the inorganic fertilisers that increase crop yields, and of the pesticides that control the insects that would otherwise compromise mono-cultural food production. The problem with both these uses is that they come with heavy environmental price tags. First, there are questions about the sustain-ability of the supplies of natural phosphates used to produce inorganic fertilisers in the quantities needed by an ever-growing world population; second, the extraction and production of phosphates create large quantities of waste products; and third, the use of phosphate fertilisers and organophosphate pesticides allows hazardous residues to enter the environment and human food chain.

When humanity finally unlocked the Pandora's Box of elemental chemistry in the nineteenth century and began to build new chemical compounds out of the existing materials provided by nature, the knowl-edge gave us the advances in medicine, industry and agriculture that produced the vast increases in population, life expec-tancy and living standards that we witnessed in the twentieth century. In agriculture, the German chemist Justus von Liebig (1803–83) discov-ered and promoted the role of chemical fertilisers (until then farmers were foolishly growing their crops by spreading human and animal manure over the soil – extraordinary but true!). He established the 'Law of the Minimum', which states that the limiting factor on crop yields is not the overall quantity of nutrients in the soil but the quantity of the least available nutrient. In other words, if the soil is short of one particular mineral, say phosphorus or potassium, no matter how much manure you pile onto it, the crop yield will not increase, unless that nutrient is part of the mix in sufficient quantities.

MAXIMUM YIELD
Justus von Liebig established the agricultural 'Law of Minimum'.

STRIPPED BARE
The phosphate-rich island
of Nauru has been
completely strip-mined.

If von Liebig was the father of artificial fertiliser, British agronomist Sir John Bennett Lawes (1814–1900) oversaw the birth of the artificial fertiliser business. Lawes was a leisured English gentleman, blessed with an inquiring mind and unencumbered by any pressing need to work for a living because of his substantial inherited wealth, including a large estate in Hertfordshire, north of London. Educated at Eton College and Oxford, he began his agricultural experiments in the 1830s. In 1842, he patented a process for producing fertiliser by treating phosphate rocks with sulphuric acid, creating the first 'superphosphate' fertiliser.

For the first half of the twentieth century, one of the world's leading suppliers of phosphate for the fertiliser industry was the Pacific island nation of Nauru. The island, which was covered in readily accessible surface deposits of phosphate minerals, was extensively strip-mined, briefly giving it one of the highest per capita incomes in the world, rivalling the wealth of the oil states, until the phosphates ran out in the 1980s, leaving the island scarred and stony (pun intended) broke. The sad fate of Nauru, which now lives off the charity of its larger Pacific neighbour, Australia, is a stark warning of what might happen more widely when the available reserves of extractable phosphate are used up, and world agricultural yields fall as a result.

GROWTH SPURT
The introduction of
phosphate fertilisers
significantly increased
crop yields.

Platinum

Platinum

Type: Precious metal

Origin: Native metal and alluvial deposits

Chemical formula: Pt

The hardest, and most expensive, of the three precious metals covered in this book, platinum was unknown in Europe until samples were brought back from the Americas, where the Native Americans of the Andean region had worked it since ancient times. In addition to jewellery, the metal's principal use is for the catalytic converters of automobiles that convert toxic engine emissions into non-toxic exhaust gases.

+ **INDUSTRIAL**
+ **CULTURAL**
+ COMMERCIAL
+ SCIENTIFIC

WHITE GOLD

One of the great puzzles of the history of the pre-Columbian Americas is the extremely mixed cultural, scientific and technological achievements of the most advanced cultures of Central and South America. In the entry on obsidian, we saw that the sixteenth-century Aztec–Mexica and Maya (in present-day Mexico, Guatemala, Belize and Honduras) remained technologically in the Stone Age, despite their extremely sophisticated gold metallurgy and their advanced mathematics and astronomy. They lacked the arch, the wheel, draft animals and the plow, and although they used copper to a degree, they had not made the technological leap from stone to metal.

In the Andean region, we see even greater contrasts. The Inca and their predecessor cultures had no written language, but made do with the *quipu* knot system to keep records; they did not have the wheel or plow, but they did have draft animals, the llama and alpaca. The Andean peoples, too, had an extremely sophisticated gold and silver metallurgy and some knowledge of copper and its alloys, but

PLATINUM STANDARD

+

In 1799, the reforming government of the first French Republic (1792–1804) created a new measurement of length, the metre, as one ten-millionth of the distance between the North Pole and the Equator at the longitude of Paris. French scientists cast a bar of pure platinum to represent the original metre. This prototype lasted until 1889, when it was replaced by a prototype made of 90 percent platinum and 10 percent iridium measured at 0°C. This metre lasted until 1960, when it was replaced in its turn by the wavelength of the krypton-86 isotope, and finally in 1983, when the metre was defined as a fraction of the speed of light (299,792,458 metres per second in a vacuum).

WITH THIS RING
Platinum is a popular alternative to gold to make wedding rings.

Modern metallurgists were long puzzled how Colombian smiths, who were particularly skilled at platinum work, were able to make jewellery and vessels in which gold and platinum were combined in a homogeneous alloy. In theory, this was impossible because there was no way in which the ancients could have heated platinum to its exceptionally high melting point (1,775°C).

The Living Rock *(1994) by Arthur Wilson*

THE CAT

✦

Platinum is a catalyst used in a catalytic converter, or 'cat', that transforms toxic pollutants produced by internal combustion engines into non-toxic substances. A modern three-way cat converts carbon monoxide into carbon dioxide, residual hydrocarbons into water, and nitrogen oxides into nitrogen. Although catalytic converters have reduced pollution from motor vehicles, especially the production of acid rain, they have led to an increase in the production of the greenhouse gas carbon dioxide.

they, too, could not be said to have made the transition into the Bronze Age proper like the cultures of Eurasia of the fourth and third millennium BCE. But perhaps more extraordinary, the native peoples of Colombia and Ecuador knew the secret of how to work platinum, a metal that was unknown in Europe until the mid-sixteenth century.

Colombian and Ecuadorian smiths alloyed alluvial deposits of platinum with gold to make jewellery, vessels, masks and ornaments that the European colonists first identified as 'white gold', but platinum remained unidentified in Europe until chemists analysed samples brought back from the New World. For many years, archaeologists were puzzled as to how the Andean smiths had managed to alloy platinum and gold, as pure platinum melts at 1,775°C (3,227°F) – a temperature that was inconceivable with the metallurgical and furnace technologies available in the Americas at the time. One possible explanation was that the Andean metalworkers incorporated small quantities of platinum into molten gold, and repeatedly hammered and melted the mixture until it alloyed at a much lower temperature than that needed to melt the platinum on its own. With the destruction of the Andean cultures, their skill at working platinum was not matched until the nineteenth century.

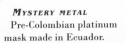

MYSTERY METAL
Pre-Colombian platinum mask made in Ecuador.

Lead
Plumbum

Type: Metal

Origin: Mineral ores, especially galena

Chemical formula: Pb

+ **INDUSTRIAL**
+ CULTURAL
+ COMMERCIAL
+ **SCIENTIFIC**

Lead working has an ancient history, not necessarily for its own sake but for the extraction of silver, with which it is often associated. In ancient times, lead, however, had many industrial and domestic applications, in plumbing, food preparation and winemaking, ceramics, paint and printing. One of its most controversial uses dates to the twentieth century, when it was added to petrol to prevent engine knocking – with disastrous environmental consequences.

DECLINE AND FALL

The expression 'the collapse of the Roman Empire' may suggest a sudden event, much like the end of British rule in the American colonies in the War of Independence (1776–83) or the French Revolution of 1789, which were sociopolitical cataclysms, maybe a long time in the making, that reached a sudden crisis that marked the passage of one state of affairs to another. Some readers might imagine that the sack of Rome by the Visigoths in 410 CE (the first since 387 BCE) signalled the end of the empire, but it survived this disaster and a second sack of the city in 455 CE. For the purposes of traditional Western chronology, the official 'fall' of the empire was signalled by the abdication of the last emperor of the West, the grandly named Romulus Augustulus (r. 475–76). However, this would not have been the perception at the time, because Roman emperors continued to rule the eastern half of the empire from their capital in Constantinople. Until the fall of the city in 1453, the Byzantine emperors maintained the fiction that they were the rulers of the whole Roman world, even when their actual authority extended to little more than the city of Constantinople itself.

PAIRED METAL
Lead is mostly found in copper- and silver-bearing ores.

Rather than a sudden event like the fall of the Nazi Third Reich in 1945, the end of the Roman Empire in the West was a protracted, slow-motion car crash that took centuries, whose causes have been debated for centuries, most famously by Edward Gibbon (1737–94) in *The Decline and Fall of the Roman Empire* (1776–98). Gibbon wrote: 'As the happiness of a future life is the great object of religion, we may hear without surprise or scandal that the introduction, or at least the abuse of Christianity, had some influence on the decline and fall of the Roman empire'. He placed a great deal of the blame for imperial decline on the rise of the Catholic Church and its effect on the martial spirit and wealth of the Roman world. Later historians have favoured a combination of economic, ideological, military, technological and environmental factors, but several medical historians (see quote, below) have looked for a more unusual explanation in the extensive use of lead in Roman times.

DEADLY PIPES
Lead may have caused the fall of the Roman Empire.

HEAVY METAL

Lead may not have the luster and value of gold or silver, or the versatility of bronze, but it is a common metallic element in Earth's crust that is soft and relatively easy to work and cast. The Romans produced large quantities of lead as part of the extraction and refinement of silver, and they found many practical uses for it. Like other heavy metals, however, lead is toxic to humans, with the acuteness of the symptoms of lead poisoning dependent on the type and length of exposure. Lead accumulates in the body, where it attacks the peripheral and central nervous systems. The symptoms of lead poisoning include neuropathy (loss of feeling and paralysis in the extremities), abdominal pain, insomnia, lethargy or hyperactivity, and, in acute cases, seizures and death; other associated effects are anemia and urinary and reproductive problems. Children under the age of 12 are particularly susceptible to its effects, and research has identified a direct link between exposure to lead in the environment and learning difficulties, ADHD and antisocial behaviour among children and adolescents.

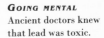

GOING MENTAL
Ancient doctors knew that lead was toxic.

The Romans used lead in two major ways that would have given them direct and prolonged exposure during their lifetimes: they made water pipes out of the metal, and they used lead containers to cook and store the fruit sweeteners *defrutum* and *sapa* that they added to food and wine. Moreover, exposure to lead would have increased with social rank, as the wealthier citizens would drink more

It wasn't the barbarians, it wasn't the Christians, it wasn't moral corruption [....] the real cause was the use of lead to prevent the souring of wine. Lead was the true source of the madness of the Caesars. Leaded wine brought the empire to ruin. *'Lead Poisoning and the Fall of Rome'* (1965) by S. Colum

plumbed water and consume more sweetened food and wine, with the most affected being the members of the imperial court itself. It must be admitted that the Romans, for all their martial prowess and administrative skills, were often ruled by homicidal maniacs whose grasp of reality was fairly notional, with the first-century emperors Caligula (12–41 CE) and Nero (37–68 CE) being prime examples. Several historians have questioned the lead-poisoning hypothesis, however, claiming that it overstates the importance of lead in the decline of Roman power. After all, they argue, lead would have been in use during the centuries of Roman ascendancy, and Roman power continued in the East for another millennium.

PRESSING MATTERS

✦

In recent centuries, lead has suffered from a rather bad press, but there is one area of human endeavour that has greatly benefited from the metal: typesetting and printing. In the fifteenth century, the West finally caught up with East Asia when Johannes Gutenberg (1398–1468) developed a system of movable type matrices, cast from an alloy of lead, tin and antimony. The discovery initiated a revolution in literacy and education by making printed matter and books cheaper and more available than ever before.

THE INFAMOUS MR MIDGLEY

Moving forward to the twentieth century, the man who will go down in history as the person who has 'had more impact on the atmosphere than any other single organism in earth's history' is the now infamous Thomas Midgley, Jr (1889–1944). He earned this unenviable reputation for not one but two scientific innovations in the 1920s: the improved synthesis of chlorofluorocarbons (CFCs) for use as refrigerants, which are now known to deplete the ozone layer; and the addition of tetra-ethyl lead (TEL; $(CH_3CH_2)_4Pb$) to petrol to prevent engine knocking – a problem caused by the uneven combustion of the petrol-

SLUGGING IT OUT
Movable type was made of lead, tin and antinomy.

oxygen mixture that can lead to poor engine performance and increased wear, and in severe cases, to damage to the piston casing or head. The addition of the tasteless, colourless and odourless TEL solved the problem, but at a very heavy environmental cost.

The first casualties of TEL were among the employees of the DuPont plant in Dayton, OH, where the additive was first manufactured. Deaths occurred there and at the General Motors Chemical Company in New Jersey, forcing the closure of the plant on safety grounds. For once, senior executives were not immune to the poisons they were manufacturing. Midgley himself had to take an extended leave of absence on health grounds, which many believe was caused by lead poisoning. TEL was not phased out in the U.S. and Europe until the 1990s, leaving a legacy of high levels of environmental lead in urban areas, especially in the immediate vicinity of busy roads and motorways.

The economist Rick Nevin has suggested that exposure to lead pollutants explains the high crime rate in many American cities in the 1980s, as well as the huge variations in crime statistics between different neighbourhoods – with the highest incidence reported in areas with the highest levels of environmental lead. He cites the experiences of countries that phased out TEL after the U.S., which saw their crime rates peak and fall slightly later. In 2002, a study of adolescent offenders in Pittsburgh, PA, revealed that they had higher levels of lead in their blood than a control group of non-offending teenagers. According to the researchers, lead poisoning caused delinquent behaviour by decreasing self-control and increasing the incidence of antisocial behaviour among the affected teens.

Plutonium
Plutonium

Type: Radioactive element

Origin: Uranium ores

Chemical formula: Pu

◆ **INDUSTRIAL**

◆ CULTURAL

◆ COMMERCIAL

◆ **SCIENTIFIC**

HOT STUFF
Plutonium is the most powerful energy source known to science.

This article on plutonium should be read with the related article on uranium (pp.202–207), as the two substances are inextricably linked by their applications in nuclear weapons and the generation of nuclear energy. Plutonium is used to manufacture nuclear missiles and munitions, and, as such, is the material creating most concern in terms of the proliferation of nuclear weapons and its possible use by terrorists to make a 'dirty bomb'.

THIS ISLAND NATION

If the British have a reputation for being an insular nation, always suspicious of the schemes of their continental neighbours, when compared to the Japanese, they are evangelical internationalists, throwing their doors open to all-comers. The Japanese, however, have an excuse, because for almost 250 years, between the early seventeenth and late nineteenth centuries, their home islands were sealed off from the outside world, except for one small opening – the port city of Nagasaki – where the Japanese feudal state, headed by the military dictator, or Shogun, in Edo (now Tokyo), tolerated the presence of a strictly limited number of foreign visitors and residents, mainly Chinese and Dutch

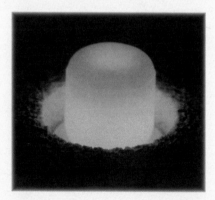

merchants. Through this portal filtered in what the Japanese state thought was worth knowing of the outside world – which was not a great deal – while the rest of the country turned in on itself, secure in the knowledge that Japanese culture was by far superior to anything the West had to offer.

The arrival of a squadron of American gunboats commanded by Commodore Matthew Perry (1794–1858) in 1853 forced the Shogunate to accept the opening of Japanese ports to foreign trade, triggering a free-for-all among the other Western powers, all eager to get a slice of the Japanese pie, just as they had been doing in China for over a decade. The shockwaves caused by the forced opening of the country led to the toppling of the Shogun and his replacement, in name only, by the Meiji Emperor (1852–1912), whose ancestors had long been relegated to a ceremonial role in the old imperial capital of Kyoto.

If the initial aim of the Meiji Restoration of 1868 had been to repudiate the unequal trade treaties and expel the foreigners from Japanese soil, its effect was the creation of a new powerful, centralised state with an internationalist, modernising agenda. Unlike China and many of its less fortunate Asian-Pacific neighbours, Japan kept her independence and poured her energy into catching up with the West technologically and militarily. By 1904, Japan had progressed enough to defeat Czarist Russia, the leading European power in the region, in a short but epoch-making war, when, for the first time since the Age of Exploration, a non-Western nation had stood up to a Western power and won a decisive victory.

THE EMPEROR AND THE FAT MAN

Unfortunately for the Japanese, they had arrived far too late at the top table of nineteenth-century colonialism and imperialism, not just missing out on the starters and main course, but also the desserts and cheeseboards, so they had to make do with the nuts and after-dinner mints. While Britain, France, Germany, Russia and even the United States had acquired considerable overseas interests, there were slim pickings left for Japan. Undeterred, the Japanese created a bijou empirette out of Formosa (now Taiwan), Korea and parts of China and Far Eastern Russia, with options on Manchuria, Southeast Asia, the south Pacific and Australia.

Although Japan had appeared too late on the world stage to establish herself as a major colonial power, she was recognised as a major player. During the World War I, she sided with the victorious Allies, but in the run-up to World War II, she unwisely threw in her lot with the Axis Powers. As Germany, Italy, Britain and France squared off in the West, the U.S., Britain and Japan prepared to do the same in the East. The Pacific War (1941–45) was bloody and cruel, and would probably have been much

If the radiance of a thousand suns were to burst at once into the sky, that would be like the splendor of the mighty one. Now I am become Death, the destroyer of worlds. *Physicist J. R. Oppenheimer (1904–67), one of the creators of the A-bomb, quoting from the Hindu classic, the* Bhagavad Gita *after the successful test of the first plutonium bomb on July 16, 1945*

longer and bloodier had it not been for the development of the atomic bomb during the war. The 'A-bomb' was in fact a term describing several nuclear weapons created by the Manhattan Project (1941–46) set up by the UK, U.S. and Canada. The 'Little Boy' bomb that destroyed Hiroshima on August 6, 1945, will be described in the entry on uranium, but this entry deals with the 'Fat Man' plutonium bomb that was dropped on Nagasaki on August 9, 1945.

The weather in Japan in August can be very warm and muggy and is often overcast. The primary target for the crew of the B-29 Bockscar bomber was the unregarded castle town of Kokura overlooking the Shimonoseki Straits between the two large islands of Kyushu and Honshu. Because of poor visibility, Bockscar diverted to its secondary

HEAVYWEIGHT
The 'Fat Man' dropped
on Nagasaki on August
9, 1945.

target of Nagasaki, the city that had traditionally been the most open to outside influences in Japan. Just before 8 AM local time, the air-raid sirens wailed their warnings of impending incendiary doom, but the all clear was given half an hour later when fire bombs failed to come raining down from the skies onto the wood and paper houses of the city. At 10:53, two B-29s were sighted high over the city, but they were ignored as reconnaissance planes. Nagasaki had literally eight minutes left. At 11:01 a break in the cloud allowed the bombardier to sight the drop zone and release the first and only plutonium bomb ever to have been dropped on a populated target.

The spherical 'Fat Man' bomb – said to be named for the character played by Sydney Greenstreet in the movie, *The Maltese Falcon*, or British premier Winston Churchill – contained a core of 6.4 kg (14.1 lb) of plutonium-239 packed inside a shell with conventional explosives, and was released about two miles off target. The bomb detonated 43 seconds later, at an altitude of 469 m (1,540 ft). The blast generated a yield equivalent to 21,000 tons of TNT, with a total destructive radius of about one mile (1.6 km), killing an estimated 40,000 people. Physicists Albert Einstein (1879–1955) and J. Robert Oppenheimer (1904–67), who had encouraged the U.S. government to develop the A-bomb ahead of the Germans, immediately realised the destructive power that they had created, and lobbied to have the new weapons banned. In effect, the reply they got, if you allow me to paraphrase, was: 'If you didn't want it, you shouldn't have opened the packet'. All hopes of a unilateral Anglo-American ban on nuclear weapons was abandoned once the Soviet Union tested its own plutonium bomb (suspiciously similar to the American Fat Man) in a test codenamed 'First Lightning' on August 29, 1949.

DEATH CLOUD
The trademark 'mushroom' cloud caused by a nuclear explosion.

The use of the atomic bomb, with its indiscriminate killing of women and children, revolts my soul. *President Herbert Hoover (1874–1964)*

Pumice

Pumiceus

Type: Igneous rock

Origin: Volcanism

Chemical formula: Mainly SiO_2 and Al_2O_3 with trapped water and CO_2

+ **INDUSTRIAL**
+ CULTURAL
+ COMMERCIAL
+ SCIENTIFIC

Now known as an oddity – the abrasive stone that floats in your bath – pumice was used in antiquity as a lightweight building material, notably in the construction of the Pantheon in Rome, one of the empire's landmark buildings that still stands today, and that has inspired imitations across the world.

THE HOUSE OF THE GODS

Anyone who wants to be transported back to the glory days of Imperial Rome should visit the Pantheon in the twenty-first-century capital of Italy. Standing amid a cluttered cityscape of later constructions, the building, though much stained by 2,000 years of use and pollution, retains much of its original grandeur and architectural impact. The visitor will be particularly struck with its huge coffered concrete dome that is pierced by a 9.1-m (30-ft) oculus at its centre, which still provides much of the light for the interior of the building. The exact purpose of the building in antiquity is unknown. Built by the Emperor Hadrian (76–138 CE) in 126 on the site of an earlier building of the same name, the Pantheon held statues of the emperor and of the major Olympian gods; hence it was probably the site for civic, religious or imperial rites.

Religion in pagan Rome followed a very different pattern from later Christian practice, although Christians took over many pagan buildings, including the Pantheon, and adapted them to their own forms of worship. The central rite of Roman religion was animal sacrifice – usually of oxen, but also of horse, sheep, goats and chickens – that was performed outside of the temples on public altars where they could be witnessed by the faithful, who would then consume the sacrificial meat in a social act of communion with the divine. The grand temple buildings housed the images of the deified emperors, heroes and gods, and stored precious offerings in their treasuries, but they were not public places of daily worship like churches and cathedrals.

ROMAN WONDER
The Pantheon's 5,000-ton dome is a masterpiece of ancient architecture.

VAULT OF HEAVEN
The concrete around the
Pantheon's oculus uses
pumice aggregate.

THE VAULT OF HEAVEN

The Pantheon's crowning glory, which has made it a
signature building of world architecture, is its dome,
which weighs just shy of 5,000 tons. It is said to represent the celestial vault of Heaven, with the sun at its
centre. Its architect used a number of technical devices
to ensure that the 43.3-m (142-ft) dome has endured
for almost 2,000 years: its thickness varies from 6.4 m
(21 ft) at the base to 1.2 m (3.9 ft) around the circular
central opening; its structure is honeycombed with
invisible spaces to reduce its overall weight; its weight
is supported by several internal and external relieving
brick arches; and finally the aggregate used to make
the concrete varies in weight, with the lightest –
ground pumice – used for the uppermost portion of
the structure. Although the knowledge of the materials and techniques used to build the Pantheon were
lost in the West for centuries, the building itself
survived the many disasters and depredations of the
Dark Ages to inspire new generations of architects,
engineers and artists in later centuries.

FLOATING ISLAND

✦

The crew of a yacht sailing
in the Tonga Islands in 2006
were so amazed to see a new
volcanic island rising from the
ocean floor that they sailed
straight into a 'sea of stone'—a
thick layer of pumice floating on
the surface of the ocean – that
clogged their engine. Pumice
'rafts' created by underwater
volcanic explosions, some as large
as 30 km (18 miles) across, form
habitats for marine animals and
also provide a means for land
species to island hop in the South
Pacific region.

**Hadrian's Pantheon is one of the grand architectural creations
of all time: original, utterly bold, many-layered in associations
and meaning [….] It speaks of an even wider world than that of
imperial Rome, and has left its stamp upon architecture more than
any other building.** The Pantheon *(2002) by W. L. Macdonald*

Quartz
Quartzeus

Type: Silicate mineral

Origin: Granite and igneous rocks

Chemical formula: SiO_2

+ **INDUSTRIAL**
+ CULTURAL
+ COMMERCIAL
+ SCIENTIFIC

The hard but relatively common quartz and quartzite were among the first minerals used by early hominids when they began to create their toolset in Africa. But in the modern twentieth century, the mineral spawned a second technological revolution in timekeeping, ending a hundred-year-old Swiss monopoly.

STONE DAWN

The Oldowan tool industry (2.6–1.7 million years BP; named for the cradle of humanity, the Olduvai Gorge in Tanzania, East Africa) is thought to represent the earliest evidence of tool manufacture by our early hominid ancestors, whether by the genus *Australopithecus* or by the first representatives of the genus *Homo*. As such, the stones show little actual elaboration, leading some anthropologists to argue that these were found objects created naturally by rockfalls rather than intentionally shaped. However, careful analysis and practical experiments have demonstrated that these fragments of rock, including hard quartzes and quartzites, which could take an edge by being struck against a hammerstone, were purposefully shaped into scrapers, awls and axes to help our ancestors obtain food, cut down trees, strip branches and prepare animal hides to be made into clothing, tents and containers. Although a long way from demonstrating the achievements of behavioural modernity, Oldowan tools mark the beginning of the hominid mastery of the environment.

POLYMORPH
Quartz takes many different forms, including semi-precious crystalline minerals.

Oldowan tools were manufactured from hard cobblestones that can be found in riverbeds and beaches. Any material that was hard enough to produce sharp edges was used including basalt, obsidian, quartz, flint and chert. The cobblestone was repeatedly struck by the hammerstone on the edge to remove flakes and to produce sharp edges.

Origin of the Human Mind *(2008) by Andrey Vyshedskiy*

DRINKER'S TALE
Amethyst goblets were
believed to prevent
drunkenness.

DRUNKARD'S TOUCHSTONE

✦

According to Greek myth, the semi-precious quartz mineral amethyst was created after the god of wine, Dionysus, was enraged after being insulted by a mortal. The irritable god swore revenge on the whole human race and created tigers to tear limb from limb the next unfortunate individual who crossed his path. But who should come skipping down the forest path but the innocent young maid Amethyst, who was on her way to make an offering to the goddess Artemis in a nearby shrine. To save her from being torn to pieces, Artemis turned her devotee into a statue made of brilliant quartz. A repentant Dionysus shed copious tears over the metamorphosed maiden, turning the clear crystal a deep shade of purple. From this fanciful tale, the ancient Greeks believed that amethyst prevented drunkenness, and they made drinking goblets from the stone.

CUCKOO CLOCKS AT DAWN

Spool the clock forward 2.6 million years, and travel north several thousand miles, to a place and time when quartz was going to trigger a no less earth-shattering revolution in an age-old industry. It is one of those strange accidents of geography and history that the Swiss, in addition to their reputation for scrupulous cleanliness, fine chocolates and the right of every male citizen to keep an automatic rifle in his garage just in case the French or Germans decide to invade, also cornered the world market in wrist-watch technology for most of the twentieth century. But in 1969, the cuckoo shot out of the clock and hit the fan when the Japanese marketed the first quartz wristwatch – the Seiko 35 SQ Astron – using a battery-powered quartz crystal resonator vibrating at 8,192 Hz, replacing the mechanical wind-up mechanism with something that was not only sturdier and cheaper but also, to add insult to injury, much more accurate.

Within a few years, Swiss watchmakers were throwing themselves from their exquisite fretwork chalet windows or falling on their alpenhorns in despair. But in 1983, they came up with a quartz watch of their own – the Swatch – that allowed them to restore their pride as the world's favourite and tidiest watchmakers, and to regain a good slice of market share.

Radium

Radius

Type: Alkaline metal

Origin: Uranium ores

Chemical formula: Ra

+ **INDUSTRIAL**
+ CULTURAL
+ COMMERCIAL
+ **SCIENTIFIC**

The discovery of radioactivity has given us the positives of x-rays, radiotherapy for the treatment of cancer, and nuclear power generation, but the negatives of nuclear terrorism, weapons and accidents. For one group of workers in the early twentieth century, the discovery of radioactive radium was a once-in-a-lifetime opportunity to die.

DEATH RAYS

When double Nobel Prize winner Marie Curie (1867–1934) discovered a new element in 1898, she was not the first to study radioactivity. However, the name she gave to the substance, 'radium', from the Latin *radius*, meaning 'ray', became the root for the word for the phenomenon that the element displayed. The practical applications of the discovery were not immediately understood even by the greatest minds of the period. Ernest Rutherford (1871–1937), the British physicist who discovered the structure of the atom, could say in 1933: 'The energy produced by the breaking down of the atom is a very poor kind of thing. Anyone who expects a source of power from the transformation of these atoms is talking moonshine'. Confirming Albert Einstein's (1879–1955) assertion of a year before that, 'There is not the slightest indication that nuclear energy will ever be obtainable. It would mean that the atom would have to be shattered at will'.

In the two entries on plutonium and uranium, we see that they were less than two decades away from being proved completely wrong with the development of both atomic reactors and of the first nuclear weapons. We owe the discovery of radioactivity to the combined work of several scientists, but the main players were the German Wilhelm Röntgen (1845–1923), who discovered Röntgen rays, now known as x-rays; the Frenchman Antoine Becquerel (1852–1908), who worked on uranium; and the Polish-French Marie Curie, who isolated and named radium and another radioactive isotope, polonium.

Radium is extremely rare and is not found as a native metal on Earth, where it is a constituent of uranium ores. Curie

PHOSPHORESCENT
In darkness, radium gives off a blue-green glow.

isolated pure radium as a brilliant white metal that oxidised quickly in contact with the air, but in the dark, she reported that it phosphoresced with an attractive blue-green glow. The dangers of radioactivity were still unknown, and Curie handled small quantities of the element, even placing it on her skin to see the effect (it caused ulceration within a few days of exposure). She kept

lumps of radium in her desks, and to this day, her private papers are stored in lead-lined cases because they are still slightly radioactive. While her husband and principal collaborator Pierre was famously killed in a traffic accident by a horse-drawn carriage, Curie herself died of aplastic anemia caused by her work with radioactive elements. In a bizarre twist to the Curie story, the second radioactive element that she discovered, polonium, was used in the murder of a Russian dissident in London in 2006.

MR AND MRS
The Curies' work on radium led to the discovery of radioactivity.

KILLER SMILES

The huge technological advances of the First and Second Industrial Revolutions brought with them many benefits to humanity in terms of improved living standards, medical care and life expectancy for the majority. However, they also came with a heavy cost for the minority who were directly exposed to many new, untried and untested toxic substances. One of the most famous cases of industrial poisoning of the early twentieth century concerned products containing Marie Curie's new wonder element, radium.

In recent years, humans have become much more suspicious of new products, chemicals and technological advances, to the point where they may have become a bit too quick to suspect that they are being intentionally poisoned by irresponsible scientists in the pay of unscrupulous corporations. However, in the light of the litany of chemical and industrial disasters linked to magic bullet drugs such as thalidomide, LSD and heroin, 'miracle' chemicals such as DDT and CFCs, and industrial poisons such as lead, mercury and asbestos, maybe a bit of excessive caution is entirely justified. However, in the teens of the last century, the positive high tide of new discoveries that were being made every year carried humanity along on a wave of unbridled optimism and a belief in a future free of disease, war and want.

KILL OR CURE
Radium was an ingredient in many nostrums and cure-alls.

Radium had an immediate appeal. The very name, which starts alarm bells ringing for us today, suggested the positive, health-promoting, healing power of sunshine, banishing the gloom of ignorance, disease and poverty. Between 1918 and 1922, the nostrum Radithor, which contained radium, was marketed as 'Perpetual Sunshine' and 'A Cure for the Living Dead'. In 1932, a prominent socialite died of radium poisoning caused by drinking Radithor, prompting the unforgettable headline in *The Wall Street Journal*: 'The Radium Water Worked Fine Until His Jaw Came Off'.

The most tragic case, however, concerned the young female employees of the U.S. Radium Corporation, who painted the dials of wristwatches made for the U.S. armed forces during World War I with a brand of phosphorescent paint known as 'Undark'. There was

Part of what made dialpainting an attractive job must have been the work with such a sensational product. The young women applied radium to their buttons, their fingernails, their eyelids; at least one, described by a friend as a 'lively Italian girl', coated her teeth with it before a date, for a smile that glowed in the dark.

Radium Girls *(1997) by Claudia Clark*

clearly some awareness of the dangers of radium, as the research staff and managers of the firm used protective clothing and lead screens when handling the radium that gave Undark its luminescence. The girls, however, were not afforded any such protection or warned about the possible dangers of working with the paint. The slim brushes that they used to paint the tiny numbers on the watch dials quickly lost their points, and the workers were taught how to reshape the tip with their lips and tongues, thereby ingesting large quantities of the toxic paint as they worked. Unaware of the dangers to which they were exposing themselves, the girls used the paint as eye makeup and nail varnish, and some even painted their teeth with Undark for dates.

Like the workers who suffered from 'phossy jaw' (p.138) the girls began to develop alarming symptoms of radiation poisoning from their exposure to the paint, particularly a necrosis of the face known as 'radium jaw'. Hundreds of workers died in terrible agony, experiencing terrible facial disfigurement, before the company was finally prosecuted and found guilty in one of the landmark lawsuits of U.S. safety law at work. The casualties of Radithor and Undark were only the first of many from the discovery of radium and radioactivity; far worse was to come with the weaponisation of nuclear fission in 1945.

DEADLY PIGMENT
Radium paint was handpainted on the dials of watches and clocks.

NUCLEAR DAWN

✦

In addition to the radium products, there was a craze for all things atomic until humanity suddenly realised how deadly its flirtation with radioactivity might become, with nuclear accidents and events such as the Cuban Missile Crisis (1962). However, until the early 1960s, inventors, corporations and scientists happily rhapsodised about the bright new nuclear future that was just around the corner, when the new miracle power source would power everything from our vacuum cleaner to the Ford 'Nucleon' family saloon in the garage.

Sand

Sabulum

Type: Rock and mineral particles

Origin: Rock erosion

Chemical formula: SiO_2

+ **INDUSTRIAL**
+ CULTURAL
+ COMMERCIAL
+ SCIENTIFIC

Although sand has no intrinsic value and its properties make it useless in its native state as a building material, it is probably one of the most important minerals dealt with in this book, ranking alongside flint, iron and coal, as one of the foundations of human civilisation. In addition to its role as a refractory in metal casting, quartz sand is the principal constituent of glass, a substance that not only keeps our homes and workplaces dry, warm and lit, but that has made possible the scientific investigations of the cosmos and the human body. The absence of glass and its associated technologies in East Asia, in particular in China, is one of the theories put forward to explain Western Europe's dominance of the world after the sixteenth century.

THE GREAT DIVERGENCE

There are several interesting questions raised by the course taken by human civilisation: Why did the First Industrial Revolution begin in the British Isles? And why did a few hundred Spanish adventurers succeed in conquering two of the world's largest and most populous empires in a few years? This book has sought the answers by looking at certain minerals and their associated technologies. This entry on a rather unexciting and common mineral substance – sand – raises a similar question: Why did China, with its vast wealth, manpower, natural resources, early advances in science and technology, and ordered, homogeneous, literate society, not continue to dominate the planet after the sixteenth century, as it had done for the previous two millennia?

Although Western Europe was too far away to feel the direct influence of Chinese civilisation, China had a huge indirect impact on the development of Europe, the Near East and India from antiquity to the early-modern period. This was thanks to the export of technological innovations – famously, paper, printing, gunpowder and the magnetic compass – and of trade goods such as tea, silk and porcelain. A few technologies and goods went the other way, of course: China learned to work iron from Central Asian smiths, but as soon as it had appropriated the new technology, it went on to improve it, making cast iron and steel long before Western Europe.

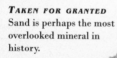

TAKEN FOR GRANTED
Sand is perhaps the most overlooked mineral in history.

WEATHERPROOF
Glass insulated scholars
from the elements.

So why are we not speaking Mandarin instead of English? And writing in Chinese characters rather than in the Latin alphabet? The Harvard historian, John Fairbank (1907–91), the most influential student of China of his generation, suggested, like Edward Gibbon had done in the context of the Roman Empire, that religion was the primary factor that explained the 'Great Divergence' – the term coined by Samuel Huntington (1927–2008) to describe the lead taken by Western Europe in the sixteenth century. In the Chinese context, this was not Christianity but Taoism.

In 2002, historians Allan Macfarlane and Gerry Martin put forward a much more intriguing theory in *Glass: A World History*, which focused on the absence of glass technology in China. The Chinese lived in semi-permanent gloom in their elegant houses and palaces, sheltered behind paper doors and windows; they carried their alchemical experiments within opaque ceramic containers that often reacted with their contents; and they did not grind lenses or mirrors to study the heavens or the microscopic world. They had acquired such a high level of sophistication in so many fields at such an early date that their success and dominance effectively stifled further development.

ENLIGHTENMENT
Western advances in science were based on instruments with glass lenses.

WINDOW ON THE WORLD
Glass gave Western
scientists and scholars an
entirely different view of
the world.

After the 1500s, the Chinese continued to improve on what they had already – refining their ceramics, lacquers, metalwork and silks beyond anything the West was ever capable of – but they did not innovate in key areas of science and technology. They did not think outside, if you'll excuse the pun, the exquisitely lacquered box. Politically, socially, artistically, religiously and after the sixteenth century, technologically and scientifically, they were content with their worldview, their capacities, their arts and architecture and their consumer goods. Even when shown the wonders of the industrial age – mechanical clocks, steam trains and ships, improved gunpowder weapons, and machine-woven cottons – the Chinese displayed polite interest, as an adult would in the muddy paintings of a child, and continued to do things in the traditional way. Until, that is, the Europeans, Americans and Japanese insisted none too politely that they change their ways. Once challenged, China entered a protracted period of political, social, and ideological decline, enduring three centuries of foreign and civil wars before she was once again able to regain her independence and her role as a global leader.

SHINING A LIGHT ON THE WORLD

The Chinese, of course, were not completely unaware of glass technology, and had developed their own glass manufacture of beads and other small object such as the disc-like *bi* during antiquity. They also imported glass products from the West in the early centuries of the Common Era. However, they never saw the need to develop glass technology beyond a certain stage, especially when most of the practical pre-industrial functions of the material could be met by ceramics.

GLASS CRAFT
A glass jug manufactured
in ancient Rome.

The history of science begins with the observation and description of the natural world, and the interpretation of these observations and descriptions, leading to the formulations of theories about the composition of matter, energy and light, and the workings of the human body. Scientific theories can become entrenched as fixed dogma, or they may be continually tested, refined and overthrown by new theories and experiments. The Chinese evolved a sophisticated worldview based on the interactions of five elementary substances, the *Wu Xing* (wood, fire, earth, metal and water), within the framework of

To see a World in a Grain of Sand And a Heaven in a Wild Flower, Hold Infinity in the palm of your hand And Eternity in an hour. *'Auguries of Innocence' by William Blake (1757–1827)*

the two opposite principles of *yin* and *yang*, which they applied to all areas of knowledge and human activity. In their understanding of human anatomy, for example, they evolved a complex theory of subtle energies circulating around the body, simplified in the West into the single concept of *qi* (or chi), and the balance of yin and yang, on which they based their diagnostic techniques, nutritional rules, pharmacology, exercise and medical treatments.

First described in detail in the *Huangdi Neijing* (*The Yellow Emperor's Canon of Internal Medicine*) written during the Han Dynasty (206 BC–220 CE), qi is not a substance that can be observed by any physical means. No matter how powerful a microscope you use, you will not see it or the channels (meridians) through which it is said to flow through the human body. But to the traditional Chinese healer treating his patient, this does not matter, as he can call on a corpus of experimental treatments dating back thousand of years. When microscopes revealed the existence of the microscopic world in the late sixteenth century, leading in the nineteenth to the germ theory of disease, the discovery did not overturn centuries of Chinese practice, which continues as a parallel form of diagnosis and treatment alongside Western scientific medicine.

MAGIC GRAINS
Common sand – the basic material needed to make glass.

Through the Looking Glass

In ancient times, glass was made from silica (SiO_2), typically the kind of yellow quartz sand found on most beaches, and an alkali such as soda or potash. When the two were heated together, they melted into a liquid that cooled into clear glass. According to the Roman historian Pliny (23–79 CE), the Phoenicians first discovered how to make glass during a beach-barbecue accident. However, it is likely that glass was discovered several times independently in different parts of the world. The most likely explanation is that glass was first produced accidentally as a byproduct of metalworking during the Bronze Age (5,300–3,200 years BP). The ancient Mesopotamians, Egyptians and Greeks all contributed to the development of glass technology, but it was the Romans who developed and disseminated glassblowing to make bottles and drinking cups. The techniques of glass manufacture were not lost when the Roman Empire collapsed in Western Europe in the fifth century, but glass technology diversified, with an Eastern tradition in North Africa and the Near East, and a Western tradition in Italy and Germany.

SOME LIKE IT HOT
Glass technology developed more slowly in the warmer climates of the Near East.

Glass has made many contributions to science and scholarship through the centuries. In the medieval period, improvements in sheet glass technology made the glazing of windows affordable. While earlier buildings had unglazed windows that let in light, they also let in the cold, wind, rain and snow, limiting the comfort and working hours of scribes and copyists. But even more significant than window glass was the development of glass spectacles that first appeared in Italy in the late thirteenth century, and quickly spread all over Europe. Henceforth the career of a scholar was not limited by the lifetime of his eyes, and was lengthened by up to 20 years. The development of glass lenses, mirrors and prisms led to an understanding of light, which itself unlocked many of the secrets of matter. Optical instruments, such as telescopes and microscopes (see box, opposite) allowed navigators, doctors and scientists to deconstruct and reconstruct the natural world and the human body. Alchemists and then chemists used non-reactive glass beakers, retorts and test tubes impervious to cold, heat, alkalis and acids, to conduct the experiments that allowed them to identify the

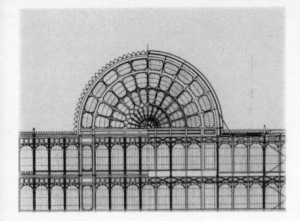

GLASSHOUSE
It is no accident that the Great Exhibition of the Works of Industry of All Nations of 1851 was held in a giant glass building known as the Crystal Palace.

chemical elements that constitute matter beyond the classical four elements of earth, fire, air and water, and rearrange them at will into new chemical compounds.

It would not be an exaggeration to say that glass was the invisible medium through which Western science finally broke free from religious dogma and alchemical magic. But do Macfarlane and Martin go too far in explaining the overwhelming dominance of the West from the sixteenth to the twentieth centuries by the invention of something as simple as glass? Rival historians have accused them of oversimplification, citing, for example, the heterogeneity of Chinese culture that stifled internal competition and the need for change, as well as the vast resources of the New World that Europe acquired in the sixteenth century. However, if we think of glass, not simply as the material for our windows, eyeglasses, laboratory equipment and optical instruments, but as a state of mind: the ability to see through and into matter – the ability, in short, to be open to intellectual enlightenment – then I would agree with their assertion that glass was a significant factor that gave the West its overwhelming advantage over the East.

A NEW LOOK AT LIFE

✦

Today we take it for granted that the world we can see with our eyes is only part of the overall picture, and that there exists both a much bigger (macro) and a much smaller (micro) world that our senses are not designed to apprehend directly but that we can see with the help of optical instruments. Lenses ground from natural glass and gems were known in antiquity, and eyeglasses were first made in Europe in the thirteenth century, but it was only in the sixteenth and seventeenth centuries that glass lenses and mirrors were used to make scientific instruments: the telescopes and microscopes that transformed our understanding of the world. Galileo Galilei (1564–1642) perfected the telescope, and his astronomical discoveries helped launch the Scientific Revolution that overturned centuries of accepted wisdom and Christian dogma. At the other end of the optical scale, Antonie van Leeuwenhoek (1632–1723) popularised the use of the microscope, and amazed his contemporaries with his drawings of magnified insects, plants and human and animal tissues.

Saltpetre
Sal petrae

Type: Mineral salt

Origin: Wood ash

Chemical formula: KNO_3

+ *INDUSTRIAL*
+ CULTURAL
+ COMMERCIAL
+ SCIENTIFIC

ELIXIR OF DEATH
Saltpetre was first used to make an alchemical elixir of eternal life.

Saltpetre (potassium nitrate) is a man-made chemical extracted from wood ash. It has had applications as a fertiliser and food preservative, but its main historical application was as a constituent of 'Black Powder', the Chinese invention that gave the world the wonders of fireworks displays, as well as the destructive power of gunpowder and gunpowder weapons.

THE CHINA SYNDROME

In the previous entry on sand, I suggested one possible answer as to why China lost its dominant place in the world in the sixteenth century, and began to lag behind the West. From the Han Dynasty (206 BCE–220 CE), which was contemporaneous with the Roman Republic and early Empire, to the first century of the Ming Dynasty (1368–1644) during the European Renaissance, China remained the uncontested world leader in many areas of technology, as well as in the fine and applied arts. In addition to the theories based on the differential development of technology and available natural resources, historians have suggested that China was primarily a victim of its own success. Once the Chinese empire had been unified, it developed into an ordered, centralised state that was so vastly superior to any of its neighbours and regional rivals that for centuries there was no external force strong enough to threaten its internal stability.

Like the Romans, however, the Chinese were perfectly capable of fighting among themselves, which they did at intervals, but the rise and fall of individual dynasties did not undermine the fundamental stability of Chinese civilisation. The history of the West, in contrast, has been marked by a series of catastrophic societal collapses, beginning with the Bronze Age Collapse (c. 1200–1150 BCE) in the eastern Mediterranean, and followed by the fall of the Western Roman Empire in 476 CE, the Islamic conquest of the Persian and southern provinces of the Byzantine Empires in the seventh century, and the fall of Constantinople to the Ottoman Turks in 1453, when the existing social order was destroyed and replaced by something completely new. If the development of the West could be compared to white-water rafting, with the raft going over the occasional waterfall, then the history of China would be more akin to a cruise on a broad, flat river with the galley of state occasionally running into stormy weather or aground on a sandbank.

During its long period of dominance, the Chinese gave the world the 'Four Great Inventions', three of which – paper, printing and the magnetic compass – are deserving of the adjective 'great' because the benefits they brought to humanity far outweigh any difficulties they may have caused. But as for the fourth, gunpowder, few will deny that its invention has been more murderous and destructive of human life, culture and potential than almost any other substance until the discovery of high explosives in the nineteenth century and of nuclear weapons in the twentieth.

Chinese alchemy, in contrast to its Western counterpart, which was largely concerned with the conversion of base metals into gold, was obsessed with the pursuit of immortality. The Chinese had recognised early on that while the accumulation of vast wealth and power was a reasonable aim for one's earthly lifetime, the real prize was to find a way of holding onto them forever.

WESTWARD PROGRESS
Gunpowder made its way to India and then the Near East and Europe.

The Egyptians believed that if they preserved the physical appearance of the body through mummification, the spirit of the deceased would live forever in the afterlife; Christians, Jews and Muslims opted for the immortality of the spirit while the body was allowed to decay; but the Chinese emperors wanted it all: absolute power, fabulous wealth and a physical body that could be transmuted into an indestructible substance that would be impervious to time. In their search for the Elixir of Life, the Chinese experimented with many elements and chemical compounds. In the process, they combined the three constituents of gunpowder – carbon in the form of charcoal, sulphur and saltpetre – with explosive results. Instead of discovering a means of prolonging life, they succeeded in creating a substance that has shortened a considerable number of human lives.

ITCHY FEET
Primitive Chinese gunpowder mines or projectiles.

CHINA'S SECRET WEAPONS

Despite their technological superiority and the Great Wall that they built to protect the vulnerable northern border of the empire from marauders from Central Asia, the Chinese fell prey to repeated barbarian incursions from the north and west during the first millennium CE, culminating in the conquest of China by the Mongols, who established the Yuan Dynasty that ruled the country from 1271 to 1368.

At first, the secret of gunpowder protected the settled, agrarian Chinese from the threat of invasion from their nomadic neighbours. Chinese alchemists probably discovered the mixture in their life-prolonging experiments in the ninth century CE, usually by setting fire to their own wood-and-paper houses. Their initial mix, known as 'black powder', which contained high proportions of charcoal and sulphur but much less saltpetre, burned fiercely but did not explode. This made the powder suitable as an incendiary, which could be combined with natural resins, oils and plant matter that the Chinese could launch against their mounted attackers by catapult from behind the safety of their city walls.

Like the Byzantines, who exploited the incendiary properties of asphalt and petroleum to protect their cities from highly mobile Arab and Central Asian invaders, the Chinese developed a range of weapons that made use of black powder, such as fire arrows, that could be launched singly with a bow, or from the first multiple 'missile launchers', as well as the first land and water mines. In the late tenth century CE, Chinese artificers invented the 'fire-lance', the remote ancestor of all subsequent gunpowder weapons and firearms. The world's first 'gun' was a paper flamethrower strapped to a lance that had a range of about 3.6 m (12 ft). With their knowledge of metal-casting technology, the

FIREPOWER
The introduction of gunpowder weapons transformed warfare.

Saltpetre, the key ingredient [of gunpowder], was isolated by Chinese alchemists, looking, ironically, for compounds that would bring bodily immortality. It appears in Song Dynasty formulas from the mid-800s, and these in turn in much older alchemical work. Gunpowder proper seems to have first appeared in 1044 A.D. in China and to have worked its way westward over the next three centuries by routes still uncertain.

A History of Greek Fire and Gunpowder *(1960) by James Partington*

Chinese soon replaced the paper casing with cast iron, which could be packed with shards of metal, pottery or poisonous arsenic balls that would be ejected when the lance was ignited.

By changing the black-powder mix, and adding more saltpetre, a cast-metal gunpowder weapon could propel a projectile at much greater range. By the twelfth century, the Chinese were making true cannons, first out of bronze and then out of cast iron. These early cannons were shaped like thick-bottomed vases and were loaded from the muzzle, with the projectile and gunpowder tightly packed into the thick metal tube, with a small touchhole at the rear of the weapon for the fuse. The Chinese made a hand-held version in around 1285 CE. But the world's first 'handgun' would not have fitted in a clutch bag or a glove compartment: it measured about 30 cm (1 ft) long and weighed about 3.6 kg (8 lb).

The gunpowder revolution, although significant, did not give the settled, civilised Chinese a permanent advantage over their enemies. Like the barbarians who lived on the borders of the Roman Empire, the Central Asian nomads gradually learned from the Chinese, unfortunately not the civilised arts of peace, but the secrets of gunpowder technology.

STARBURST
Fireworks are one of the few peaceful applications of gunpowder.

In the thirteenth century, the Mongols overcame Chinese resistance to establish their own barbarian state across most of Eurasia, from China in the East to the borders of the Byzantine Empire in the West. The Mongols pushed westwards, defeating all the states they encountered until they reached Europe, where the Byzantines succeeded in halting their advance. The vast, borderless Mongol Empire facilitated the transfer of technologies from East to West, and gunpowder weapons finally reached to the Near East and Europe in the fourteenth and fifteenth centuries.

THE WILD, WILD WEST

Western Europe in the fifteenth century was a patchwork of some 500 states: holy empires, kingdoms, principalities, dukedoms, religious states and independent cities, all fighting endless petty wars. Faced by the might of a world-conquering superpower, there should have been only one outcome: the annihilation of the West. But the Mongol war machine, sated by their conquest of China, northern India and the Islamic world, stalled when it reached the Mediterranean world. Sheltered behind the massive walls of Constantinople, which could resist any weapon in the Mongol arsenal, including its Chinese gunpowder technology, the West survived the Mongol invasions.

As soon as Europeans acquired gunpowder weapons through their contact with the Mongols and the Islamic world, they were quick to improve on the Chinese originals. The Germans developed the muzzle-loaded matchlock musket in the last quarter of the fifteenth century. As the principal pastime of the European states between the twelfth and twentieth centuries was warfare, there was a constant drive to improve military technology, with the development of the wheel-lock musket, and the more reliable flintlock, that quickly made all other projectile weapons obsolete. Gunpowder technology not only transformed war on the battlefield and at sea; it also transformed siege warfare. From antiquity until the fifteenth century, city walls had been proof against almost anything a besieging army

HIGH AND DRY
A perennial problem of gunpowder was how to keep it dry.

GUNSLINGER
By the seventeenth
century, Western firearms
were the best in the world.

could throw against them. Constantinople owed its survival to a formidable double line of land walls and moats, built by the ancient Romans, which could not be breached until the Ottoman Turks developed giant long-range cannon.

Gunpowder weapons, combined with steel, gave Western Europe the edge over its rivals during the Age of Exploration. As we saw in the entry on gold, it enabled small forces of European adventurers to conquer the most advanced and populous empires of the New World. Starting in the eighteenth century, it would help England, a small, under-populated and under-resourced island on the northern fringe of Europe, to dominate the world.

Salt

Salio

Type: Mineral salt

Origin: Evaporation of seawater and rock salt deposits

Chemical formula: NaCl

+ INDUSTRIAL

+ CULTURAL

+ COMMERCIAL

+ SCIENTIFIC

S alt is a mineral that is so basic to life and culture that modern humans have long ago forgotten the role that it played in the development of early civilisation. Salt-producing areas and salt mines are responsible for the locations of many of our roads, ports and cities. In the modern period, food manufacturers add so much salt in processed food that it is adversely affecting human health, but once it was so vital for the preservation of food supplies that it was used as a form of currency. In the early twentieth century, salt played a major role in the struggle for Indian independence.

THE UNPLANNED CONQUEST

On January 30, 1948, Mohandas Gandhi (b. 1869), known to many as Mahatma ('Great Soul'), or more affectionately as Bapu ('Father'), fell victim to an assassin's bullet as he addressed a prayer meeting in New Delhi, capital of the newly independent Republic of India. Ironically, the man who murdered Gandhi was a Hindu nationalist, who should have been one of his victim's most fervent supporters. Among the young assassin's objections was that India's liberation had been achieved with a lot less blood (specifically English blood) than would have been the case had Gandhi been an advocate of violent struggle. However, even if independence was achieved with little death and destruction, the partition of the subcontinent into the republics of India and Pakistan (then consisting of both Pakistan and Bangladesh) cost an estimated one million lives.

India's official incorporation into the British Empire dated to 1858, after the Indian Mutiny of 1857, which was one of the bloodiest revolts of native troops against British rule during the nineteenth century. But the beginnings of direct British involvement in the subcontinent were already a century old by then. India's liberation from its

STAFF OF LIFE
Salt is not just a flavouring, it is vital to life and wellbeing.

Ye are the salt of the earth: but if the salt have lost his savour, wherewith shall it be salted? it is thenceforth good for nothing, but to be cast out, and to be trodden under foot of men.

Matthew 5:13, King James Bible

colonial status took decades of political activism, which included in 1930 a campaign of civil disobedience concerned with one of the least glamorous or controversial of commodities: table salt.

The takeover of India is something of an anomaly in the annals of imperialism and colonialism. India was not annexed or conquered by a national government but acquired piecemeal over decades by a private corporation, the British East India Company, established in 1600 to trade with the East during the reign of Queen Elizabeth I (1533–1603). The company initially struggled to survive in the face of competition from European rivals at a time when the term 'trade war' did not mean a bad-tempered dispute with an exchange of strongly worded communiqués and the creation of tit-for-tat protectionist legislation, but full-on encounters between naval and land forces. During the seventeenth century, the British succeeded in holding their own against the Dutch, Portuguese and French, establishing permanent bases in India, and forming alliances with local elites until they had become the dominant foreign power, administering whole provinces of the country, while nominally acknowledging the fiction of the sovereign authority of the Mughal emperor in New Delhi.

When the British first arrived, India was ruled by the descendants of the Mughal Timur (Tamerlane; 1336–1405), who had established a Central Asian empire in imitation of his world-conquering forebears. The Mughals established their rule in Northern India in 1526, and gradually expanded southwards to claim most of the subcontinent by the early eighteenth century. However, the size and diversity of the

GOING DOWN TO THE SEA

✦

At 423 m (1,388 ft) below sea level, the Dead Sea – located between Israel, the Palestinian Territories and Jordan – is the lowest place on the surface of planet Earth. Although called a 'sea', this 67-km (42-mile)-long body of water is a salt lake that is cut off from the Mediterranean and the Red Sea. Fed by the Jordan River, the Dead Sea has a salinity of 33.7 percent, with a density of 1.4 kg of salt per litre of water, making it one of the few bodies of water where it is extremely difficult (though not impossible) to drown.

empire, which consisted of Muslim, Sikh and Hindu states, created insurmountable problems for the Mughals, who struggled to control their dominions, and had to deal with increasingly powerful European adventurers, acting sometimes for themselves and for their home governments, but who always demanded ever greater privileges, preferential trading treaties, and were quite happy to back their commercial demands with military force.

The East India Company skillfully exploited the weakness of the divided Mughal state, encouraging subversion among its subjects, while fighting military campaigns against its European rivals, with whom the British state was often at war during the eighteenth century. The company, in theory an independent corporation, was an instrument of British imperial policy while at the same time dictating it to suit its own commercial ends. It was not a situation that could last forever, and maybe it is amazing that it endured as long as 100 years. The equivalent might be if a large American corporation – Microsoft, for example – took over a large country to further its business aims.

Like China, India had been a global superpower since antiquity and it had achieved a high degree of cultural and technological sophistication centuries before western Europe. Unlike the native peoples of the New World, the Indians were not technologically backwards. They had led the world in many fields, notably iron metallurgy and gunpowder technology, and in the sixteenth and seventeenth centuries, India was more than a match militarily for Portugal, Holland, France and England, whose ships sailed to her ports around Africa once the fall of Constantinople in 1453 had closed the overland trading routes to China. Yet at the very height of its power, at the beginning of the eighteenth century, Mughal India was entering a period of decline. As with the decline of China, historians have put forward a range of theories – economic, ideological, religious and social – to explain why

FLAT RATE
Boycotting government salt was an unexpected but successful tactic.

India failed to maintain her lead over Europe, given the size of her population, high levels of literacy, and the wealth of natural resources at her disposal.

The Raj, as the British administration in India became known, endured until 1948, though with mounting opposition and growing calls for home rule or full independence that escalated after the World War I. After 1915, one of the principal leaders of the independence movement was the soft-spoken Gandhi, whose entire life would be devoted to establishing the independence of his native land.

THE NON-VIOLENT FIGHTER

Those who might have met the young Gandhi would not have predicted his extraordinary political career. Born in a well-to-do, high-caste Hindu family, Gandhi received a solid education in India, though without excelling or distinguishing himself academically. After graduating from high school, he went to London to study law, where he qualified as a courtroom advocate, or barrister. In England, he did not stand out from his contemporaries. He returned to India but failed to find a job at home. Instead in 1897, he took up a post in South Africa, then a province of the British Empire, and already a state built on deeply racist principles, with distinctions between whites and non-whites, and gradations of discrimination between native Africans, people of mixed heritage, and South and East Asians. Gandhi's political conscience awoke in South Africa after he experienced both personal and state-sponsored discrimination. He organised the local Indian community to resist discriminatory legislation, evolving his own particular philosophy of non-violent resistance and civil disobedience inspired by the teachings of Hinduism.

Although Gandhi and his supporters faced continuous persecution and violence from the authorities, and Gandhi himself was arrested and imprisoned on several occasions, their non-violent stance won them the respect and admiration of liberal white opinion in South Africa and Britain. The South African government must have been overjoyed and relieved when, in 1915, Gandhi decided to return to India to campaign for Indian independence.

MONOPOLY
Indian salt production was a monopoly controlled by the British Raj.

The Raj, by the standards of European colonial rule, could have been considered to be fairly enlightened. When compared to Spanish rule in the Americas, with its murderous repression of local elites, suppression of native religions and cultures, or Dutch rule in the East Indies (now Indonesia), British rule, though paternalistic and undeniably racist, was relatively benevolent. There were no forced conversions to Christianity, racial pogroms or intentional genocides. But until the beginnings of the twentieth century, the British were confident in the superiority of Anglo-Saxon culture, and of their right to rule the 'lesser' races, while they also protected their political and economic interests against the Russians.

RUBBING SALT INTO IMPERIAL WOUNDS

When Gandhi decided to launch his first major campaign of political protest against British rule, his choice of target surprised many of his followers, and initially caused a certain amount of hilarity among the British administration. Gandhi had chosen to attack the government monopoly on the production and sale of table salt. Salt is possibly not the substance that comes to mind first in a discussion of great social movements and revolutions, but the salt that you and I take so much for granted that we do not even notice it unless it is missing from our restaurant table was once a key staple of daily life, and thus, its control, supply and taxation was a major concern of governments. Although taxes are never popular with the population, the taxation of commodities is probably the most resented. In France, the gabelle, a tax on salt first instituted in the thirteenth century, was the cause of many revolts against the crown, and was one of the many grievances cited by the revolutionaries of 1789.

> **Is not birth, beauty, good shape, discourse, Manhood, learning, gentleness, virtue, and such like, the spice and salt that season a man?**
> Troilus and Cressida *(1602) by William Shakespeare*

Apart from its use as a flavouring in cooking, sodium chloride has a wide range of industrial applications, but its main historical use was as a food preservative, which was particularly important before the invention of canning and refrigeration. Until the early nineteenth century, the salting of meat and fish was the best way to preserve these important foodstuffs, and even today, many forms of meat processing across the world make use of salt as a preservative.

Gandhi considered salt to be the ideal target for both economic and symbolic reasons: It is a staple used by all peoples, of whatever social class, caste or religion, whether rich or poor, and it could only be obtained legally from the government. In terms of revenue, the salt taxes amounted to about eight percent of the receipts of the Raj. In March

PRESERVATIVE
Before refrigeration, salt played a vital role in food preservation.

WE SHALL OVERCOME
Gandhi led the Salt March
until imprisoned by the
British.

1930, Gandhi began a march from his home of Ahmedabad in northern India to the coastal village of Dandi, some 390 km (240 miles) away. Along the route of his march, Gandhi illegally produced his own salt by boiling up seawater, encouraging others to do the same, to buy illegal salt, and to boycott government-produced supplies. The movement quickly won national and international attention, and millions in India joined in the protest.

NATURE'S BOUNTY
Gandhi taught the
protesters how to make
their own salt.

As with the civil rights movement of 1960s America, the authorities could only respond with brutal, repressive force: They arrested and imprisoned Gandhi and the leaders who came forward to take his place. When this did not end the salt marches, illegal production, and boycotts, they were forced to arrest tens of thousands of ordinary Indians who were openly breaking the law. When peaceful protesters blockaded a salt works, the soldiers guarding the gates were ordered to hold them off with force if necessary. Gandhi had instructed his supporters not to resist but to sit down in the middle of the road when confronted, which caused the enraged soldiers to turn on them in full view of the world press. Although the protests were brutally repressed, with many killed and injured, Gandhi scored a major moral victory over the British, who had to acknowledge that it was only a matter of time before they would have to grant full Indian independence.

Flint

Silex

Type: Nodules in
sedimentary rocks

Origin: Low-temperature,
low-pressure metamorphism

Chemical formula: SiO_2

+ **INDUSTRIAL**
+ **CULTURAL**
+ COMMERCIAL
+ SCIENTIFIC

The hominid tool kit is at least 2.6 million years old. Alongside organic materials such as bone, antler and wood, humans used several types of hard stone that they learned to shape into a range of tools. One of the best materials they found was flint, a hard sedimentary rock that is found in large nodules in chalk deposits. Flint was extensively mined in prehistoric and historic times, with the larger deposits having the value of major oil fields today. Unlike later materials technology, the working of flint and other stones is open to all, although it requires a high degree of skill to do well. Hence, Stone Age societies are thought not to have had the marked distinctions of caste and class that were associated with societies based on more complex technologies.

THE FIRST HUMANS

There are many things we don't know about our early hominid ancestors. For one thing, we don't know who among the early ape-like creatures, the australopithecines – who evolved in Africa around 5.5 million years BP – or even among the first representatives of the genus *Homo*, who date back 2.3 million years, are our direct ancestors. I am not with the creationists who would rather believe that humans stand apart from the animals, magically fashioned from clay by a benevolent creator; it is simply that, as paleoanthropologists will themselves admit, we have far too few specimens and too great a time span between them and the first *Homo sapiens* to identify with 100 percent certainty the first human.

According to creationism, *Homo sapiens* could be 200,000–250,000 years old, in line with evolutionary theory, but emerging *ex nihilo* out of the hands of the deity, or possibly as little as 6,016 years old, if they accept Bishop James Ussher's (1581–1656) chronology, which states that Adam was created in 4004 BCE, on the evening of Saturday, October 22, when the creator had a few hours to spare – Saturday nights can be so quiet, especially for an omnipotent being with no one else to talk to. Of course, there weren't

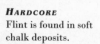

HARDCORE
Flint is found in soft
chalk deposits.

any Saturdays or evenings back then, as the concept of time is something humans created, when they needed to know whether they were wasting it or spending it wisely.

Some men and women of faith would rather believe in the unlikely miracle of creation than accept the even more miraculous idea that an animal not that different from a modern chimpanzee could, over millions of years, have developed the ability to make and use tools, learned how to control and later make fire, and created complex social interactivity, language, religion and art. Tool use, as we have seen in earlier entries, was once thought to be a defining human trait, but we now know that the great apes, and several birds, mammals and cephalopod species use objects as simple tools; similarly, language, emotion and self-awareness are no longer considered to be unique to humans. However, with the appearance of *Homo habilis* (the 'handyman') around 2.3 million years BP, the human tool kit begins to surpass anything used by non-human species, as well as the tools used by early hominids, as humans began intentionally to shape flakes of flint, obsidian and quartz into recognisable implements.

TOOL KIT
The human stone tool kit became ever more sophisticated.

AXEMAN
The flint axe allowed our ancestors to dismember animal carcasses.

THE AGES OF STONE

The term 'Stone Age' can be misleading. Because humans still use stone in their daily lives, in some sense, they are still living in the Stone Age, just as much as they are still in the Copper and Bronze Ages. They have just supplemented these materials with many more. However, for the sake of argument, the Stone Age lasted for 2.6 million years – give or take 7,000–10,000 years. Considering that we consider a product to be obsolete in a matter of years, it is difficult to imagine a technology that lasted for that length of time. Naturally, the design and range of tools changed, from very roughly altered pieces of stone, with only a very passing resemblance to the functional terms used to describe them, to extraordinarily and beautifully worked axes, knives and scythes, that anyone would be able to recognise as manufactured objects. As we have seen in the entry on obsidian, the Stone Age can be said to have lasted well into the historic period in some parts of the world, and still describes the technology of some hunter-gatherer societies today, in the most remote areas of the planet, although few of them do not make use of the products of industrial civilisation when these come their way.

The Stone Age is so long that archaeologists have divided it into several sub-periods, such as the Acheulean and the Mousterian – terms coined in the eighteenth and nineteenth centuries from the places where different Stone Age 'industries' were first discovered, which is not the same thing as saying that these were their places of origin.

HUNTER-GATHERER
Stone arrows and spearheads gave humans the edge while hunting.

Early harvesting tools were made of wood or bone into which razor-sharp flint blades were inserted. Later tools continued to be made by chipping and flaking stone, but during the Neolithic period stone that was too hard to be chipped was ground and polished for tools. People developed sickles, scythes, forks, hoes, and simple plows to replace their digging sticks.

Anthropology: The Human Challenge (2010) by William Haviland et al

The sites of Saint-Acheul and Le Moustier are both in France. Later research has placed the origin of tool manufacture in East Africa, from where it radiated across the planet with our ancestors during their repeated waves of migration. The nomenclature for different tool industries is encompassed within broader epochal terms: the Paleolithic (old), the Mesolithic (middle) and the Neolithic (new) Stone Ages, terms that were coined in the early eighteenth century.

In 1969, Graham Young added his own five stages of stone technology (modes 1–5), which occurred in the same sequence in different world regions, though not necessarily at the same time. Modes 1 to 5 show greater and greater elaboration, as well as the development of new types of tools. There is no absolute chronology for the development of Stone Age tools, as in certain regions they continued to be made well into the historic period. Mode 1 tools show the least elaboration, with one usable end, and the rest of the stone in its natural state (for example, Oldowan, 2.6–1.7 million years BP). Mode 2 tools show two complete faces (such as Acheulean, from c. 1.75 million years BP). Mode 3 features smaller, knife-like tools (such as Mousterian, c. 300,000–c. 30,000 years BP), while mode 4 features long-bladed tools (such as Aurignacian, c. 47,000–41,000 years BP). The characteristic of mode 5 is the abundance of microliths, small flakes of flint or obsidian that were affixed to a wooden shaft to make composite tools and weapons (such as Magdalanian, 17,000–9,000 years BP).

THE EGALITARIAN MATERIAL

The manufacture of tools long precedes the development of behavioural modernity in humans, which some archaeologists believe took place around 50,000 years BP, though some of the evidence presented in the entry on ochre suggests that this could have occurred up to 30,000 years earlier. The most interesting question, however, may not be how humans discovered the use of stone tools, but why, after millions of years of uninterrupted use, they stopped making them and began to produce metal implements that

CUTTING EDGE
Flint knives were used to prepare meat and to collect edible plants.

STONEWALL
In parts of Europe, flint is still used as a strong, durable building material.

were far more difficult to source and manufacture, and which, at the beginnings of metallurgy at least, were not that much better than the tried-and-tested stone alternatives.

In Australia and parts of the Americas, the Stone Age did not end until the arrival of European explorers in the sixteenth and seventeenth centuries. In the Andean region of South America, for example, where the Inca and their predecessor cultures evolved sophisticated metallurgical techniques sometimes well in advance of the Old World (as we have seen with platinum), the Stone Age extended into the sixteenth century. The discovery of a new, more advanced, technology, it seems, did not entail the automatic disappearance of an earlier technological stage, as it has done in the industrial period, for example, where we see a succession of technologies and materials.

The evolution of human technology from stone to metal that was once seen as a linear progression through set developmental stages of civilisation with its associated technologies is now seen as only applicable to the history of one particular region of the world: Europe, which is also the region where the idea of the smooth progression from stone to copper, bronze and then iron first originated. The pattern followed in the Americas was very different: The Classic Maya who lived in Mexico, Belize, Honduras and Guatemala during the first millennium CE developed sophisticated mathematics and astronomy, a calendar that still prompts the writing of best-

WEAPON OF WAR
Flint blades were probably used as the first weapons.

sellers, superb artistic achievements in the fields of sculpture, painting, ceramics and architecture, all achieved with Stone Age technology.

The presence of certain minerals, and even the knowledge of how to manufacture new materials such as metals, does not alone explain why certain cultures developed new technologies while others chose not to, or why they decided to remain at a certain technological stage. India and China were well placed to host the First Industrial Revolution but failed to do so, while England, with far fewer advantages in terms of natural resources and population, led the world technologically for a century. It has been suggested that what made metal so much more difficult – its rarity and the complexities of its extraction and manufacture – is also what made it so attractive to human societies as they began to become socially stratified.

Although the best flints and obsidians were mined and traded over a wide geographical area in Neolithic times, establishing the first long-distance trading networks, they were not the only varieties of stones that could be made into tools. Stone is by its nature an egalitarian material freely available to all. But metal ores, especially those used to make the alloys of tin and copper, bronze and iron, had to be traded over long distances, and the production of the metals was a skilled process that entailed the existence of a caste of specialist metalworkers, and a class of powerful men and women with sufficient wealth to commission and purchase metal artifacts. Metals, in other words, are the products of hierarchical societies in which the surpluses are controlled by the political and warrior elites. However, as we have seen on the entry on obsidian, metallurgy is not a prerequisite for the development of a complex hierarchical society: The Aztec-Mexica and the Maya, for example, developed highly stratified societies without bronze and iron.

MATCHLESS

♦

You don't have to be a boy scout to know that starting a fire in the open – in the wind and rain – even with matches, can be quite tricky. Our early ancestors, unless they were lucky enough to come across a fresh lava flow or forest fire that was not life-threatening, had to rely on rubbing two sticks together until they noticed the sparks flying from the flint nodules that they were fashioning into tools. However, even with considerable skill and a supply of dry kindling, starting a fire in this way can take several minutes. The first great advance in fire-making was the invention of the tinderbox, which consisted of a metal container containing inflammable material and a piece of steel that would be struck against a sharpened flake of flint to make a spark. The tinderbox, with some refinements, remained in use until the invention of matches.

LIGHTER
The tinderbox remained in use until the nineteenth century.

Steel
Stahl

Type: Metal alloy

Origin: Iron ores

Chemical formula: Fe with varying amounts of carbon (C)

+ **INDUSTRIAL**
+ CULTURAL
+ **COMMERCIAL**
+ SCIENTIFIC

INDUSTRIAL METAL
The modern world
is literally built
of steel.

The main driver of the development of iron and steel metallurgy was military technology. From the very earliest times, ironsmiths produced steel, but they did not understand the chemical processes by which alloying different quantities of carbon with wrought iron changed its properties. They produced blades with sharper edges than bronze weapons but that could also be flexible, but their discoveries were achieved through trial and error and experience, and their knowledge was more akin to magical lore than technological know-how. Although armour had been made from bronze, sheet iron made stronger and lighter armour, but at a higher cost. The extra resources and time required to make steel plate armour changed the nature of warfare. Now that the soldier carried so much extra weight, he needed to be mounted to remain mobile. Thus a warrior required considerable wealth to buy his armour and a suitable mount. Beginning in late antiquity, large armies of lightly armoured infantrymen made way for elite forces of heavily armoured mounted cavalrymen who would evolve into the medieval knight in shining armour.

'WE BAND OF BROTHERS'

Friday October 25, 1415, was the date of the Battle of Agincourt, which inspired one of William Shakespeare's most stirring patriotic compositions. King Henry V (1386–1422) delivers the 'Band of Brothers' speech in a play named after its lead character, which Shakespeare wrote almost two centuries after the king's death. Agincourt, fought between the French and English on a muddy field in northern France, was only one of many such engagements during the long drawn-out conflict between the two countries that later became known as the Hundred Years' War (1337–1453). Although portrayed as a war between two nation states, the causes and origins of the conflict show that this is an oversimplification made up by historians to serve the propaganda needs of later conflicts.

After the conquest of Anglo-Saxon England in 1066 by the Normans, themselves the descendants of Viking raiders who had settled in northern France, the various dynastic claims through marriage between the

English Norman and French nobility, combined with the relationships between feudal lords and their subjects, became inextricably confused with issues of national allegiance and territorial claims. The result, after centuries of conflict, was the emergence of two recognisably national entities – France and England – that would remain natural rivals until the beginning of the nineteenth century. The exact course of the war, its triumphs and disappointments, are not what concern us in this entry on steel, though for the benefit of my American readers I can reveal that though the English won many of the major battles, ultimately, they lost the war and had to renounce their territorial claims in France.

The significance of the Battle of Agincourt for this book is the role, both positive and negative, that iron plate armour played in the outcome of the battle. On the eve of the confrontation, the French were convinced that they were going to score an easy victory over the English. Henry was leading a small force of between 6,000 and 9,000 men, consisting of armoured knights supported by lightly armoured

ARMOUR-PLATED
Agincourt signalled the beginning of the end for the knight in armour.

Great armies were created using steel [....] Those who were vanquished, were entirely destroyed; their cities looted and burned, and the whole country, laid waste. At the time an entire country went to war [....] Gradually, the method of working steel became so excellent that armour could be made which would resist the attacks of all known weapons, but as armour cost a great deal and was hard to get, it developed into a few armed men doing all the fighting for their people.

Four Military Classics *(1999) by David Jablonsky*

archers – the famed English longbowmen – in a retreat north towards the safety of the English-held port of Calais on the French coast. The pursuing French army, estimated at between 12,000 and 36,000 fighting men, including 1,200 heavily armoured mounted knights, was keen to avenge earlier losses against the English. Although gunpowder weapons were already in use at the time, they didn't play a major role in the battle that would be a match between French plate armour against the English longbow.

THE DREADFUL ARITHMETIC OF WARFARE

Although we think of knights in armour as being quintessentially Western European and medieval, the origins of heavy cavalry were far older, dating back to antiquity, with origins in the East. The immediate ancestor of the medieval knight was the late Roman and Byzantine *kataphraktoi* (cataphract), a heavy cavalryman armed with an iron lance, mace and sword, who wore a full helmet, and whose body was protected by a surcoat of overlapping metal scales worn over chain mail. The Byzantine cataphract was himself inspired by Iranian and

METAL MAGIC
The quality of a steel blade was dependent on the skill of the smith.

UPPER CUT
The best steel sword blades
are still produced in Japan.

Central Asian heavy cavalry, which had proved itself against Roman infantry and light cavalry in several major campaigns between Sassanid Persia and Rome.

In the dreadful arithmetic of warfare, which is still being calculated today in Iraq and Afghanistan, strategists had to weigh the relative value of the protection afforded to the soldier by armour against the loss of speed and manoeuvrability in armouring personnel or vehicles. For the French at Agincourt on that day, the sums would not work out at all. Although they had the advantage of numbers on their side (although by exactly how many they outnumbered the English has recently been questioned), the battlefield was hemmed in by woodland that would not allow them to outflank their more lightly armoured opponents or to make best use of their numbers. The English had prepared defensive positions, burying sharpened stakes into the ground to protect themselves against the shock and awe of a French massed cavalry charge. When the French launched their first attack against the English, the French knights were protected by their armour against the English arrows and crossbow bolts, but their horses were not.

With their mounts dead, wounded or panicked, the French knights were forced to run towards the enemy across heavy ground, transformed into mud by the fall rains. When they reached the English lines, they were so exhausted that they were unable to fight. Many of the knights fell and were unable to get up. Once lying helpless on the ground, they

THE UPPER CUT

✦

The *katana*, the long sword carried by Japan's samurai warriors, is acknowledged to represent the very best of the swordsmith's art. Unlike a Western sword, which has a straight, double-edged blade, the katana has a slightly curved blade with a single cutting edge, which dictates how the sword is worn and drawn. Samurai wore the katana in their *obi*, or sash, cutting edge uppermost, and were trained to draw and strike in one deadly movement. Varying in length from 60 cm (23.6 in) to 73 cm (28.7 in), the katana owed its distinctive shape, flexibility and superb cutting edge to a unique manufacturing process that used two grades of steel in the blade. Hard carbon-rich steel made up the core of the blade, while softer low-carbon steel that could keep a sharp edge was folded around it. The curve was given to the sword not during the forging process but by the way the blade was quenched within a protective layer of clay and ash that was thinner along the blade's cutting edge.

were either easily captured or slaughtered by the
English infantrymen and archers, most of whom were
not encumbered by plate armour. The second French
attack, this time mainly on foot, met the same fate.
The French lost between 7,000 and 10,000 men,
including many knights, while English losses have
been estimated at fewer than 200. Although Agincourt exposed the weaknesses of plate armour, it is a
tribute to the conservatism of the military mind that
it did not signal the end of its use in warfare. Steel
armour would evolve but it continued to have a role
on the battlefield until the World War I.

THE STEEL AGE

Although smiths were making steel tools and weapons
as soon as they had begun to smelt iron, they did not
understand the chemistry that made one alloy of iron
and carbon harder but more brittle and another more
malleable but more easily blunted. In addition to the
composition of steel, ironsmiths discovered that they
could change the physical properties of the metal by
'quenching', that is, immersing the red-hot blade in
water, or a mixture of water and oil. The quenching
process altered the structure of the metal, making it
harder and giving it a much sharper cutting edge.

STEEL TEARDROP
The Chicago skyline is
reflected on the surface of
Cloud Gate.

Although swordsmiths from Syria and Spain were famous for their blades in the medieval period, the world's finest steel blades were made in Japan for the samurai elites (see box, p.185). However, because Japan remained closed to the outside world for almost 250 years until the late nineteenth century, the excellence of Japanese swords was only revealed to the world long after military tactics had moved on from one-to-one combats between armoured swordsmen.

A full understanding of the steel manufacturing process was not achieved until the middle of the nineteenth century, when it was perfected in Britain, America and Germany, which, as a result, became the leaders of the industrial age. The First Industrial Revolution was powered by coal (pp.66–71) and with machines made of cast and wrought iron. However, iron is subject to metal fatigue, which in extreme cases could lead to disastrous failures. During the first half of the nineteenth century, there were several high-profile disasters including the collapse of iron bridges and the failure of iron railway tracks. In 1856, Henry Bessemer (1813–98) perfected the 'Bessemer process' that allowed the manufacture of plentiful quantities of cheap steel.

The metal provided the material base for the Second Industrial Revolution, creating a world of railways, steamships, automobiles, mechanised factories and metal-framed buildings. Although our materials technology has moved on with the invention of plastics and aluminium alloys, a quick glance around our homes and workplaces will reveal how much we still depend on steel in daily life. The framework of the chair on which I am sitting, the bolts, screws and nuts that hold my desk together, the armature of the computer that I am using to write this book, even the frame of the glasses I need to see the screen clearly as I type are all made with different types of steel.

REINFORCED
The steel girder is a major component of modern buildings.

Tin

Stannum

Type: Metal

Origin: Mineral ores and alluvial deposits

Chemical formula: Sn

+ **INDUSTRIAL**
+ CULTURAL
+ **COMMERCIAL**
+ SCIENTIFIC

The industrial and commercial history of humanity begins with the manufacture of the first metal alloy, bronze. Before the Bronze Age, humanity consisted of disparate, isolated groups of hunter-gatherers, pastoralists and settled agriculturalists with only sporadic contacts with one another. The manufacture of bronze called into being international trading networks linking the peoples of northern Europe to those of the Mediterranean and the Near East. The first long-distance maritime traders in world history were the Phoenicians, who explored the coasts of Africa and Europe; they were also the first Mediterranean people to reach the fabled Isles of Tin in northern European waters.

'TAKE ME TO YOUR LEADER'

When the first Phoenician traders arrived by ship in Cornwall in southwest England, during the first millennium BCE, to purchase tin from the Celtic inhabitants of the British Isles, the encounter must have been as extraordinary as if a flying saucer had landed in an American backyard to ask the homeowner for directions to the White House. Historians once referred to the Phoenician heartland as the 'Levant' – the coastal region now occupied by the modern countries of Syria, Lebanon and Israel – where they lived in several independent city-states, the best known of which were the ports of Tyre, Byblos, Beyritus and Sidon.

Like the Greeks, who were their main commercial rivals in the Mediterranean, the Phoenicians did not seek to establish large territorial empires, but set up colonies at key locations along their trade routes. They gradually migrated westwards, establishing bases along the North African coast, on the Balearic Islands and in southern Spain, while the Greeks founded their colonies in southern Italy, Sicily and southern France. The geopolitical shape of the ancient world would be dictated by these early efforts at colonisation. The Greeks would civilise the tribes of Italy, one of which, the Latins, would go on to found the city of Rome. The Phoenicians would establish their largest western colony at Carthage, in modern-day Tunisia.

The Phoenicians lived in a crowded world surrounded by

MYSTERY METAL
The Phoenicians guarded the secret of tin, sometimes with their lives.

LONG-DISTANCE MINERAL
Tin trading involved contacts
between the British Isles and
the Levant.

THE FINE METAL

+

After bronze, the most common
historical use of tin was in the
manufacture of another alloy,
pewter. Pewter is a soft, dull grey
metal, made up of 85–90 percent
tin mixed with varying amounts of
copper, antimony or lead. The
alloy has a low melting point and
is easy to work. Although pewter
objects are known from antiquity,
its main period of use was
between the twelfth and nineteenth centuries, when it was
made into tableware, cutlery,
drinking vessels and food and
beverage containers. There are
three main alloys called pewter:
'fine metal', which contained
about one percent copper; 'trifle
metal', which contained about
four percent lead; and 'lay metal',
which contains the most lead at
around fifteen percent. Modern
pewter no longer contains lead, as
its presence was recognised to be
a cause of lead poisoning. Pewter
remained popular until the
development of cheap glassware
and porcelain tableware in the
nineteenth century. The metal
now has niche uses as a material
for decorative items.

larger, more powerful empires and restless neighbours:
To the south was Egypt, to the west the many peoples
of Canaan and beyond them Mesopotamia, and to the
north Assyria. Through diplomacy and trade, the
Phoenicians succeeded in maintaining their independence for centuries, until they were finally absorbed
into the Persian Empire. Although Phoenicia itself
may have been conquered, its colonies retained their
independence and created their own empires in the
western Mediterranean. The rivalry
between the Greeks and the Phoenicians in the eastern Mediterranean
would be played out between
their heirs, the Carthaginians
and the Romans. The great
city of Carthage, in what is
now the North African country
of Tunisia, established its own
colonies in southern Italy,
Sicily, the Balearic Islands
and southern Spain. And one
of the sources of wealth that
Rome and Carthage fought
over was the trade in tin, the
metal that was alloyed to
copper to make bronze.

TIN POT
Tin was used to manufac-
ture pewter tableware.

THE ISLES OF TIN

As we saw in the entry on bronze, tin and copper are very rarely found together, and the supplies of alluvial tin and tin-bearing ores are relatively rare. The largest deposits in Western Europe are located in northern Spain, Brittany in northwest France and most plentifully in Cornwall in southwest England. During the Bronze Age (5300–3200 BCE), northern European tin made its way to the Mediterranean and Near East, and, at first, the metal would have been traded indirectly through many intermediaries, which not only increased the time it took the tin to reach its final destination, but also vastly increased its cost as each intermediary took his cut.

CORNISH TRADITION
Tin was mined in Cornwall from antiquity to the twentieth century.

The Phoenicians and Greeks both searched for the sources of north European tin, and it was the Phoenicians who first discovered the Cornish mines. They naturally were very protective of the secret of their supply, wishing to keep the lucrative trade to themselves. Before the Roman conquest of Britain in the first century CE, a Carthaginian captain, who was being followed by a Roman ship, preferred to wreck his own vessel rather than reveal his destination to his rivals. Early Greek geographers knew very roughly which region tin came from, but they could not pinpoint its exact location. They called this tin-producing land the Cassiterides, which they identified as either an archipelago or a single large island, placing them anywhere from Spanish to English waters.

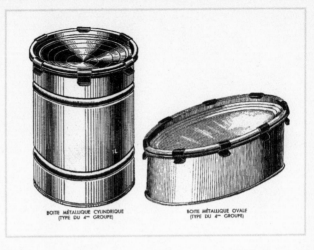

BOÎTE MÉTALLIQUE CYLINDRIQUE
(TYPE DU 4ᵉ GROUPE)

BOÎTE MÉTALLIQUE OVALE
(TYPE DU 4ᵉ GROUPE)

ARMY RATIONS
The tin can was designed to provide supplies for the military.

The Greek geographer and historian Diodorus Siculus, who was active in the first century BCE (see quote, below), correctly identified the Cassiterides as Cornwall, though much of the detail of his description has never been confirmed by archaeology. The growth of Roman power in the Mediterranean led to the elimination of the Carthaginians as the Western Mediterranean's long-distance traders. The Romans fought three wars against the North African kingdom of Carthage between 264 and 146 BCE. In the third, they came very close to defeat at the hands of the Carthaginian general Hannibal (247–182 BCE), who famously crossed the Alps with war elephants. Despite Hannibal's annihilation of the Roman army at Cannae in 216 BCE, Rome ultimately triumphed, razing Carthage to the ground, and through this ruthless act of military terrorism, established its pre-eminence in Europe and North Africa for the next five hundred years.

RARE AS GOLD
Cassiterite ore is now extremely rare.

The inhabitants of Britain who dwell about the promontory known as Belerium are especially hospitable to strangers and have adopted a civilised manner of life because of their intercourse with merchants of other peoples. They it is who work the tin, treating the bed which bears it in an ingenious manner.

The Library of History *by Diodorus Siculus (fl. c. 50 BCE) trans. by W. Thayer*

Sulphur

Sulphur

Type: Non-metal

Origin: Native sulphur and mineral ores

Chemical formula: S

Sulphur has been in use since antiquity, but it was only in the eighteenth century that it was understood to be an element in its own right. Used in a range of industrial, domestic, military and agricultural applications, sulphur is also the basic ingredient of sulfutric acid – one of the most important industrial chemicals in use in the modern world.

ARTIFICER'S ELEMENT
Sulphur was a key ingredient of gunpowder and Greek Fire.

FIRE AND BRIMSTONE

According to the Bible, a vengeful god 'rained upon Sodom and upon Gomorrah brimstone and fire'. (Genesis, 19:24; King James Bible). 'Brimstone', meaning 'burning stone', was the traditional name given to the inflammable element sulphur. The association of sulphur with divine wrath falling from the skies comes from its occurrence in areas of active volcanism, which remain the main sources of mined sulphur for industrial use. An important historical area of production was Sicily, which provided much of the sulphur for the First Industrial Revolution. In the modern period, since the growth of the petroleum economy in the mid-twentieth century, large quantities of sulphur are created as a byproduct of oil refining.

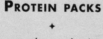

SALT OF THE EARTH
Sulphur accumulates around volcanic vents.

PROTEIN PACKS
✦

Like magnesium and potassium, sulphur is an essential nutrient that plays an important role in metabolism. Sulphur is a component of two amino acids, thus is present in many proteins and enzymes within the body, and in two essential vitamins: vitamin H and vitamin B1, which both play a role in the repair of cells and their protection from free radicals. Eggs are one of the best sources of dietary sulphur.

We have seen in earlier entries that sulphur was an ingredient in two incendiary weapons. Along with charcoal and saltpetre, sulphur is a constituent of black powder, or gunpowder, first discovered by Chinese alchemists (who were seeking the elixir of life), and later exported to the West with gunpowder weapons. Sulphur is also thought to have been an ingredient of Greek Fire, the inflammable mixture that the Byzantines sprayed onto enemy ships. As both weapons played a major role in warfare, sulphur would have been a valued commodity, keenly sought after both by states and free-lance arms dealers.

One of the main uses of sulphur is to manufacture sulphuric acid, whose applications we shall review in the next section. But sulphur is the base for many other important chemicals. It finds many applications in agriculture, animal husbandry and viticulture as a fertiliser, pesticide, bacteriocide and fungicide. Because elemental sulphur is considered to be a natural substance, it can be used in organic farming. It has been used to dust crops to prevent blight and mildew on fruit and vegetables, as well as to kill insect pests that attack crops. Sulphur has also played an important role in medicine. In antiquity, as in the modern period, it has been used to treat skin disorders, and it was a common ingredient of preparations used to treat adolescent acne.

FIRE AND BRIMSTONE God destroys Sodom with a rain of sulphur.

ACID BATH

In common usage, the word 'acid' does not suggest particularly positive associations. At best, it describes a none-too-pleasant taste – the acidity of lemons or vinegar, for example; at worst, it is linked to acid attacks and murders. Historically, sulphuric acid was known as oil of vitriol, giving us the adjective 'vitriolic', referring now to extremely abusive language but

In some translations of the Bible, sulfur is referred to as brimstone, which, along with fire, destroyed the famed cities of Sodom and Gomorrah. It was this reference that may have resulted in sulfur's nickname, 'the Devil's Element'. Sulfur *(2007) by Aubrey Stimola*

reminding us that vitriolic attacks were often more than just verbal. Men who cannot accept a woman's right to choose the man she will marry have been known to use acids in particularly gruesome revenge attacks. Now very rare, though not unknown in the West, such disfiguring assaults with sulphuric acid have been reported from the Indian subcontinent and Southeast Asia.

Sulphuric acid has also been linked with murder – notably, with the English career criminal turned serial killer, John Haigh (1909–49), better known as the 'acid bath murderer', who claimed to have killed nine people. In order to steal his victims' property, Haigh murdered them and then dissolved their bodies in barrels of sulphuric acid, believing that without a corpse, he could not be found guilty of homicide. Although he had destroyed the bodies and therefore much of the evidence of his crimes, Haigh could not dispose of absolutely everything. In the sulphuric-human sludge at the bottom of one barrel, the police found part of a denture that was identified as belonging to one of Haigh's victims. He was condemned for the murder of six people and went to the gallows after one of the most sensational trials of the twentieth century.

BURNING PASSION
Sulphuric acid was used by jilted lovers in revenge attacks.

VULCAN'S MOON
Jupiter's moon Io is covered in sulphur compounds.

Yet another negative connation of the word acid is in the term 'acid rain'. Known since the mid-nineteenth century, acid rain only became a major environmental concern in the last quarter of the twentieth century, when its deleterious effects on forests, lakes and rivers were widely publicised by environmental campaigners. Man-made emissions of carbon dioxide, sulphur dioxide and nitrogen oxides from the burning of fossil fuels, in particular gasoline in motor vehicles, are the main causes of acid rain, which, in addition to affecting plant and animal life, also damages metal structures and limestone and marble buildings. A 2006 report revealed that up to one-third of China, which generates much of its energy from coal-fired power stations, is affected by acid rain. In the developed world, strict emissions controls, the fitting of catalytic converters to cars, and the shift to nuclear, natural gas and renewable energy, has noticeably improved the situation, with the recovery of formerly affected lakes, rivers and forests.

THE HARDWORKING ACID

Sulphuric acid was known in antiquity and the Middle Ages, but its use dramatically increased during the First Industrial Revolution, when several new methods revolutionised its manufacture, increasing production and reducing its cost. Sulphuric acid is made in several strengths, which are used in different industrial applications. The weakest is known as 'dilute sulphuric acid' and contains ten percent acid; 'battery acid' is a solution of about 30 percent sulphuric acid, and 'concentrated sulphuric acid' is between 95 and 98 percent pure acid. One of the main uses of sulphuric acid is in the manufacture of phosphate fertilisers, when phosphate-bearing rocks are treated with acid at a concentration of 93 percent to release the phosphorus in the rocks. Other important applications included iron and steelmaking, aluminium production, the manufacture of nylon and other synthetic fibres, paper-making, petroleum refining, dying and the treatment of wastewater.

SURREY SALTS

✦

In the seventeenth and eighteenth centuries, the town of Epsom in the county of Surrey on the outskirts of London was a popular spa town where fashionable Londoners would go and take a dip in the waters and socialise in the town's pump rooms. According to local lore, the virtues of the mineral-rich Epsom waters were discovered by a farmer who noticed its beneficial effects on his cattle. When reduced by boiling, the water produces a residue of magnesium sulphate ($MgSO_4$), which became known as 'Epsom Salts'. The salts are now mainly used as an ingredient for bath preparations, which are said to be good for the skin and to relieve muscular aches and pains.

HIGH PLAINS
Bolivia's Atacama Desert is stained yellow by ancient sulphur deposits.

Talc

Talc

Type: Metamorphic mineral

Origin: Metamorphic rocks

Chemical formula:
$Mg_3Si_4O_{10}(OH)_2$

ROCK TALC
Steatite, or soapstone, is a source of talc.

Mention the word talc and most readers will think of the talcum powder that is used on the skin after baths and showers. Talc, or magnesium silicate, however, has many industrial applications including food manufacture, ceramics and papermaking.

+ **INDUSTRIAL**

+ CULTURAL

+ COMMERCIAL

+ SCIENTIFIC

SAVING BABY

Nappy rash is not the most distressing of complaints (unless you're a baby, of course); in the greater medical scheme of things, it probably ranks quite low as a public health concern. In the nineteenth century, when the population of Western European and American cities mushroomed, as displaced agricultural workers moved to take up jobs in the new factories, the plight of children soon became critical and rates of infant mortality soared. In the mid-century, if your parents were factory workers, you'd be lucky to see your first birthday, but you'd have to be even luckier to celebrate your fifth birthday. High rates of child mortality reduced average life expectancy among sections of the urban working class to 20 years.

Much of the death toll was due to epidemic diseases caused by poor sanitation, overcrowded conditions, infected water supplies and made worse by insufficient diets. Of those who did not succumb to epidemics in childhood, many died from industrial accidents and occupational diseases. The late nineteenth century was not a good time to be a working-class baby. Conditions such as nappy rash were indicative of low standards of hygiene in the care of babies. Although today we have effective treatments for the skin infections that can be caused by nappy rash, in the days before antibiotics or hydrocortisone creams, such infections could lead to serious complications. Without effective treatments, prevention was the only way forward.

UNKINDEST CUTS

+

According to a 2010 report published by the Centre of Public Health at Liverpool John Moores University, talc, or talcum powder, is a common bulking agent used to adulterate or 'cut' illicit drugs. The drugs identified as containing talc included amphetamines and metamphetamines and MDMA (ecstasy). Other studies have found that talc is also used to bulk up cocaine, as well as counterfeit versions of legal drugs. Although talc is considered to be safe for external use, and as a food additive, when inhaled it can cause inflammations and infections of the lungs, and it has been linked to certain types of cancer.

SNUG AND DRY

The first mass-produced cloth nappy in the United States was produced in 1887; until then, babies had been dressed in any type of material available, however difficult to keep clean or unfit for purpose. Until the 1940s, when the first disposable nappys were introduced in Europe and North America, avoiding nappy rash meant frequently changing and washing the cloth nappies. However, poor hygiene and infrequent changes meant that nappy rash led to more serious infections. In 1894, Johnson & Johnson Inc., then a pharmaceuticals company, manufactured its first consumer product aimed specifically at babies: 'Baby Powder', a preparation of powdered talc that absorbed excess moisture and reduced friction between the skin and nappy to tackle the incidence of nappy rash. Although not an innovation as radical as vaccination in the fight to bring down child mortality, the appearance of specialist baby products signalled a major change in attitudes to the care of babies and infants throughout society.

Nerves are the most delicate things in baby's make-up and lie just under baby's skin. A comfortable skin is an aid to quiet nerves. And mothers have found that using Johnson's Baby Powder keeps baby's skin cool and soft and relieves itching and chafing. *Johnson's Baby Powder print advertisement from 1921*

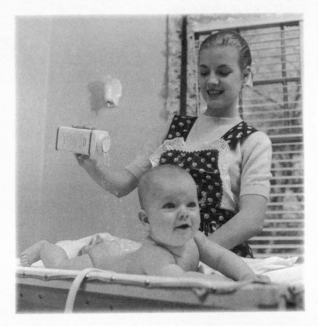

BABYCARE
Baby powder signalled a change in the care of babies and infants.

Titanium

Titanium

Type: Transition metal

Origin: Igneous and sedimentary rocks

Chemical formula: Ti

+ *INDUSTRIAL*
+ CULTURAL
+ COMMERCIAL
+ *SCIENTIFIC*

Although the metal titanium was first identified in the eighteenth century, the difficulty and high cost of extracting it from mineral ores meant that it remained a laboratory curiosity until the mid-twentieth century. In the postwar period, it has found a role in the aerospace industry, where its high strength-to-weight ratio makes it an attractive alternative to steel alloys.

SPACE-RACE METAL

On October 4, 1957, the American public was shocked to hear that the Soviet Union, the U.S.'s main ideological and military rival in the post-World War II era, had succeeded in launching the first man-made object into Earth's orbit. By the standards of later spacecraft, *Sputnik 1* was an extremely simple piece of machinery: little more than a battery-powered radio transmitter inside a metal sphere. However, as the first artificial satellite in Earth's orbit, it was a presage of bigger and better, or possibly, nastier, things to come. The alloy used to make *Sputnik*'s heat shield consisted primarily of aluminium (93.8 percent) with magnesium (6 percent) and titanium (0.2 percent).

Compared to many of the elements and minerals featured in this book, titanium is a very recent discovery. Titanium was first isolated in the late eighteenth century, but it was only at the turn of the twentieth century that titanium metal was produced. However, the process was time-consuming, expensive and produced small amounts of the metals. Like aluminium in the mid-nineteenth century, titanium was a scientific curiosity that was too expensive and scarce to have any practical application. In 1940, the Kroll process finally made titanium available in larger quantities and at a relatively affordable price.

World War II witnessed the dawn of rocket and missile technology, pioneered by the Germans, and taken up by the Americans and Russians immediately after the war, and the development of the first jet fighters by the Germans and British, spurring their adoptions for civilian and military use by the victorious Allies. Both these developments made titanium, which was stronger

A MODERN METAL
Titanium metal was first made in the twentieth century.

than steel while being much lighter, a very desirable material. It was the Soviet Union that was to take the lead in the development of titanium and its alloys, using it in its aerospace programmes and its fleet of nuclear submarines.

In April 1961, the Soviet Union scored another space first when Yuri Gagarin (1934–68) became the first human to orbit Earth in *Vostok 1*, a second titanium spacecraft. Russia's lead in space seemed unassailable, prompting President John F. Kennedy (1917–63) to pledge that the U.S. would put a man on the moon before the end of the decade. The space race had begun in earnest, and it would be run with spacecraft that made increasing use of titanium. The Apollo programme would probably have made it to the moon without the metal, but it might have taken longer and with more accidents on the way. Since the 1970s, every major space vehicle, including Russia's

Soyuz; the U.S.'s shuttle fleet; the unmanned probes that have been sent to survey the planets of the solar system; and the International Space Station, have made use of titanium components for their structural elements and engine components.

'WE CAN REBUILD YOU'

+

The lead character in the 1970s U.S. TV series *The Six Million Dollar Man* is literally rebuilt after an aeroplane crash. His implants – left eye, right arm and legs – give him superhuman abilities. What the show does not reveal, however, is what the implants are made of. While in the 1970s the technology described in the show was pure science fiction, with recent developments in medicine, electronics and materials science, we are probably not that many years away from matching the bionic man's implants, though probably at a much higher cost than $6 million. Because of its strength, biological inertness and its resistance to corrosion, titanium (or titanium alloyed with aluminium or with aluminium and vanadium) is used to repair and replace damaged bones and joints. The metal is also used to make heart valves, pacemakers and dental implants.

THE PAINTED ASTEROID

TITANIC ORE
Martin Klaproth named the metal after the mythological Titans.

HIGH-TECH CLADDING
The Guggenheim Museum, Bilbao, is clad with titanium alloy.

In September 2002, an amateur astronomer discovered an unidentified object in Earth's orbit. The object, given the designation J002E3, was first thought to be a small rocky asteroid, but the orbit was all wrong for a natural object. Astronomers concluded that it must be a spacecraft that had been launched from Earth in the recent past; however, this, too presented problems, as no launches in the past decade matched J002E3's size and trajectory. A spectral analysis of J002E3 revealed the presence of white titanium dioxide (TiO_2) – a pigment used to manufacture domestic white paint.

Like elemental titanium, the compound titanium dioxide is a relatively recent discovery, dating back to 1821. Like titanium, it remained in the laboratory because it was difficult to produce in any quantity and at too high a cost for it to have any practical uses. Scientists, however, noted its high opacity and whiteness, and a refraction index that was higher than that of diamonds. It was only in 1916 that the Norwegian Titan Company and the American Titanium Pigment Corporation independently succeeded in making titanium dioxide paint for commercial applications, by combining it with another white pigment, zinc oxide. In 1921, the first artist's grade titanium white was produced to replace the toxic lead-based alternative.

Titanium and titanium alloys are used in the manufacture of planes, jets, helicopters, missiles, space shuttles and satellites. All of these must be able to withstand the intense pressure experienced while taking off, flying, orbiting and landing [....] A Boeing 777, for example, contains approximately fifty-eight tons of titanium metal. The A380 Airbus – the largest passenger airliner in the world – contains approximately seventy-seven tons. Titanium (2008) by Greg Rosa

Another modern application of titanium dioxide that takes advantage of its high refractive index is in commercial sunscreen preparations, when it is often combined with zinc oxide and other UV-absorbing compounds. Titanium oxide is used in high-factor sunscreens for people with sensitive skin because it is less likely to cause irritation than other chemicals.

As it was unlikely that a passing alien craft had decided to whitewash a small asteroid or spray it with sunblock (although to some UFO aficionados, this was probably just as believable as the alien origin of crop circles), scientists began to look to spacecraft launches further back in time, and vehicles that might have been painted with titanium dioxide paint. They finally identified J002E3 as being the third stage of the Apollo 12 Saturn V rocket, NASA's second manned mission to land on the moon, which had left Earth in November 1969. The third stage, which should have been placed in solar orbit, must have strayed back into Earth's orbit 33 years after its initial separation from the Command and Lunar Modules. It remained in orbit until June 2003 and may make a return visit in another 30 years.

EXOTIC FRAMES

✦

As an avid cyclist who has road-raced in his time, I know that weight is a critical factor in cycling competitions. Traditional bike frames were made of steel, which is strong, while still allowing the frame some flexibility. This is perhaps less important for road bikes that race over smooth road surfaces, but is crucial for mountain bikes, which have to handle rough terrain and repeated impacts from jumps and potholes. However, steel is heavy and corrodes when exposed to air and water. Aluminium, while much lighter, would be too soft. Steel can be alloyed to reduce its weight, but in recent years manufacturers of high-end racing bikes have come up with an alternative: titanium frames, which are extremely strong while being much lighter than steel. Titanium frames are easy to spot as they are made of larger-diameter tubing than their steel counterparts. Although undoubtedly superior to steel and alloy frames, titanium has the drawback of being much more difficult to work and much more expensive.

Uranium

Uranium

Type: Actinide metallic element

Origin: Mineral ores

Chemical formula: U

✦ **INDUSTRIAL**

✦ CULTURAL

✦ COMMERCIAL

✦ **SCIENTIFIC**

Without the pressing needs of war, it is unlikely that nuclear weapons and reactors would have ever been developed as early as the 1940s, when the world was just emerging from the Great Depression. The cost alone would have been prohibitive and the returns too uncertain. In the related entry on plutonium, we saw that although the 'Fat Man' that destroyed Nagasaki had been tested successfully, the bomb dropped on Hiroshima a few days earlier, the uranium 'Little Boy' had not. In the event, it was Little Boy that killed more people and caused more devastation. In an attempt to steer the world away from nuclear weapons proliferation and reassure the public about the dangers of nuclear war, President Eisenhower launched the Atoms for Peace programme in 1952.

THE ROAD TO MANHATTAN

In historical and scientific terms, the road to the Manhattan Project (1942–46), which succeeded in creating the first nuclear weapons, was extremely short. The structure of the atom and the existence of radioactivity were unknown until the turn of the twentieth century. The first clue that certain substances emitted unknown forms of energy was the discovery of x-rays by the German physicist Wilhelm Röntgen (1845–1923) in 1895. In 1896, Antoine Becquerel (1852–1908), who was studying phosphorescence, placed a sample of uranium salts on a photographic plate, and recorded that where the salts had been in contact with it, the plate had darkened – the first evidence of what would later become known as 'radiation'. Finally, in 1898, Marie Curie (1867–1934) and her husband Pierre (1859–1906) isolated two radioactive elements: polonium and radium. During the following decades, physicists discovered the processes of 'radioactive decay' through which one element was transmuted into another by emitting or capturing subatomic particles.

POOR METAL
Natural uranium has to be enriched to be used in nuclear weapons.

By the 1920s, theoretical physicists were discussing the feasibility of artificially splitting the atom in manmade nuclear fission. However, not everyone was convinced. In 1932, Albert Einstein (1879–1955) could still assert that nuclear fission (and therefore nuclear reactors and bombs) was impossible. Two years later, the Italian physicist

EVERYONE'S GONE MAD

✦

The aptly named 'MAD' – mutually
assured destruction – described the
state of affairs that existed between
the U.S. and its nuclear allies,
Britain and France, on one side, and
the USSR on the other, from the first
test of a Soviet A-bomb in 1949 to
the collapse of the Soviet Union in
1991. Unfortunately, the demise of
the USSR did not entail the end of
nuclear weapons. During those four
Cold War decades, a number of
other states acquired nuclear
weapons technology, including the
People's Republic of China (1964),
India (1967), Israel (1969), Pakistan
(1972) and South Africa (1979).
Despite strenuous efforts to prevent
proliferation, North Korea is the
latest country to have acquired
nuclear capability, with Iran thought
to be not too far behind. Far from
decrying this state of affairs, a few
neo-con strategists have welcomed
nuclear proliferation, asserting that
MAD maintained peace between the
U.S. and the USSR for 42 years and
discouraged Chinese aggression
against its East Asian neighbours.
However, MAD only works if the
people in charge of the nuclear
button are not themselves mad
enough to deploy them, whatever
the consequences, which cannot be
guaranteed for the leaders of certain
'rogue' states, whose political
ideologies and religious values are
very different from our own.

Enrico Fermi (1901–54) came close to proving him
wrong, but just missed out on observing fission when
he was experimenting with uranium in Rome. That
prize would go to two German scientists, Otto Hahn
(1879–1968) and Friedrich Strassmann (1902–80),
who bombarded uranium with neutrons, confirming
nuclear fission experimentally in 1938. They demonstrated that once triggered, fission could be sustained
through a chain reaction, as the splitting of one
atomic nucleus produced more neutrons that would
continue the process until all the available fuel had
been used up. This proved that fission could power a
nuclear reactor to produce energy, but also that fission
could also occur explosively, with the sudden release
of the huge amounts of energy locked up in the
atomic nucleus of fissile uranium.

Hahn, Strassman and Fermi's research could have
given Nazi Germany and its ally, fascist Italy, the
A-bomb before the Allies, and thus changed the
course of the World War II and postwar history. It

This new phenomenon [nuclear fission of uranium] would also lead to the construction of bombs, and it is conceivable – though much less certain – that extremely powerful bombs of a new type may thus be constructed. A single bomb of this type, carried by boat and exploded in a port, might very well destroy the whole port together with some of the surrounding territory. *Letter from Albert Einstein (1879–1955) to President Franklin D. Roosevelt (1882–1945) written on August 2, 1939*

was fortunate for the world (though not for the scientists concerned) that Adolf Hitler's (1889–1945) racist beliefs led him to persecute Jews in Germany and Austria, which Benito Mussolini (1883–1945) imitated in Italy, denying the Axis powers nuclear weapons. Many of the leading physicists working in the field in Germany, Austria and Italy were either Jewish or horrified by Hitler's anti-Semitic policies. Rather than face internment or death in the concentration camps, many of Germany and Italy's physicists followed Albert Einstein into exile to Britain and the U.S.

On the eve of the declaration of war in Europe, in August 1939, Einstein had revised his opinion about the feasibility of nuclear weapons. He and other leading physicists wrote to President Franklin D. Roosevelt (1882–1945) warning him that the Nazis were attempting to make nuclear weapons and urging the U.S. to do the same. Although the U.S. would not enter the war until December 1941 after the Japanese attack on Pearl Harbour, in June 1941, Roosevelt signed an executive order creating the research programme that would become the Manhattan Project.

THE ROAD TO HIROSHIMA

If the discovery of nuclear fission had taken the relatively short interval of three decades, its weaponisation by the U.S., Britain and Canada took a mere four years, reflecting the huge resources that the Allies devoted to the project, which involved dozens of universities, military research establishments and private corporations in the three countries. The bulk of the practical work was conducted in the U.S. at the three reactor sites of Oak Ridge, TN, Argonne, IL and Hanford, WA, and the main weapons site at Los Alamos, NM. With what was at the time an almost unlimited budget of $2 billion, and a total workforce of 130,000, the project succeeded in making two types of nuclear bombs by 1945.

Because of the difficulties in enriching enough uranium to the necessary weapon's

ONE-OFF
There was only enough enriched uranium to make one bomb.

grade (a difficulty now encountered by the Iranians, who seventy years on are recreating the Manhattan Project in bunkers and nuclear facilities scattered across Iran), the uranium-235 Little Boy could not be tested. The bomb had been designed without the fail-safes built into later atomic weapons, and any number of factors, such as a lightning strike, could have set off the nuclear reaction. Little Boy was a 'gun-type' fission bomb, in which a conventional explosive charge fired a sub-critical uranium-235 'bullet' down a hollow tube into a uranium-235 'target', triggering the nuclear reaction. The trick was to keep the two masses of uranium apart and sub-critical to prevent premature detonation.

In the entry on plutonium we charted the rise of Imperial Japan from 1868 to its alliance with Germany in 1941. After initial successes, with the attack on Pearl Harbour in 1941 and the capture of the Philippines and Singapore the following year, the tides of war slowly began to turn against Japan. The U.S.'s full mobilisation after Pearl Harbour meant that it was only a matter of time before an overextended Japanese military, fighting simultaneously on three fronts – in the Pacific, in China and in Southeast Asia – would become exhausted and be forced to retreat back to Japan. As the Americans were also fighting on several fronts in Europe and the Pacific, it took the Allies three years and many tens of thousands of lives to push the Japa-

NON-FISSILE
Natural uranium only contains 0.7 percent of fissile uranium-235.

nese forces back to Japan's home islands. The fiercely fought battles for
the Japanese islands of Iwo Jima (February–March 1945) and Okinawa
(April–June 1945) taught the Americans that Japan's declaration that
it would fight to the last man, woman and child was no mere bluff.

The war in Europe had ended in April 1945 with Hitler's suicide and
the capture of Berlin by the Soviet Red Army. In Germany's case, the
Nazis and the war were so inextricably linked that the end of hostilities
naturally entailed the end of the regime. The political and ideological
situation in Japan was completely different. The imperial institution in
whose name the Pacific War had been fought
was almost 800 years old, and the role of the
reigning Showa Emperor (1901–89) was quite
different to the dictatorships of Hitler or
Mussolini. After the war, the emperor was
revealed to be a shy and retiring scholar, who
was politically both inept and ineffectual.
The government that acted in his name was led by militarists who were
incapable of negotiation or surrender. They turned down the surrender
terms offered by the Allies in the Potsdam Declaration of July 1945 that
demanded the disarmament of Japan in return for a guarantee of Japanese sovereignty over the home islands.

**As the bomb fell over Hiroshima and exploded,
we saw an entire city disappear. I wrote in my
log the words: 'My God, what have we done?'**

*Captain Robert Lewis (1917–83), co-pilot of the B-29
that dropped the bomb on Hiroshima.*

The U.S. claimed that the Japanese rejection of Potsdam and the prospect of many more months of hostilities, with the resulting loss of Allied lives, justified the atomic bombing of Japan. As the provisions of the Geneva Convention protecting non-combatants only came into force after the war in 1949, the U.S. was not breaking international law when it bombed Hiroshima and Nagasaki. Although the two bombs caused an estimated 70,000 deaths in Hiroshima and 40,000 in Nagasaki on the days of the bombing, with many more dying from their injuries and radiation sickness over the next few months, in terms of overall destruction and loss of life, they were comparable to the bombings with conventional explosives and incendiaries carried out by the Allies against Japan and Germany in the closing years of the war. The real horror of the new weapons was that they would carry on killing for decades to come. As of August 2011, the official death toll directly attributed to the bombings had climbed to 430,000.

NATURE'S OWN THREE MILE ISLAND

✦

Most people would imagine quite correctly that a nuclear reactor is an extremely complex piece of machinery and not something that could be assembled by pure chance – just as you wouldn't expect nature spontaneously to generate a plasma TV, for example. However, in 1972, evidence for up to 16 'natural' nuclear reactors came to light in Gabon, West Africa. What nature created, however, was not a building, complete with smoke-stacks and control rooms. Around 1.7 billion years BP, groundwater flooded underground ore deposits particularly rich in fissile uranium-235, triggering a nuclear chain reaction. The heat generated by the natural reactor boiled the water dry, stopping the reaction until the water had been replenished. Geologists estimate that the reactors remained active in short bursts for hundreds of thousands of years until there was no longer enough uranium-235 to sustain them. Could such a thing happen today? No: 1.7 billion years ago, uranium ores contained 3.1 percent uranium-235 (roughly the same as the fuel for man-made reactors), but in the modern day, due to the equally natural processes of radioactive decay, this has fallen to 0.7 percent – much too little to trigger natural fission.

HIGH EXPLOSIVE
A handful of enriched uranium has the explosive capacity of thousands of tons of conventional explosives.

Jade

Venefica

Type: Metamorphic rock

Origin: Jadeite and nephrite

Chemical formula:
Jadeite: $NaAlSi_2O_6$; nephrite: $Ca_2(Mg,Fe)_5Si_8O_{22}(OH)_2$

+ INDUSTRIAL
+ CULTURAL
+ COMMERCIAL
+ SCIENTIFIC

J ade refers to two semi-precious minerals of similar appearance: nephrite, which is the jade of the Asia-Pacific region, and jadeite, the jade of Meso-america. This entry will concentrate on jadeite, and in particular the artifacts created by one of the most mysterious cultures of the first millennium CE, the Classic Maya. To the Maya, jade symbolised both royalty and eternal life; hence the Maya kings adorned their bodies with jade ornaments in life and were surrounded by it in death.

THE HUMAN EXTRATERRESTRIALS

What is particularly striking about the Classic Maya, who lived in southern Mexico, Guatemala, Belize and Honduras between the middle of the third and ninth centuries CE, is how alien they appear to us in their customs, dress and beliefs – literally like beings from another planet. Even in their physical appearance, they went out of their way to look different from their neighbours. It was the custom of the Maya elites to elongate their skulls by squeezing them between pieces of wood during infancy. The strangeness of the Classic Maya has led some to assert that alien visitors were the true authors of their culture and advanced astro-nomical knowledge. Although this may seem to be a harmless fantasy, it is a form of racism no less insulting and injurious than to suggest that Maya civilisation was the product of contact with Eurasian cultures.

When reports and images of Classic Maya cities reached North America and Europe in the mid-nineteenth century, there were many who refused to believe that a Native American people could have attained a high level of civilisation on their own. At that time, the explanation was sought not in alien visitations but in the arrival of traders or colonists from Eurasian cultures – Mesopota-mians, Israelites, Phoenicians, Indians (from the Indian Subcontinent) and most popularly, from the other civilisation that is known for its pyramids and hieroglyphic script: ancient Egypt. While superficially believable, because of the apparent simi-

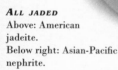

ALL JADED
Above: American jadeite.
Below right: Asian-Pacific nephrite.

STONE IDOLS
Jadeite was used for statuary all over Mesoamerica, as in this Olmec figurine.

larities between the two cultures, which both created stone bas-reliefs covered in images of divine kings and gods surrounded by hieroglyphic texts and built palaces and pyramids, even a cursory examination of the writing systems, architecture and artistic styles of the two regions should make it obvious that there could be no link between them.

There was another important difference between the ancient Egyptians and the Classic Maya. Whereas the Egyptians, like many other Eurasian cultures, valued gold above all other minerals and interred their pharaohs with vast quantities of the stuff, the Maya had no use for the precious metal until post-Classic times (ninth to sixteenth centuries). The material the Classic Maya valued most was jade, in their case the hardest of the two minerals given that name, jadeite. They shared this admiration of jade with an

GREENSTONE WATER

✦

To the Maori people of New Zealand, the country's South Island is *Te Waipounamu*, which translates as 'The Greenstone Water' (or more colloquially, the Land of Greenstone). *Pounamu* now refers to green nephrite jade, though historically it was the name given to several varieties of hard green stones. Pounamu was carved into tools, weapons and ornaments that have become important cultural properties of the Maori people. Like other visitors to Te Waipounamu, I bought a greenstone souvenir, a *koru* – a stylised fern frond that symbolises new life and new beginnings, as well as the bond between husband and wife and parent and child. The second most popular traditional pounamu design is the *hei matau*, the fishhook – a symbol of prosperity for a people who have long depended on the country's rich marine resources, which was also believed to protect the wearer as he or she travelled over water.

PAJAMAS OF ETERNITY
Chinese aristocrats were
buried in jade suits.

important East Asian culture: China. Both the Maya
and Chinese made ritual and decorative objects from
jade, and the mineral played an important role in the
burial customs of both cultures (see box, left).
However, to my knowledge, the two cultures have
never been linked, although in prehistoric terms, the
closest links between Eurasia and the Americas are
through East Asia, as the original settlers of the
Americas came across the Alaskan land bridge around
20,000 years BP.

NOT LOST BUT MISLAID WORLDS

It is difficult to lose something as large as a city,
unless, like the Roman town of Pompeii in southern
Italy, it is suddenly buried under several million
tons of volcanic ash and pumice. Even after its
disappearance, people knew where Pompeii had
been and what had happened to it from the writings
of Latin authors. It is a conceit of European and
North American scholars and explorers to say that
the Maya cities were 'lost' and then 'rediscovered'.
From the first decades of colonial rule, Spanish
settlers knew of several Classic sites, including
Palenque in Mexico and Copan in Honduras, but as
the goal of the Catholic Church and the colonial
authorities was to eradicate Maya culture and
religion, they did not encourage investigations or

research into a glorious native past. Additionally, the inhabitants of the area would have known of the ruined palaces and pyramids in their rainforests. However, as was usually the case during the nineteenth century, the knowledge of local informants about the locations of giant lakes and waterfalls, the source of famous rivers, or the locations of lost cities did not count.

TRICOLOUR
Three colours of jade.

The Classic Maya cities, with the exception of the isolated site of Lamanai in Belize, had all been abandoned by the ninth century, setting Mayanists one of the most challenging problems in world archaeology. The Maya established their cities in areas that were often extremely disadvantaged ecologically. The great city of Tikal in the Petén region of Guatemala, for example, was built in the middle of swamps and rainforest, in an area with very few obvious advantages, especially as the site had no dependable natural water supply during the dry season, when the city had to survive with rainwater collected and stored in a vast network of cisterns. However, at its height, the population of the city and its suburban zones is thought to have reached between 80,000 and 120,000.

Although the evergreen ecological collapse theory for the disappearance of the Maya is the most likely, they managed to sustain high population densities for centuries through intensive agricultural techniques.

LORDS OF JADE
To the Classic Maya, jade was more precious than gold.

And cities that had ecological advantages in terms of permanent water supplies, lower population densities, and good soil fertility also succumbed during the collapse. Hence, while ecological factors must have played an important role in the process, they form only part of the explanation. Other possible explanations put forward by Mayanists include peasant revolutions that overthrew the Maya elites, drought, epidemics and foreign invasions.

Jade gods

If recent protests in Wall Street and the City of London have underlined the social inequalities in our own societies, these are insignificant when compared to the social gulf that separated the Maya elites and the general population that supported them. Bill Gates may have billions in the bank, but we know that he is a mortal man, no different from the other seven billion human beings on this planet. Many cultures have deified their rulers, but few to the degree of the Classic Maya. As kingship developed through the pre-Classic into the Classic periods, the ruler and his extended kin group became more and more remote from their subjects. They lived in the ceremonial centres that formed the core of the sprawling Maya cities. Although many of the structures in Tikal, Palenque, Calakmul and Copan are described as 'palaces', they combined both residential and administrative functions. And visitors to Tikal, in particular, must wonder why anyone would want to live in the cramped, dark, dank, airless rooms of its palaces.

> For the ancient Maya, jade was the most precious of stones, and jade carving represents the finest examples of lapidary art. Mineralogical studies of Maya jades show that they are jadeite, which differs in chemical composition from nephrite, the most common Chinese jade.
>
> The Ancient Maya (2006) by Robert Sharer and Loa Traxler

The Maya rulers were not only intermediaries with the divine world of gods and ancestors, they were divine themselves – living incarnations of the gods and cultural heroes who had founded Maya civilisation. The visible symbol of their divinity was jade. Green jadeite was associated

DEATH'S HEAD
The Maya king Pakal was buried with a splendid jade mask.

with the Maize god, one of the principal deities of the Maya pantheon because maize was the staple crop of the Maya – and with vegetation generally and rebirth. For most of their history, the Maya had no metal tools, and one of their greatest technical accomplishments was the carving and polishing of jadeite – the hardest of the two types of jade – which they achieved with rope saws, wood and bone picks and natural abrasives. With these primitive materials, they rivalled anything produced by Chinese craftsmen who had access to metal tools.

FUNERARY TEMPLE
King Pakal's tomb was discovered below the Temple of the Inscriptions.

We have seen above that Mayanists rejected any possible link between Egypt and the Maya because of the visible difference in their architecture, especially the design of their pyramids. The steep-sided Maya pyramids are platforms for shrines that were accessed by stairs, like the ziggurats of Babylonia, whereas the pyramids of Egypt are for the most part true geometric pyramids that were built as tombs. However, the assertion that Maya pyramids did not contain burials was overturned in 1952 by the discovery of the tomb of the ruler of the city of Palenque, K'inich Janaab' Pakal (603–83), within the pyramid known as the Temple of the Inscriptions. Subsequent archaeological finds at other Maya sites have confirmed that the practice was fairly common, though even when they contained royal burials, pyramids functioned primarily as temples.

BREASTPLATE
Jade ornaments were made for both the living and the dead.

In death, Pakal was surrounded by a cache of jade objects, beads and jewellery, and his face was covered with a jade mask. The presence of so much jade symbolised the ruler's rebirth as a god. His internment underneath a temple was not unlike Christian burial in a churchyard, to ensure that the deceased would be close to their god for the Day of Resurrection; Pakal had become a god, and his descendants could interact with him through a 'psychoduct' – a thin tube that connected his tomb with the shrine above it.

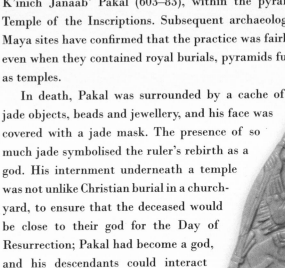

Tungsten

Wolfram

Type: Transition metal

Origin: Wolframite and other tungsten-bearing ores

Chemical formula: W

The incandescent lightbulb, which was commercialised at the end of the nineteenth century and perfected in the first decade of the twentieth, transformed daily life. Once dimly lit by candles, oil lamps and town gas, and always in danger from fires and explosions, homes were brighter and safer than they had ever been. One of the vital elements of the modern lightbulb is the tungsten filament, which created a brighter, longer-lasting lightbulb.

A BURNING ISSUE

When elders talk about 'incandescent lightbulbs', their children, born in the early years of the twenty-first century, will probably look at them pityingly, as we do our grandparents and parents who reminisce about good old vinyl LPs and cassette tapes. For them, after incandescent bulbs are phased out in most parts of the world by the end of the next decade, domestic lighting will be provided by compact fluorescent lamps, which are currently made up of linked tubes or spirals that look nothing like the conventional arrangement of a filament inside a glass bulb.

In the UK, which began its phaseout of incandescent bulbs with the rest of the EU in 2009, the voices of reaction have already been heard, grumbling that their god-given right to high-energy lightbulbs are being infringed. In historical terms, however, that right is an extremely recent one, as the first tungsten filament was introduced exactly 100 years ago. Our true light heritage consists of the oil lamps and candles that were used for millennia. The industrial revolution gave us two new ways of lighting our homes, workplaces and cities: kerosene, distilled from petroleum, and town gas produced from coal. The drawback of these materials was that they depended on a naked flame, which provided little illumination, caused air pollution and, on occasion, exploded.

HARD NOSED

+

The alloy of tungsten and carbon, tungsten carbide (WC), or simply carbide, is one of the hardest alloys in use today, with a Mohs scale rating of 8.5–9 (diamond being 10). Its hardness and high melting point (5,200°F/2,870°C) make it suitable for drill bits and high-performance tools used to machine carbon steel and stainless steel. The second major application of carbide is in armour-piercing ammunition that has been in use since the World War II for small-arms and aircraft rounds used against tanks and other armoured vehicles.

SAFETY LAMPS

Although Thomas Edison (1847–1931) is usually credited with the invention of the lightbulb, he was one of over 20 inventors and scientists who contributed to its development. The first practical demonstration of the principle came in 1802, when the British chemist Humphry Davy (1778–1829) passed an electrical current through a platinum wire, but without enclosing it in a protective glass bulb. Davy's light experiment was just a scientific curiosity, not a commercial venture. The light he produced was not very bright; the platinum filament was expensive and burned out quickly; and the demonstration had taken place in an age long before large-scale electricity generation was technically feasible.

Edison's genius was not the invention of the lightbulb, but its successful commercialisation. Admittedly, he had a good product: a bulb with a carbonised bamboo filament that could burn for 1,200 hours and that outshone and outlasted most of its rivals. But there were several further stages needed before the world got the 100-watt incandescent lightbulb. In 1904, a Hungarian company produced the first tungsten filament, which improved on the carbon alternatives. Finally, in 1906, William Coolidge (1873–1975) of General Electric developed 'ductile tungsten', which allowed the wire to be tightly coiled like a miniature spring. This not only extended the life of the filament, but it also produced a much brighter light. The last refinement was to fill the bulb with an inert gas that increased the bulb's luminosity and reduced blackening. By 1914, GE's tungsten-filament light bulbs were the market leaders, outlasting and outselling all their rivals.

R.I.P.
The 100w incandescent tungsten lightbulb.

The fragility of the [lightbulb] filament was one of the most serious difficulties [....] Tungsten seemed ideal, but from 1884 to 1909 the search for a means of making it sufficiently ductile proved abortive. Then, in 1909, Coolidge in the U.S.A. found how to make it ductile by swaging and sintering. The Social History of Lighting *(1958) by William O'Dea*

Zinc

Zink

Type: Transition metal

Origin: Sphalerite and zinc-bearing ores

Chemical formula: Z

+ **INDUSTRIAL**

+ **CULTURAL**

+ **COMMERCIAL**

+ **SCIENTIFIC**

Historically, zinc was alloyed with copper to make brass, which was used to make ornaments, weapons, coins and containers. The most common modern application for metallic zinc is to protect iron and steel from corrosion through the process known as galvanisation. Galvanisation is itself the product of a biological experiment in 1800 that led to the invention of the first electrical battery.

RUNNING LOW
World stocks of zinc may be exhausted by 2055.

FROG WITH BATTERY INCLUDED

Sometimes a scientific invention has an unlikely genesis, but the one that must rank as one of the oddest is the discovery of the electrochemical cell (electrical battery), by Alessandro Volta (1745–1827), which was inspired by an experiment conducted on a frog's leg by fellow scientist Luigi Galvani (1737–98). There are several versions of the story: that Galvani was passing an external current through a dead frog's leg and noticed that it began to twitch; that he was dissecting a frog's leg attached to a copper hook with an iron scalpel, again causing the leg to twitch; or that it was his assistant who touched an exposed nerve in the frog's leg with a metal scalpel, triggering the contraction of the dead muscles. Whichever is correct, Galvani concluded that the animal tissue contained 'bio-electricity'.

ELECTRICIANS
Volta (left) and Galvani (right), the inventors of the battery.

Upon hearing of the accidental experiment, Volta came to a very different conclusion. He theorised that the frog's leg did not contain electricity but merely conducted it, and that the electrical effect that Galvani had noticed was caused by a reaction between the two metals present facilitated by the frog. In order to prove his theory, Volta built the first electrochemical cell. The 'voltaic pile', as the device was known,

A thin coating of zinc is used to protect steel from rust. This is called galvanization. The zinc forms a barrier between the iron and steel and the air. Even if some of the zinc is scratched off, the surrounding zinc still protects the steel underneath. *Zinc (2006) by Leon Gray*

was not something that you could put into your TV remote or transistor radio. First made in 1800, the pile consisted of stacks of zinc and copper discs separated by cardboard soaked in brine. The discs were the electrodes and the brine was the electrolyte – the electrical conductor. When the top and bottom discs were connected by wire, an electric current flowed through the pile.

DRY ELECTRICITY

During the next eight decades, inventors improved on Volta's 'wet' battery design and experimented with other materials. Zinc continued to be a permanent fixture, featuring in the Daniell cell of 1836, the Grove cell of 1844 and the Leclanché cell of 1866. Finally in 1886, Doctor Carl Gassner patented the first dry battery, which replaced the liquid electrolyte with plaster of Paris, used a zinc cup as the negative terminal, and used carbon powder containing manganese dioxide as the positive terminal. Zinc-carbon batteries are still in use today, and being the cheapest to manufacture, they are usually the ones that are packed with products that are advertised as having 'batteries included'.

In the modern version, the tubular outer shell of the battery is made of zinc with a metal plate at the bottom (the minus terminal), with ammonium chloride paste as the electrolyte surrounding a carbon rod sheathed in manganese oxide, which is attached to a metal cap (the plus terminal) at the top of the battery. Today, you can still buy several updated versions of Gassner's battery: the zinc-carbon battery just described; the very common alkaline (zinc-manganese dioxide) battery that you're probably using in your consumer electronics; and the high-end nickel oxyhydroxide (zinc-manganese dioxide and nickel oxyhydroxide) battery.

HIGH ENERGY
(Opposite) The world's first battery: the voltaic pile.

Further Reading

Bernstein, Peter (2004) *The Power of Gold: The History of an Obsession*, Hoboken, NJ: John Wiley & Sons

Chaline, Eric (2008) *Traveller's Guide to the Ancient World: Greece in the Year 415 BCE*, London: David&Charles

Chaline, Eric (2009) *History's Worst Inventions and the People Who Made Them*, New York: Fall River Press

Chaline, Eric (2011) *History's Worst Predictions and the People Who Made Them*, London: History Press

Chaline, Eric (2011) *Fifty Animals That Changed the Course of History*, London: David&Charles

Chen, Ke Lun (2003) *Chinese Porcelain: Art, Elegance, and Appreciation*, San Francisco, CA: Long River Press

Cirincione, Joseph (2008) *Bomb Scare: The History and Future of Nuclear Weapons*, New York: Columbia University Press

Clark, Claudia (1987) *Radium Girls: Women and Industrial Health Reform, 1910–1935*, Chapel Hill, NC: University of North Carolina Press

Cobb, Cathy and Goldwhite, Harold (2001) *Creations of Fire: Chemistry's Lively History from Alchemy to the Atomic Age*, London: Basic Books

Collis, John (1984) *The European Iron Age*, New York: Schocken Books

Cooke, Stephanie (2009) *In Mortal Hands: A Cautionary History of the Nuclear Age*, New York: Bloomsbury

Cooper, Emmanuel (2010) *Ten Thousand Years of Pottery*, Philadelphia, PA: University of Pennsylvania Press

Crump, Thomas (2007) *A Brief History of the Age of Steam: From the First Engine to the Boats and Railways*, Philadelphia, PA: Running Press

Del Mar, Alex (2004) *A History of Precious Metals from the Earliest Times to the Present*, Whitefish, MT: Kessinger Publishing

Drew, David (1999) *The Lost Chronicles of the Maya Kings*, London: Wiedenfeld & Nicolson

Drews, Robert (1995) *The End of the Bronze Age: Changes in Warfare and the Catastrophe ca. 1200 BC*, Princeton, NJ: Princeton University Press

Durand, Françoise, Lichtenberg, Roger, and Lorton, David (2006) *Mummies and Death in Egypt*, Ithaca, NY: Cornell University Press

Enghag, Per (2004) *Encyclopedia of the Elements: Technical Data, History, Processing, Applications*, Hoboken, NJ: John Wiley & Sons

Gordon, Andrew (2010) *A Modern History of Japan: From Tokugawa Times to the Present*, New York: Oxford University Press USA

Gray, Leon (2005) *Zinc*, London: Marshall Cavendish

Gray, Theodore and Mann, Nick (2009) *The Elements: A Visual Exploration of Every Known Atom in the Universe*, New York: Black Dog & Leventhal Publishers

Gruber, Nicholai (ed.) (2000) *Maya: Divine Kings of the Rain Forest*, Cologne: Könemann

Hally, Cally (2002) *Smithsonian Handbooks: Gemstones*, London: DK Adult

Havilland, W. et al (2010) *Anthropology: The Human Challenge*, Andover, Hants: Cengage Learning

Heinberg, Richard (2005) *The Party's Over*, Forest Row, East Sussex: Clairview Books

Hodder, Ian (2006) *Çatalhöyük: The Leopard's Tale: Revealing the Mysteries of Turkey's Ancient Town*, London: Thames & Hudson

Johnsen, Ole (2002) *Minerals of the World*, Princeton, NJ: Princeton University Press

Keay, John (2000) *India*, London: HarperCollins

Kurlansky, Mark (2003) *Salt: A World History*, New York: Penguin

MacDonald, William (2002) *The Pantheon: Design, Meaning, and Progeny*, Cambridge, MA: Harvard University Press

Macfarlane, Allan and Martin, Gerry (2002) *Glass: A World History*, Chicago, IL: University of Chicago Press

Morley, Neville (2007) *Trade in Classical Antiquity*, Cambridge: Cambridge University Press

Moss, Norman (2000) *Managing the Planet*, London: Earthscan Publications

Partington, James (1999) *A History of Greek Fire and Gunpowder*, Baltimore, MD: Johns Hopkins University Press

Pellant, Chris (2002) *Rocks and Minerals (Smithsonian Handbooks)*, London: DK Adult

Peltason, Ruth (2010) *Living Jewels: Masterpieces from Nature: Coral, Pearls, Horn, Shell, Wood & Other Exotica*, New York: Vendome Press

Ponting, Clive (2005) *Gunpowder*, London: Chatto & Windus

Prescott, William and Foster Kirk, John (2004) *History of the Conquest of Mexico*, New York: Barnes & Noble Publishing

Rapp, George (2009) *Archaeomineralogy*, London: Springer

Raymond, Robert (1986) *Out of the Fiery Furnace: The Impact of Metals on the History of Mankind*, Philadelphia: Pennsylvania State University Press

Rosa, Greg (2008) *Titanium*, New York: Rosen Central

Schoff, W.H. (ed.) (1912), *The Periplus of the Erythraean Sea: Travel and Trade in the Indian Ocean by a Merchant of the First Century*, New York: Longman's Green and Co

Schumann, Walter (2008) *Minerals of the World*, 2nd ed., New York: Stirling

Simmons, Allan (2011) *The Neolithic Revolution in the Near East*, Tuscon, AZ: University of Arizona Press

Stimola, Aubrey (2007) *Sulfur*, New York: Rosen Central

Thomson, Charles (2002) *Alchemy and Alchemists*, Mineola, NY: Dover Publications

Turrell, Kerry (2004) *Tungsten*, Glasgow: Benchmark Books

Vyshedskiy, Andrey (2008) *Three Theories: Uniqueness of the Human Mind, Evolution of the Human Mind, and the Neurological Basis of Conscious Experience*, Boston: Mobile Reference

Weatherford, Jack (1998) *The History of Money*, New York: Three Rivers Press

Weightman, Gavin (2010) *The Industrial Revolutionaries: The Making of the Modern World 1776–1914*, New York: Grove Press

Wilson, Arthur (1994) *The Living Rock: The Story of Metals Since Earliest Times and Their Impact on Civilization*, Cambridge: Woodhead Publishing

USEFUL WEBSITES

American Museum of Natural History
www.amnh.org

British Museum
www.britishmuseum.org

Coal and coal mining
www.cmhrc.co.uk

Environmental Protection Agency
www.epa.gov

Food and Drug Administration
www.fda.gov

Geology on line
www.geology.com

Hibakusha (victims of the atomic bombings of Hiroshima and Nagasaki
http://wn.com/Hibakusha

History of aluminum
www.historyofaluminum.com

International Atomic Energy Agency
www.iaea.org

Mineral and locality database
www.mindat.org

Mundo Maya
www.mayadiscovery.com

NASA
www.nasa.gov

National Geographic
www.nationalgeographic.com

Natural History Museum
www.nhm.ac.uk

Phoenicia online
www.phoenicia.org

Precolumbian jade
www.precolumbianjade.com

Quartz page
www.quartzpage.de

Roman Empire online
www.roman-empire.net

Salt in history
www.saltinstitute.org

Science Museum
www.sciencemuseum.org.uk

Smithsonian Institution
www.si.edu

United Nations Environment Program
www.unep.org

United States Geological Survey
www.usgs.gov

Wikipedia
www.en.wikipedia.org

World Health Organization
www.who.int

Index

IMAGE CREDITS

4, 153	© J J Harrison | Creative Commons (CC)
5&12	© Jonathan Zander
6	© Vladvitek | Dreamstime.com
7	© JVCD | Creative Commons
8	© Apttone | Dreamstime.com
11	© Gump Stump | Creative Commons
13 Left	© Gerbil | Creative Commons
13 Right	© Bullenwächter | Creative Commons
14	© Eric Guinther | Creative Commons
15	© Daniel Schwen | Creative Commons
16	© Massimo Finizio | Creative Commons
17	© Plismo | Creative Commons
18	© Mountain | Creative Commons
19 Top	© Editor at Large | Creative Commons
19 Bottom, 70, 78, 209 Top, 177 Bottom	© Getty Images
20	© Andrzej Barabasz | Creative Commons
21	© Dave & Margie Hill | Creative Commons
22	© P. Fernandes | Creative Commons
23	© David Dennis | Creative Commons
24, 51 Top, 188	© Dirk Wiersma | Science Photo Library
25	© Dan Brady | Creative Commons
26, 35, 37 Top, 40, 58 Top, 61, 64 Bottom, 133 Top, 136 Both, 143 Top, 172, 189 Top, 200 Bottom, 210	© Creative Commons
27	© Steve Allen | Dreamstime.com
29	© 2011 Bloomberg
30, 51 Bottom, 56, 63 Top, 96 Both, 100, 140 Top, 145 Top, 152 Left, 191 Bottom, 196	© Rob Lavinsky | iRocks.com
31	© Farbled | Dreamstime.com
32 Bottom	© Mary Evans | The National Archives
34	© Hannes Grobe
36	© Jeany Fan | Creative Commons
37 Top	© GFDL | Creative Commons
37 Bottom	© Manfred Heyde | Creative Commons
38, 142, 198	© Heinrich Pniok | Creative Commons
41 Top	© Armin Kübelbeck | Creative Commons
41 Bottom	© Eigenes Bild | Creative Commons
44	© Siim Sepp | Creative Commons
45	© Petr Novák | Creative Commons
46 Bottom	© Angelogila | Dreamstime.com
47	© Andy Gilham | Creative Commons
48	© Andrew Silver | Creative Commons
52	© Mark Schneider
53	© Carsten Tolkmit | Creative Commons
54	© Jacopo Robusti Tintoretto
58 Bottom	© Martin St-Amant | Creative Commons
59	© Madman2001 | Creative Commons

62	© David Monniaux | Creative Commons
63 Bottom	© -wit- | Creative Commons
64 Top	© Trevor Clifford | Science Photo Library (SPL)
65	© Cupcakekid | Creative Commons
66	© dgmata | istockphoto.com
69 Top	© Tony Hisgett | Creative Commons
72 Top	© Alan64 | Dreamstime.com
72 Bottom	© Misszet | Dreamstime.com
73, 103	© Parent Géry | Creative Commons
76	© Saddako123 | Dreamstime.com
79	© Dean Dixon | Art Libre 1.3
81 Top, 199 Top	© LoKiLeCh | Creative Commons
81 Bottom	© Artifacts | Creative Commons
82	© Dendeimos | Dreamstime.com
83 Bottom	© Dennis Jarvis | Creative Commons
86, 168	© Geni | Creative Commons
87 Bottom	© Derek Ramsey | GNU License 1.2
88 Bottom	© Parksy 1964 | Creative Commons
89	© Peter Hendrie
90 Left	© Beatrice Murch | Creative Commons
91 Left	© World Imaging | Creative Commons
92	© Donkeyru | Dreamstime.com
93 Top	© Charles Humphries | iStockphoto
93 Bottom	© Marie-Lan Nguyen | CC
94	© Daniel Schwen | Creative Commons
95 Bottom	© Icefront | Dreamstime.com
97	© ERproductions Ltd
98	© David Jones | Creative Commons
99 Top	© Eric Le Bigot | Creative Commons
99 Bottom	© Lindom | Dreamstime.com
101, 160 Bottom	© Sailko | Creative Commons
102 Top, 109, 126 Right, 128, 158, 170, 182, 187 Bottom	© Dreamstime.com
104, 154	© Astrid & Hanns-Frieder Michler | SPL
105 Bottom	© David | Creative Commons
106	© Luis Miguel Bugallo Sánchez
108 Bottom	© David Gaya | Creative Commons
110 Left, 157	© John Solie | iStockphoto.com
110 Right	© =mc2 | Creative Commons
112 Bottom	© Jasmin Awad | iStockphoto.com
114	© Valery2007 | Dreamstime.com
115 Top	© Rkburnside | Dreamstime.com
116	© André | Creative Commons
117	© Thutmoselll | Creative Commons
118	© Manfred Werner | Creative Commons
120	© Igorius | Dreamstime.com

121	© Dea | G. Dagli Orit
122, 211 Bottom	© Michel Wal | Creative Commons
123 Top, 194 Top	© Mary Evans Picture Library
123 Bottom	© Bildarchiv Steffens Henri Stierlin
127	© Trzaska | Dreamstime.com
131 Bottom, 156, 159 Bottom	© Rama | Creative Commons
135	© Walter Siegmund | Creative Commons
137	© Bryant & May | Creative Commons
140 Bottom	© Zelfit | Dreamstime.com
141	© Stahlkocher | Creative Commons
144	© Willi Heidelbach | Creative Commons
145 Bottom	© Science Photo Library
148 Bottom	© Los Alamos National Laboratory
150 Top	© Rekemp | Dreamstime.com
150 Bottom, 151 Top	© Plotnikov | Dreamstime.com
152 Right	© Christian Jegou | Science Photo Library
155 Bottom	© Vitold Muratov | Creative Commons
162	© Hans Bernhard | Creative Commons
165 Bottom	© BabelStone | Creative Commons
171	© Tomas Senabre | Creative Commons
174	© Sushant Savla | Creative Commons
176	© Andreas Trepte | Creative Commons
177 Top	© Lillyundfreya | Creative Commons
180 Top	© Nick Stenning | Creative Commons
180 Bottom	© Opodeldok | Creative Commons
181	© Theo V. Bresler | Creative Commons
186	© Tifonimages | Dreamstime.com
187 Top	© Spanish School | Getty Images
189 Bottom	© Mariobonotto | Dreamstime.com
190	© N P Holmes | Creative Commons
193	© Peter Willi | Creative Commons
195	© Jbroome69 | Dreamstime.com
197	© Grundy | Getty Images
202	© Thedore Gray | Science Photo Library
205 Top	© Gamma-Keystone | Getty Images
205 Bottom	© Vladvitek | Dreamstime.com
207	© US Dept Of Energy | SPL
208 Top	© efesan | iStockphoto.com
208 Bottom	© Arpad Benedek | iStockphoto.com
211 Top	© Simon A. Eugster | Creative Commons
212	© Wolfgang Sauber | Creative Commons
213 Top	© Jan Harenburg | Creative Commons
213 Bottom	© John Hill | Creative Commons
214	© Alchemist-hp | Creative Commons
215 Bottom	© KMJ | Creative Commons
217	© Luigi Chiesa | Creative Commons